ISSUES IN
SCIENCE AND THEOLOGY

ISSUES IN
SCIENCE AND THEOLOGY

This series is published under the auspices of the
European Society for the Study of Science and Theology (ESSSAT)

Editor

NIELS HENRIK GREGERSEN
Research Professor in Theology and Science
University of Aarhus, Denmark

Advisory Board

Design and Disorder

Design and Disorder: Perspectives from Science and Theology

Editors

NIELS HENRIK GREGERSEN

ULF GÖRMAN

T&T CLARK
A Continuum imprint
LONDON • NEW YORK

T&T CLARK LTD

A Continuum imprint

59 George Street
Edinburgh EH2 2LQ
Scotland

www.tandtclark.co.uk

370 Lexington Avenue
New York 10017–6503
USA

www.continuumbooks.com

First published 2002

ISBN 0 567 08868 5

British Library Cataloguing-in-Publication Data
A catalogue record for this book is available from the British Library

Typeset by Waverley Typesetters, Galashiels
Printed and bound in Great Britain by MPG Books Ltd, Bodmin, Cornwall

Contents

Preface and Acknowledgements

This volume is motivated by the fundamental assumption that the old debate between design theorists and proponents of natural law and chance needs re-examination. In a physical perspective, order and disorder are no longer seen as alternatives; rather order and disorder coexist, and it may well be that we have a high degree of order at the level of fundamental physics while we have vast areas of unpredictable outcomes at the level of complex particulars such as weather systems and ecosystems, not to speak of human cultures. Also in biology we see a coexistence of strict chemical pathways with the more loose principles of variation and selection. If we add to this received picture the insights of the complexity sciences into the self-organizing principles of matter, we again see a mathematical order which pervades the biological world and yet brings evolution to teem in a wide array of directions.

But also from a theological perspective it can be doubted whether a theology standing in the Judeo-Christian tradition should necessarily adopt a theory of an all-determining divine design. Some relaxation might be called for in the hostile debates between design theorists and proponents of nature's capacity for self-organization. It is indeed possible to affirm the idea of a divine design of the constants of physics without claiming that everything within evolution, from bacteria to bees, has to be intelligently designed for specific purposes. The openendedness of reality, sheltered and at the same time propagated by general laws and principles, might provide a better environment for religious thought than the alternatives of pure order or pure chance.

From 14 to 19 April 2000 the European Society for the Study of Science and Theology (ESSSAT) organized its Eighth European Conference around the issue of *Design and Disorder*, or with the French twist, *Sens et Hasard: Perspectives en science et en théologie*. The site chosen for the conference was Lyon, the seat of Bishop Irenaeus, the church father for the Catholic, the Orthodox and the Reformation Churches. We should express our gratitude to the Faculties of Theology, Science and Philosophy of the Catholic University of Lyon for hosting the around two hundred participants, and in particular to Dr Bernard Michollet who was in charge of the local organization of the conference. (Together with the editors of this volume, Bernard Michollet will also edit a French version of the plenary lectures of the conference which is planned to appear next year.)

What is contained in this volume are extended versions of the plenary lectures (by Barrow, Brooke, Gregersen, Stengers and Theobald) with three important presentations from the conference programme at large (by Drees, Nesteruk and Puddefoot). We hope to have provided a volume that shows how the issue of design can be discussed in other frameworks than that of an anti-naturalist approach to design.

A conference of this pan-European sort could not have been undertaken without substantial support from a number of sponsors. In particular we want to thank the John Templeton Foundation for its generous support of the speaker's programme and the Ministère de Culture et Communication, France, and Centre Français des Patrons Crétiens for supplying us with the basic funding of the conference. We also want to thank and honor the Radboud Foundation and the Counterbalance Foundation for sponsoring the two ESSSAT Prizes.

Last but not least we express our gratitude to Anne Marie Baden Olesen and Bente Stœr at the Department of Systematic Theology, Aarhus, who have worked meticulously at the editing of the manuscript. They also took care of the other selection of papers from the conference that have appeared in *Studies in Science and Theology* 8 (2001).

This is the second volume of *Issues in Science and Theology* (IST). The third volume will have the provisional title, *Creating Homo*

S@piens, and is going to deal with values and ethical issues in the interface between theology, science, and technology. The mutual interaction between theology and the sciences seems ever widening, and it is a pleasure for us to be able continue this discussion in the always easy and joyful collaboration with the staff of the T&T Clark publishing house.

List of Contributors

JOHN D. BARROW is Professor of Mathematical Sciences and Director of the Millennium Mathematics Project at Cambridge University. He previously held positions at the Universities of Oxford, California at Berkeley, and Sussex. He has received the Locker Award, the Kelvin Medal, and an honorary doctorate from the University of Hertfordshire for his contributions to astronomy. His research interests are in cosmology and gravitation physics and he is the author of more than 310 papers and thirteen books, the most recent of which are *The Book of Nothing* (Pantheon Books 2001) and *Constants of Nature* (2002). He is also well known for his work on the Anthropic Principle in modern cosmology.

JOHN HEDLEY BROOKE is the Andreas Idreos Professor of Science and Religion and Director of the Ian Ramsey Centre at the University of Oxford. He has been President of the British Society for the History of Science and of the Historical Section of the British Association for the Advancement of Science. In 1995, jointly with Professor Geoffrey Cantor, he gave the Gifford Lectures at the University of Glasgow. His main books are *Science and Religion: Some Historical Perspectives* (Cambridge University Press 1991); *Thinking About Matter: Studies in the History of Chemical Philosophy* (Ashgate 1995); and (with Geoffrey Cantor) *Reconstructing Nature: The Engagement of Science & Religion* (T&T Clark 1998).

WILLEM B. DREES holds the chair in philosophy of religion and ethics at the Department of Theology, Leiden University, The Netherlands. He has been Executive Director of ALLEA, the federation of academies of sciences and humanities in Europe, and part-time extraordinary professor on the Nicolette Bruining chair in philosophy of nature and technology at Twente University, The Netherlands. He is the author of *Creation: From Nothing until Now* (Routledge 2001); *Religion, Science and Naturalism* (Cambridge University Press 1996), and *Beyond the Big Bang: Quantum Cosmologies and God* (Open Court 1990).

ULF GÖRMAN is Professor of Ethics at Lund University in Sweden. He has been President of ESSSAT, the European Society for the Study of Science and Theology, 1996–2002, and formerly Secretary of Societas Ethica: Europäische Forschungsgesellschaft für Ethik. His research focuses on bioethics and on ethical issues in science and religion. He is currently heading a research project where Swedish ethicists investigate ethical aspects of postgenomic research, as well as a multidisciplinary project at Lund on religious mobility. Current publications include *Towards a New Understanding of Conversion* (ed.) (Lund University 1999), and articles on ethics and biotechnology (in Swedish).

NIELS HENRIK GREGERSEN is Research Professor in Theology and Science at the University of Aarhus, Denmark. He is a leader of the Danish Science–Theology Forum and was a Vice-President of the European Society for the Study of Science and Theology, 1996–2002. He has published widely in theology and has edited or co-edited more than ten books in science and religion, most recently *From Complexity to Life: On the Emergence of Life and Meaning* (Oxford University Press 2002). In 1999 he was a recipient of the $100,000 Templeton Research Award for his work on theology and the sciences of complexity.

ALEXEI V. NESTRUK was born in St Petersburg in Russia in 1957. He received his education in physics and philosophy in Russia, and in theology in England. At present he is a lecturer of Mathematics at the University of Portsmouth and a research associate at the Institute for Orthodox Christian Studies in Cambridge. His main research interests are in the foundations of cosmology and quantum physics, as well as in science and Eastern Orthodox theology. He is a recipient of several awards from the John Templeton Foundation and is finishing his book, *Logos and Cosmos: An Eastern Orthodox Perspective in Science and Theology*.

JOHN C. PUDDEFOOT is Head of Mathematics and honorary chaplain at Eton College in the UK. He writes on general issues in philosophy, philosophy of religion, and religion and science, as well as on theology and mathematics, information theory, artificial intelligence, and theological issues related to extraterrestrial life. Apart from numerous papers on the science and theology of mathematics and information he has published *God and the Mind Machine: Computers, Artificial Intelligence and the Human Soul* (SPCK 1996).

ISABELLE STENGERS, b. 1949, has a doctorate in the philosophy of science. Her works are centred on the problems of physics confronted by the issues of time and irreversibility (*Order out of Chaos*, with Ilya Prigogine), on the issue of the power of scientific concepts (*The Invention of Modern Science*), on the vexed history of the relation between psychoanalysis and the sciences (*A Critique of Psychoanalytical Reason*, with Léon Chertok) and on the relations between scientific expertise and democracy (*Power and Invention*).

CHRISTOPH THEOBALD, SJ, is Professor of Fundamental Theology and Dogmatics at the Faculty of Theology of the Centre Sèvres in Paris, editor of *Recherches de Sciences Religieuses* and a member of the board of the international review, *Concilium*. His publications include contributions to the history of exegesis, the history of dogmatics, systematic theology and the theology of spirituality, and include *Maurice Blondel und das Problem der Modernität* 1988; *Histoire des dogmes 4* (with B. Sesboüé), 1996; *Le devenir de la théologie catholique depuis le Concile Vatican II* 2000 (Histoire du Christianisme 13), and *La Pensée musicale de Jean-Sébastien Bach* (with Philippe Charru), 1993.

1

Introduction

ULF GÖRMAN

How does the discussion on design and disorder affect science and theology? Probably we all have something we may call a received view in these matters. Let us start by looking at that.

In a traditional Christian understanding, order characterizes the world as created by God. Accordingly, the goodness of God becomes manifest in the victory over chaos and disorder, which are seen as expressions of evil, the enemies of God. Life and harmony are among the different forms in which order is expressed. Sin and death are expressions of the evil forces, still with a perceptible influence on the world of creation. But these evil powers are only temporarily capable of inferring disorder in the creation. At last order will prevail and disorder be eliminated.

Also in a traditional scientific understanding, reality is regarded as in principle ordered. Order means here, among other things, regularity. In this sense any kind of order may be analysed and described, and with detailed enough knowledge, it can be given a mathematical form. This order, however, does not necessarily indicate that there is design in the sense that some kind of intention lies behind the regularities, and that order is an expression of this intention. Instead order is often regarded as a brute fact or a result of chance.

The tensions involved already in these two traditional views lead to a number of interesting questions. For instance: What is the relation between the scientific presupposition of order on the one hand, and the religious idea of intelligent design on the other? Are they in opposition to each other, or should they rather be regarded as two very similar interpretations of reality? If so, what does a religious understanding of nature add to a non-religious understanding?

However, recent trends in science as well as theology have challenged these traditional interpretations of order. Chaos theory shows that our received view of determinism may be far too limited. It seems that either we have to reinterpret our concept of determinism, meaning that determinism is something much more subtle, complex and open than we have imagined, or we will have to leave it as a general framework for the understanding of reality, because it is far too limited to understand reality when not in equilibrium. What, then, does chaos theory mean to the received image of God? Must not the understanding of God's providence, pre-knowledge, and predestination be understood in new ways in the light of chaos theory?

Correspondingly, what is the relation between chaos and chance? Does 'chance' mean a lack of determinism or does it mean only a lack of knowledge of the way things are part of causal networks? Is chance still to be understood as a keyword for a secular non-religious interpretation of the world? Should not also Christian theology integrate the idea of God as acting by means of chance?

Thus it would appear that the traditional Christian concept of divine activity has been too much associated with an idea of causal determinism connected with seventeenth-century scientific ideas, which are nowadays abandoned by science. Some theologians have already offered reinterpretations on this line. What should the reaction from scientists be to that?

Isn't it hubris to claim to understand a wholeness of which our minds are only a tiny part? Among other issues, this means: Is it at all possible for a human mind to create a theory of everything, be it scientific or religious? And at the same time it seems to be part of the core effort of science as well as religion to set up all-embracing theories about how all things might be interrelated in the web of reality.

What does, in this context, 'design' at all mean? Is it possible to imagine a world with life, which does not look as if it were designed? So, is apparent design an argument for real design? By the way, what would be the difference? Is design in the eye of the observer or is it a part of reality? But isn't the observer himself or herself part of reality?

Accordingly, what do we understand by 'order'? Is order necessarily harmonious? Can we imagine a disorganized harmony or a harmonious disorder? Can we conceive of a disharmonious order? If we can, then we turn traditional positions upside down. If we cannot, what would follow from that? Does it tell us something about nature in general, or does it only say something about human psychology?

Another kind of challenge comes from the biological sciences. Suffering and death are generally considered to be bad things in a religious framework, except perhaps as tools for educating the soul or as a gate to heaven. But modern biology describes suffering as a necessary tool for living creatures to orient themselves in reality, or as by-products of this capacity. And death is necessary for evolution through variation and selective retention. So, in a biological interpretation the death of the individual is nothing contrary to nature, but instead belongs to its very core. This understanding may inspire theologians to reconsider traditional positions.

Another concept that has attracted the attention of many is the idea of emergence. This concept may imply that new properties of reality start to exist, for instance through evolution to greater complexity. But does this really mean that something new comes into existence? Was it not there already in a sense before it emerged? Emergence may be 'nothing but' the expression of already existing properties. But if so – in what sense did they already exist? Did they exist in the same sense before emergence as after?

Emergence may be the expression of potentialities. But what is then a potentiality? The glass breaks in my hand – does this express its potentiality to break? Are the other glasses examples of un-expressed potentialities? Is a potentiality something that is realized unless an obstacle comes in between? Or is it only something that may happen in a lucky or an unlucky coincidence? Only one out of millions of pollen from the birch tree in my garden realizes its potentiality to fertilize a birch and contribute to the development of a seed. Only one out of millions of birch seeds realizes its potentiality to become a birch. Is it a potentiality of seed to feed birds? Is it a potentiality for a seed to fall apart and become mould? We may choose to say so. But then other questions appear. If every possible development is the expression of a potentiality, what is then not a potentiality? The concept of potentiality may become without content. If it is not the case that every possible change is the expression of a potentiality, how can we know when there is a potentiality behind, and when not?

Emergence may mean that something new appears or that an already existing potentiality expresses itself. But is the difference between these two alternatives really as large as we tend to think? How well can our words and concepts fit reality?

New ideas like these are challenges, not only to religion, but also to the very framework and presuppositions of science itself. While biology traditionally has not accepted the idea of intentionality in nature, it seems that the idea of function is indispensable. But what are the relations between function, design, intentionality and teleology? How far is function from intention? Is function a part of reality or is it an unavoidable tool for human understanding of reality? And what would follow from that? This raises the still more general question: Is meaning inherent in reality, or is it in our eyes? What would be the difference? Are not our eyes parts of reality?

The Contents of this Volume

This has been a long journey among questions. Its aim is evident: to indicate that the meaning of design and the meaning of disorder and the relations between them are much more subtle, complicated and interesting than one may think at first glance. In the understanding of this, theology as well as science have interesting contributions to offer.

This volume of *Issues in Science and Theology* (IST) bears upon material presented at the Eighth European Conference on Science and Theology, arranged by ESSSAT, the European Society for the

Study of Science and Theology, and held in Lyon, France, in April 2000. The theme for this conference was 'Design and Disorder: Perspectives from Science and Theology', and its aim was to cast new light on the relation between these two concepts. This book contains the plenary lectures as well as a selection of papers discussed in the parallel workshops. The different contributions touch upon a number of the questions asked above. Together the different authors give an insight into the interesting multiplicity of aspects by means of which current science, theology and world-views make design and disorder fascinating food for thought.

Physicist **John D. Barrow** starts by introducing us to this complexity by discussing how chaos coexists with order. Is the universe simple or complicated? he asks, and by making the distinction between the laws of nature and their outcomes, he shows that simplicity and complexity coexist. The search for simplicity and order has directed the development of science during the last 300 years. This search for simpleness leads to the physicist's search for a Theory of Everything. However, complexity is not simple. The fundamental laws of nature are based upon the preservation of symmetry. But the outcomes of these symmetrical laws need not possess the symmetries of the laws themselves. Simple laws may have very complicated outcomes, among them organized complexity, such as feedback, self-organization and non-equilibrium behaviour. Consequently, chaos and order coexist in a curious symbiosis. There are many natural and man-made systems that are chaotic at the microscopic level but combine to maintain a semblance of equilibrium. In connection with this Barrow also gives an illuminating comment on the 'design' argument for the existence of God. His distinction between simple laws and complex outcomes helps him discern two different kinds of design arguments. Traditional design arguments until the late seventeenth century were characterized by their emphasis upon outcomes. With the development of Newton's laws of mechanics and gravitation, a new form of design argument emerged, one that focused upon the mathematical form of the laws of nature, rather than their outcomes.

Two centuries later the design argument met with a new challenge. Darwin had provided a naturalist explanation to design through evolution. For many, this made it more difficult to believe in the unfolding of a divine plan. In his contribution to this volume, the historian of science **John Hedley Brooke** takes a new look into the received view of Darwin's relation to religion. What did Darwin himself have to say on order and design? Brooke's return reveals that Darwin's relation to natural theology seems to have been a complex one. He read Paley with admiration, and his earliest notebooks reveal him as a reformer rather than a destroyer of natural theology. His later writings, however, show that he has lost his Christian faith. How do we account for his loss of faith? The standard view is one of linear progression from theism over deism to agnosticism, based on scientific considerations. However, Brooke points out and discusses a number of personal reasons for his change of mind, above all the loss of a beloved daughter. In his old age Darwin was happy with the idea that one could have order without design. On the road to this position, the theodicy problem seems to have offered him important arguments, reasons connected with personal experiences.

Theologian **Niels Henrik Gregersen** approaches the relation between order and design from another angle. He draws attention to the recent discussion within theoretical biology, whether the Darwinian principles of variation and selection need to be supplemented by mathematical principles of self-organization. Extremely simple physical laws can be responsible for the production of highly complex structures. Gregersen points to self-organized criticality and complex adaptive systems theory as steps towards an understanding of the world as self-organizing. What would a theological reaction to this be? Does (natural) self-organization replace (divine) design, or would the former presuppose the latter? Gregersen proposes a theology of self-organization and self-productivity, a new theology for God's continuous creation. One of the leading ideas in his proposal is the theological assumption that a creative Logos is built into the mathematical order of the universe. (This suggestion has interesting connections with the proposal of Alexei

Nesteruk in this volume.) Instead of a causal approach, which attempts to make an inference to God from processes in the world, Gregersen presents a qualitative approach, which presupposes the reality of God on pre-scientific grounds and aims then to recognize the works of God in the world of nature.

Mathematician **John C. Puddefoot** starts by looking at human discourse from a surprising angle, not by focusing on its substance in terms of statements, arguments, etc., but instead by interpreting the type of discourse itself. He tries to understand the laws that govern human discourse as a complex and dynamical system or, as he puts it, a landscape. This outlook proves to have relevance for the question of realism versus constructivism: Is human discourse configured by the topics it addresses, or does it configure them? Puddefoot suggests that the human mind, as well as human discourse, is only superficially linear, but may be more like complex adaptive systems, with multiple attractors and a multiplicity of endpoints, susceptibility to arbitrarily small fluctuations, and non-computable although deterministic. This paves the way for an understanding of theological as well as scientific discourse, where endless emergence and dissolution of stable configuration creates long-term stability and vitality.

Philosopher **Isabelle Stengers** brings up similar questions: What is the relation between science and theology as interpretations of the world? She starts by calling attention to Alfred N. Whitehead, who resisted the modern dichotomy between nature conceived of as blind, and the human subject, free and the source of all value, a dichotomy Whitehead deemed an inconsistency. He considered it a disaster that religion has lost its power in the modern era, and he believed that religion will not regain its old power until it can face change in the same spirit as science does.

Will the idea of complementarity help religion regain its power? Is it, for instance, satisfactory to say that science deals with 'how', and religion with 'why'? In her tentative answer Stengers suggests, first, that science and religion are complementary. This is, however, not a complementarity of two descriptions, but between two kinds of practice and their requirements. Science as a practice is infused with values. It is not a negation of human freedom, neither a submission to the power of facts against interpretation. Instead it is relative to a very particular value: only that statement has value that can survive controversy. The practice of science is oriented towards proof, but only proof which has a capacity for progression. She suggests that the complementary practice of religion is one of possibility: it is the difference that it is possible to make to the other, and with the other, which commits and obligates. But, secondly, there may be also something in common, beyond complementarity, where science and religion 'face change in the same spirit'. This, Stengers suggests, is trust. It is not a matter of authority, but trust in the creativity in each practice and in the possibility that contradictions can be overcome. In order to achieve this, we should learn to start from the unknown, not from what we know.

Theologian **Christoph Theobald** discusses the idea of finality in creation theology. While seeking for an alliance between theology and recent cosmology in this respect, he articulates certain reservations. The 'anthropic cosmology' is a very limited approach compared to the faith in a creator God. Theobald looks carefully at the philosophical and ideological positions that create this limitation. Biology as well as physics has had to combat anthropomorphism and redefine the concept of teleology. These thoughts have lately been challenged. The frontier between science and myth has proved to be movable. But, contends Theobald, to introduce teleology in biology and physics is a problematic enterprise, because of the claims to completeness inherent in these sciences. 'Does the theologian need finality?' is the question Theobald takes the task to investigate – and his final answer is in the negative. Proper theological reflection should have a different basis, the messianic opening of the universe.

Mathematician **Alexei V. Nesteruk** is a Russian Orthodox, and he uses this background in his approach to the problem of design in the universe. In modern cosmology the argument from design has been reinvigorated. The fine-tuning of the universe is often used as an argument for design. Nesteruk discusses the question whether the physical universe bears the pattern of design at its ontological level, or whether this is rather the design of our intellect. As a philosopher, Immanuel Kant has set up many of the presuppositions for modern thinking. According to him, the ground for the world order can be found in the ideal. Kant's idea of intelligible reality is subjective and deprived of an independent ontology. Nesteruk argues that Kant was a strictly monistic philosopher, which stopped him from finding a theistic argument from design. The thinking of Kant is still the basis of, and is reflected in, the modern scientific world-view. Divine design cannot be discovered in any of these concepts, as they exclude divinity by their very presuppositions.

In contrast to this view, the Greek patristics pursue a different approach to the understanding of God. The patristic fathers start with the Word of God. They do not try to deduce God from a scientific world-view. Instead the reality of God is presupposed. Contemplation of the *logoi*, the eternal principles of created things, is a way of communion with the divine Logos – the Word of God. Nesteruk finds interesting connections between patristic thought and the current attempt by Roger Penrose to solve the riddle of temporal flow in modern physics. Penrose suggests that the present state of the universe has its origin in boundary conditions in the remote past of the universe. Here Nesteruk finds an interesting parallel to the idea of the *logoi*.

In the final contribution to this volume, physicist and theologian **Willem B. Drees** opens up for future discussions a number of different matters with his ten theses on disorder and the ambitions of 'science and theology'. His main message is that disorder in nature is a reality, which can even be considered as if it were designed to call humans to responsibility. Theists face the complex situation to handle the tension between emphasis on the goodness of creation and the need for redemption. Arguments from design tend to be too optimistic and to neglect this ambivalence. Science does not support this view. Further, religions are not just peculiar cosmologies. They also have a moral dimension, and a mystical aspect that surpasses our understanding. Every faith contradicts reality in some way. A prophetic religion relates to the experience of a discontinuity between values and facts. In Christianity there is not only a theology of divine presence, but also of divine absence. This makes a natural theology, based on order and design, problematic. In contrast to consonance, bridge building and realism, Drees wants to stress the inaccessibility of the Holy. In relation to technology, he thinks that natural theologies tend to over-emphasize the way things are, and he asks for more focus on transformation as a central theological theme. A theologically adequate view should attempt to disclose the possibilities for transformation of the natural order.

In different ways all the authors in this volume try to handle challenges to the conception I named 'the received view'. The relation between design and disorder is not a simple one. They are not strictly opposites. Nature does not only contain harmony, but also on a very foundational level possibilities of ambivalence, conflicts, suffering, and other traits we use to connect with disorder. Disorder may be enclosed in the design of nature. Our under-standing of design or disorder is also dependent not only on our views of life but on very basic presuppositions set up by our situation as human beings. This calls for an ongoing openness for reinterpretation in science as well as theology. It is our hope that this volume will contribute to that process.

2

How Chaos Coexists
with Order

JOHN D. BARROW

Introduction

The view of the universe revealed by our discoveries in physical science provides the basis for many attempts to interpret its significance and our place within it. Here, we are going to take a look at two contrasting views of nature which have both been much in the news over recent years, as scientists from very different disciplines have trumpeted dramatic developments through the media and in works of popular science. For the outsider, these different messages can be confusing and disjointed: on the one hand, there are the physicists talking of 'Theories of Everything' and the rapid convergence of our investigations of nature towards a single all-encompassing mathematical theory of exquisite simplicity, while, on the other hand, we are told of chaos, unpredictability and a well of bottomless complexity all around us.

These messages have each inspired extrapolations into the philosophy of science and theology as commentators seek to evaluate what each has to tell us about who we are, why we are, and where we might be going. Our aim, here, is one of explanation: to ask whether the universe is simple or complicated, and to show that the question is a subtle one. We will see why order and complexity coexist in nature and then look further into the folklore surrounding chaotic behaviour to assess some of the practical consequences of such behaviour for the long-term stability of macroscopic systems. In line with other themes in the conference, we will also draw some lessons about the nature of traditional 'design' arguments in the light of what we learn about order and chaos in nature.

Simplicity

If you were to engage some passing particle physicists in a conversation about the nature of the world, they might soon be regaling you with a story about how simple and symmetrical the world really is, if only you look at things in the right way. But, when you return to contemplate the real world, you know that it is far from simple. Nor would many other scientists agree with the verdict of the particle physicists. For the psychologist, the economist, the botanist, or the zoologist, the world is anything but simple. It is a higgledy-piggledy of complex events, whose nature owes more to their persistence over time, in competition with other alternatives, than to any mysterious penchant for symmetry or simplicity. So who is right? Is the world really simple, as the particle physicists claim, or is it as complex as everyone else seems to think?

Our belief in the simplicity of nature springs from the observation that there appear to exist 'laws' of nature. The idea of laws of nature has a long history rooted in monotheistic religious thinking and in practices of social government. For our purposes, it is most instructive to consider the concept of scientific law and order in the broadest context. This involves some developments in mathematics and computer science that provide some discrimination between order and randomness.

Suppose you encounter two sequences of digits. The first has the form

$$...000100010001000100010001...$$

while the second has the form

$$...010001011010101111010010...$$

Now you are asked if these sequences are random or ordered.

Clearly, the first appears to be ordered. The reason you say this is because it is possible to 'see' a pattern in it; that is, we can replace the sequence by a rule that allows us to remember it or convey it to others without simply listing its contents. In line with this, we will call a sequence *non-random* if it can be abbreviated by a formula or a rule shorter than itself. If this is so, we say that it is *compressible* (Chaitin 1980, 1987). By contrast, if, as appears to be the case for the second sequence (which was generated by tossing a coin), there is no abbreviated formula, pattern, or rule which can capture its information content, then we say that it is *incompressible*. If we want to tell our friends about the incompressible sequence then we simply have to list it in full. There is no encapsulation of its information content shorter than itself.

This simple idea allows us to draw some lessons about the scientific search for a so-called 'Theory of Everything' (Barrow 1991). We might define science as the search for compressions. We observe the world in all possible ways, and gather facts about it; but while this is necessary for science it is not sufficient for science. We are not content simply to gather up a record of everything that has ever happened, like manic micro-historians. Instead, more like real historians, we look for patterns in the facts, compressions of the information on offer, and these patterns we have come to call the laws of nature. The search for a Theory of Everything is the quest for an ultimate compression of the world. Interestingly, Greg Chaitin's proof of Gödel's incompleteness theorem, using the concepts of complexity and compression, reveals that Gödel's theorem is equivalent to the fact that one cannot *prove* a sequence to be incompressible. We can never prove a compression to be the ultimate one; there might still be a deeper and simpler unification waiting to be found.

Our discussion of the compressibility of sequences has taught us that pattern, or symmetry, is equivalent to laws or rules of change. Classical laws of change, like Newton's laws of motion, are equivalent to the invariance of some quantity or pattern. These equivalences only became known long after the formulation of the laws of motion prescribing the allowed changes in terms of causes and effects. This approach strikes a chord with the traditional Platonic tradition which places emphasis upon the unchanging, atemporal aspects of the world as the key to its fundamental structures. These timeless attributes, or 'forms' as Plato called them, seem to have evolved, with the passage of time, into the laws of nature, and the invariances and conserved quantities (like energy and momentum) of modern physics.

Since 1973, this focus upon symmetry has taken centre stage in the study of elementary particle physics and the laws governing the fundamental interactions of nature. Symmetry is now taken as the primary guide into the structure of the elementary particle world, and the laws of change are derived from the requirement that particular symmetries, often of a highly abstract character, be preserved. Such theories are called 'gauge theories' (see Pagels 1985; Zee 1986; Weinberg 1983; and Greene 1999). The currently successful theories of four known forces of nature – the electromagnetic, weak, strong and gravitational forces – are all gauge theories. These theories require the existence of the forces they govern in order to preserve the invariances upon which they are based. They are also able to dictate the character of the elementary particles of matter that they govern. In these respects, gauge theories differ from the classical laws of Newton which, since they governed the motions of all bodies, could say nothing about the properties of those bodies. The reason for this added power of explanation, is that the elementary-particle world, in contrast to the macroscopic world, is populated by collections of identical particles ('once you've seen one electron you've seen 'em all' as Richard Feynman once remarked). Particular gauge theories govern the behaviour of particular subsets of all the elementary particles, according to their attributes. The use of symmetry in this powerful way enables entire systems of natural laws to be derived from the requirement that a certain abstract pattern be invariant in the universe. Subsequently, the predictions of this system of laws can be compared with the actual course of nature. This is the opposite route to that which was followed a century ago. Then, the systematic study of events would have led to systems of mathematical equations giving the laws of cause and effect. Only later would the fact that these rules of change are equivalent to the requirement that some other quantity does *not* change be recognized.

This generation of theories for each of the separate interactions of nature has motivated the search for a unification of those theories into more comprehensive editions based upon larger symmetries. Within those larger patterns, smaller symmetries respected by the individual forces of nature might be accommodated in an inter-locking fashion that places some new constraint upon their allowed forms. So far, this strategy has resulted in a successful, experimentally-tested, unification of the electromagnetic and weak interactions, and a number of purely theoretical proposals for a further unification with the strong interaction ('grand unification'), and candidates for a four-fold unification with the gravitational force to produce a so-called 'Theory of Everything' or 'TOE'.

A favoured candidate for a TOE is a variant of 'superstring' theory, first developed by Michael Green and John Schwarz (see Green et al. 1987). Elementary description of superstring theory can be found elsewhere (see Green 1986; Bailin 1989; Davies and Brown 1988; Barrow 1992). But these early investigations have recently been developed into a more compelling synthesis, called 'M theory', wherein the superficially different editions of superstring theory are revealed to be different limits of some (as yet unfound) deep underlying theory (Greene 1999) linked to each other by mathe-matical invariances of the underlying theory. Superficially, there appeared to be a large number of different superstring theories, but it begins to look as if they are just different mathematical repre-sentations of a small number of theories – or even just one theory. Suffice it to say that the enormous interest that these theories attracted over the last nineteen years can be attributed to the fact that they revealed that the requirement of logical self-consistency – previously suspected of being a rather weak constraint upon a TOE – turned out to be enormously restrictive. At first, it was believed that it narrowed the alternatives down to just two possible sym-metries underlying the TOE. Subsequently, the situation has been found to be rather more complicated than first imagined and super-string theories have been found to require new types of mathematics for their elucidation.

The important lesson to be learned from this part of our discussion is that 'Theories of Everything', as currently conceived, are simply attempts to encapsulate all the laws governing the fundamental forces of nature within a single law of nature derived from the preservation of a single overarching symmetry. We might add that, at present, four fundamental forces are known, of which the weakest is gravitation. There might exist other, far weaker, forces of nature. Although too weak for us to measure (perhaps ever), their existence may be necessary to fix the logical necessity of that single Theory of Everything. Without any means to check on their existence we would always be missing a crucial piece of the cosmic jigsaw puzzle.

It is this general pattern of explanation in terms of a smaller number of laws governing the fundamental force fields of nature, culminating in a single unified law, that lies at the heart of the physicist's perception of the world as 'simple'.

There is a further point that we might raise regarding the quest for a Theory of Everything – if it exists. We might wonder whether such a theory is buried deep (perhaps infinitely deep) in the nature of the universe, or whether it lies rather shallow. If it lies deep below the present appearances of things, then it would be a most anti-Copernican over-confidence to expect that we would be able to fathom it after just a few hundred years of serious study of the laws of nature, aided by limited observations of the world by relatively few individuals. There appears to be no good evolutionary reason why our intellectual capabilities need be so great as to unravel the ultimate laws of nature, unless those ultimate laws are simply a vast elaboration of very simple principles, like counting or comparing (Barrow 1992) which are employed in local laws. Of course, the unlikelihood of our success is no reason not to try. We just should not have unrealistic expectations about the chances of success or underestimate the magnitude of the task.

A Digression on Initial and Final Causes

When drawing lessons of a philosophical or theological kind from the nature of physical laws it is important to be aware of the fact that it is possible for laws of nature to have different mathematical formulations which have the same physical content yet quite different philosophical implications. For example, it is possible to write equations of motion in the form of differential equations with prescribed initial conditions. Thus, the future is determined uniquely and completely by the conditions specified initially. If we were seeking to draw a philosophical lesson from this state of affairs it would be that the world appeared to be causal and there are no final causes. However, in the eighteenth century the French scientist Moreau de Maupertuis (with a lot of help from Euler) realized that laws of motion could be derived from action principles. Suppose we want to know the path taken by a body moving between two points A and B under the influence of certain forces. A mathematical quantity can be defined (the action) so that if we require that this quantity be a minimum for the path actually taken by moving bodies then the path taken will be identical to that prescribed by the deterministic laws of Newton. All the laws of motion can be derived from the action perspective. In effect, it imagines all the possible paths that could be taken between the points A and B and reveals that the path with minimum value of the action is the one taken in a world governed by Newton's laws. Operationally, it makes no difference whether one adopts the causal laws or the action principle. The same paths will be found. However, philosophically, the action picture seems quite different. There are now initial (A) and final (B) conditions prescribing the motion and there is a teleological aspect to the situation that was absent in the initial value plus laws prescription. Despite their similar physical consequences these two equivalent prescriptions are philosophically divergent.

Complexity

The simplicity and economy of the laws that govern nature's fundamental forces are not the end of the story. For, when we look around us we do not observe the laws of nature; rather, we see the *outcomes* of those laws. There is world of difference. Outcomes are much more complicated than the laws that govern them because they do not have to respect the symmetries displayed by the laws. By this means, it is possible to have a world which displays complicated asymmetrical structures yet is governed by very simple, symmetrical laws. Consider the following simple example: suppose I balance a ball at the apex of a cone. If I were to release the ball, then the law of gravitation will determine its subsequent motion. But gravity has no preference for any particular direction in the universe; it is entirely democratic in that respect. Yet, when I release the ball, it will always fall in some particular direction, either because it was given a little push in one direction or as a result of quantum fluctuations which do not permit an unstable equilibrium state to persist. So here, in the outcome of the falling ball, the directional symmetry of the law of gravity is broken. Take another example. You and I are, at this moment, situated at particular places in the universe, despite the fact that the laws of nature display no preference for any one place in the universe over any other. We are both (very complicated) outcomes of the laws of nature, which break their underlying symmetries with respect to positions in space. This teaches us why science is often so difficult. When we observe the world, we see only the broken symmetries manifested as the outcomes of the laws of nature; from them, we must work backwards to unmask the hidden symmetries which characterize the laws behind the appearances.

We can now understand the answers that we obtained from the different scientists in the street. The particle physicist works closest to the laws of nature themselves, and so is especially impressed by their simplicity and symmetry. That is the basis for his assertion about the simplicity of nature. But the biologist or the meteorologist is occupied with the study of the complex outcomes of the laws, rather than with the laws themselves. As a result, she is most impressed by the complexities of nature, rather than by her laws.

The law-focused perspective represents the development of the Platonic approach to the world, with its emphasis upon the unchanging elements behind things – laws, conserved quantities, symmetries – whereas the outcomes focus, with its stress upon time and change and the concatenation of complex happenings, is the fulfilment of the Aristotelian approach to understanding of the world. Until rather recently, physicists have focused almost exclusively upon the study of the laws, rather than the complex outcomes. This is not surprising, for the study of the outcomes is a far more difficult problem, that requires the existence of powerful interactive computers with good graphics for its full implementation. It is no coincidence that the study of complexity and chaos (Gleick 1987; Stewart 1989) in that world of outcomes has advanced hand in hand with the growing power and availability of low-cost personal computers.

We see that the structure of the world around us cannot be explained by the laws of nature alone. The broken symmetries around us may not allow us to deduce the underlying laws and a knowledge of those laws may not allow us to deduce the permitted outcomes. Indeed, the latter state of affairs is not uncommon in fundamental physics and is displayed by the current state of superstring theories. Theoretical physicists believe they have the laws (that is, the mathematical equations) but they are unable at present to deduce the outcomes of those laws (that is, find the solutions to those equations). This division of things into laws and outcomes reveals why it is that, while Theories of Everything may be necessary to understand the world we see around us, they are far from sufficient.

Of those complex outcomes of the laws of nature, much the most interesting are those that display what has become known as *organized complexity*. A selection of these are displayed in Figure 1, in terms of their size (gauged by information storage capacity) versus their ability to process information (the rate at which they can change one list of numbers into another list). Increasingly complex entities arise as we proceed up the diagonal, where increasing information storage capability grows hand in hand with the ability to transform that information into new forms. These complex systems are typified by the presence of feedback, self-organization and non-equilibrium behaviour. There might be no limit to the complexity of the entities that can exist farther and farther up the diagonal. Thus, for example, a complex phenomenon like high-temperature superconductivity (Gough 1991) which relies upon a very particular mixture of materials, brought together under

FIGURE 1: THE POWER AND INFORMATION STORAGE CAPACITY OF A VARIETY OF
COMPLEX NATURAL AND ARTIFICIAL STRUCTURES

(from Barrow 1992, adapted from Moravec 1988)

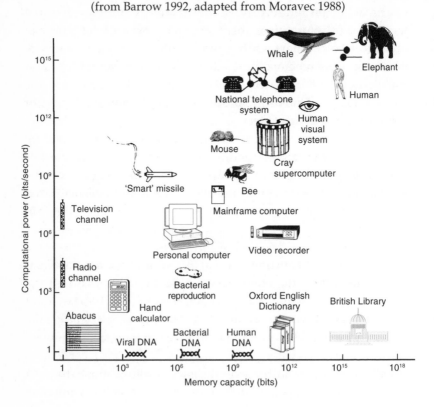

special conditions, might never have been manifested in the
universe before the right mixtures were made on Earth in 1987. It is
most unlikely that these mixtures occur naturally in the universe,
and so that variety of complexity called 'high-temperature superconductivity' relies upon that other complexity called 'intelligence'
to act as a catalyst and midwife for its creation. We might speculate
that there exist new types of 'law' or 'principle' which govern the
existence and evolution of complexity defined in some abstract
sense (Lloyd and Pagels 1988). These rules might be quite different
from the laws of the particle physicist and not be based upon
symmetry and invariance, but upon principles of logic and information processing. Perhaps the second law of thermodynamics is as

close as we have got to discovering this collection of rules that govern the development of order and disorder.

The defining characteristic of the structures in Figure 1 is that they are more than the sum of their parts. They are what they are, they display the behaviour that they do, not because they are made of atoms or molecules, but because of the way in which their constituents are organized (Davies 1987; Barrow 1991). It is the circuit diagram of the neutral network that is the root of its complex behaviour. The laws of electromagnetism alone are insufficient to explain the working of a brain. We need to know how it is wired up and interconnected. No Theory of Everything that the particle physicists supply us with is likely to shed any light upon the workings of the human brain or the nervous system of an elephant.

Design Arguments

Our distinction between the nature of laws and their outcomes is also an important guide to understanding the nature of traditional design arguments for the existence of God or of some other teleological imperative in the universe. Up until the late seventeenth century these arguments were characterized by their emphasis upon the fortuitous correlations between different outcomes of the laws of nature. For example, the construction of the human eye, the way in which animals appeared to be tailor-made for their habitats, and so forth. With the development of Newton's contributions to our understanding of the laws of mechanics and gravitation there emerged, with Newton's blessing, a new form of design argument – one which focused upon the mathematical form of the *laws* of nature rather than their outcomes. Thus, writers like Richard Bentley (1693) and William Paley (1802) would wax eloquently about the life-supporting consequences of the inverse-square law of gravity or the nature of light. These, eutaxiological design arguments are quite different to those based upon fortuitous outcomes and are immune from the impact of the theory of evolution by natural selection which undermined the basis of design arguments based upon outcomes. However, the unsound argument from outcomes retained its popular appeal because it was so easy to state and appeared common sense to most who heard it – surely the markings of animals were designed to provide them with just the right patterns of camouflage?! The eutaxiological argument from laws, by contrast, did not suffer from the same logical defects but required a sophisticated scientific knowledge in order to appreciate its basis and import. It is a little known fact that the second half of Paley's famous book *Natural Theology* (1802) was devoted to the design argument based upon Newtonian laws applied to astronomy, yet almost all commentators ignore this part of the book and concentrate upon the first part which advocates the naive design arguments based upon functionality in living things. Paley personally preferred these biological examples, stressing their closeness to observational science and their suitability for the use of argument by analogy, both features that were dear to his heart.

On the Edge of Chaos

Until quite recently, sciences like physics emphasized the deduction and confirmation of the laws and regularities of the world. The teaching of science was built around simple, soluble, problems that could be dealt with using pencil and paper. During the last decade, there has been a change. The advent of small, inexpensive, powerful computers with good interactive graphics has enabled large, complex, and disordered situations to be studied observationally – by looking at a computer monitor.

Experimental mathematics has been invented. A computer can be programmed to simulate the evolution of complicated systems, and their long-term behaviour observed, studied, modified, and replayed. One can even construct virtual realities obeying laws of nature that are not our own, and simply explore the consequences. By these means, the study of chaos and complexity has become a subculture within science. The study of the simple, exactly soluble, problems of science has been augmented by a growing appreciation of the vast complexity expected in situations where many competing influences are at work. Prime candidates are supplied by systems that evolve in their environment by natural selection, and, in so doing, modify those environments in complicated ways.

As our appreciation for the nuances of chaotic behaviour has matured by exposure to natural examples, novelties have emerged. Chaos and order have been found to coexist in a curious symbiosis. Imagine a very large egg-timer in which sand is falling, grain by grain, to create a growing sand-pile. The pile evolves in an erratic manner. Sandfalls of all sizes occur, and their effect is to maintain the overall gradient of the sand-pile in equilibrium, just on the verge of collapse. This self-sustaining process has been dubbed 'self-organizing criticality', by its discoverer, the Danish physicist, Per Bak (1991, 1996).

At a microscopic level, the fall of sand is chaotic. If there is nothing peculiar about the sand, which renders avalanches of one size more or less probable than others, then the frequency with which avalanches occur is proportional to some mathematical power of their size (the avalanches are said to be 'scale-free' processes). There are many natural systems – like earthquakes – and man-made ones – like stock market crashes – where a concatenation of local processes appear to combine to maintain a semblance of equilibrium in this way. Order develops on a large scale through the combination of many chaotic small-scale events that hover on the brink of instability. The sand-pile is always critically poised, and the next avalanche could be of any size; but the effect of the avalanches is to maintain a well-defined overall slope of sand. The course of life on planet Earth might even turn out to be described by such a picture. The chain of living creatures maintains an overall balance despite the constant impact of extinctions, changes of habitat, disease and disaster, that conspire to create local 'avalanches'. Occasional extinctions open up new niches, and allow diversity to flourish anew, until equilibrium is temporarily re-established. A picture of the living world poised in critical state, in which local chaos sustains global stability is nature's subtlest compromise. Complex adaptive systems thrive in the hinterland between the inflexibilities of determinism and the vagaries of chaos. There, they get the best of both worlds: out of chaos springs a wealth of alternatives for natural selection of sift; while the rudder of determinism sets a clear average course towards islands of stability.

We have introduced these ideas to highlight a change of scientific perspective on the world, which, for so long had emphasized the regularities and commonalities behind the appearances. This search for simplicity and order, under the assumption of common laws that link the present to the future and the past, has directed the development of science during the last 300 years. But complexity is not so simple. Only with the coming of new studies of the complex, by means provided by new technologies, has science appreciated the problem of explaining diversity, asymmetry and irregularity.

How Can You Predict Anything about a Chaotic System?

The standard folklore about chaotic systems is that they are unpredictable. They lead to out-of-control dinosaur parks and out-of-work meteorologists. There have also been attempts to exploit the unpredictability of chaotic systems as a way to allow a deity to act in the world without doing violence to free will or determinism (Polkinghorne 1995). However, before signing up to these offers it is important to appreciate more fully the nature of chaotic systems.

Classical (that is non-quantum mechanical) chaotic systems are not in any sense intrinsically random or unpredictable. They merely possess extreme sensitivity to ignorance. Any initial uncertainty in our knowledge of a chaotic system's state is rapidly amplified in time. This feature might make you think it hopeless even to try to use mathematics to describe a chaotic situation. We are never going to get the mathematical equations 100 per cent correct for something like weather – there is too much going on – so we will always end up being wildly inaccurate in our predictions. Remarkably, this need not happen. It has been found that whole collections of equations can possess shared properties regardless of their very specific form. If the problem we are studying is merely described by one of the equations in that broad class, then there will often be a simpler version of it which we can find that falls into the same class. It is easier to study and can be shown to have the same properties as the true equation. Mathematicians thus focus attention upon properties shared by *almost all* equations of a certain type.

Another important feature of chaotic systems is that, although they become unpredictable when you try to determine the future from a particular uncertain starting value, there may be a particular stable statistical spread of outcomes after a long time, regardless of how you started out. Finding the probability that a particular range of values will be visited is an important thing to know because most mathematical equations exhibit different degrees of sensitivity for different values of the control parameters governing the system.

The most important thing to appreciate from the existence of this stable statistical distribution is that often what really matters about a chaotic system in many practical situations is simply whether it possesses long-term stable average behaviour. As a simple example, take a volume of moving molecules (their average energy of motion determines what we called the gas 'temperature') and think of the individual molecules as little balls. The motion of any single molecule is chaotic. Each time it bounces off another molecule any uncertainty in its direction is amplified exponentially. This is something you can check for yourself by observing the collisions of marbles or snooker balls. In fact, the amplification in the angle of recoil, in the successive collisions of two identical spherical molecules, is well described by a bounce-rule like:

$$n + 1 = (d/r) \, n$$

where d is the average distance between collisions and r is the radius of the spheres. You can apply this rule to snooker balls as well as molecules. One knows from bitter experience that snooker or pool exhibits sensitive dependence on initial conditions: a slight miscue of the cue-ball produces a big miss! If the balls are bouncing around a frictionless snooker table in a perfect vacuum (otherwise they will just stop moving after one or two collisions) then we might typically have $d = 1$ metre and $r = 3$ cm. The growth in recoil angle uncertainty in the trajectory of a ball as it bounces off other balls is therefore pretty dramatic. Very soon the uncertainty in the angle grows larger than 360°. Chaos occurs whenever d is larger than r in systems like this. In fact, if you hit the ball as accurately as Heisenberg's quantum uncertainty principle allows any physical process to be determined by observation, then only about thirteen collisions are needed to amplify this uncertainty up to more than 360°!

The motions of gas molecules behave like a huge number of snooker balls bouncing off each other and the walls of their container (made of denser, more closely packed molecules). Unlike the snooker balls they won't slow down and stop. They give us a nice example of how some chaotic systems can have simple, predictable, average properties. All the motions are individually chaotic, just like the snooker balls, but we still have simple rules like Boyle's law governing the pressure P, volume V, and temperature T, of the gas molecules:

$$PV/T = constant$$

The velocities of the molecules will also tend to attain a particular probability distribution of values, called the Maxwell–Boltzmann distribution, after many collisions regardless of their initial values. The lesson of this simple example is that chaotic systems can have stable, predictable, long-term, average behaviours. However, it is often very difficult to predict when they will. The mathematical conditions that are generally sufficient to ensure it are very difficult to check in practice and much weaker conditions will usually suffice in particular situations. You usually just have to explore numerically and discover whether the computation of average quantities converges in a nice way or not.

These examples show that there is a form of the design argument that was never investigated by eighteenth- and nineteenth-century natural theologians. One thing that counts about a life-supporting complex environment is its long-term stability. In a dynamical situation that is being monitored by statistical sampling this amounts to the existence of long-term stable averages. Interestingly, the first person to appreciate the significance of this for the design argument was the nursing pioneer, Florence Nightingale. She was one of the earliest students of statistics and realized its importance as a tool to study which treatments and hygienic procedures were the most efficacious. But she also wrote about how it was the maintenance of stable ordering in the world over long periods that constituted the most interesting aspect of 'design', citing the continued balance between the number of males and females in the human population as a typical example.

Conclusions

We have seen how the issue of order versus complexity in nature is a subtle one that requires a clear distinction to be made between the laws of nature and their outcomes. At present all the fundamental laws of nature are based upon the preservation of a symmetry. The ongoing search for larger and larger embeddings of these symmetries into a single over-arching pattern constitutes the physicists' search for a so-called Theory of Everything. However, the outcomes of these symmetrical laws need not possess the symmetries of the laws themselves. They are much less symmetrical and far more complex. This process of symmetry breaking is the way in which nature manages to display innumerable complicated asymmetrical states yet be governed by a very small number of simple symmetrical laws. It enables order and disorder to coexist. We saw how this division between laws and outcomes allows one to understand why workers in different sciences take a different view of the nature of reality, according as to whether their work focuses upon finding laws or deducing outcomes. We also saw that this same division sheds light upon the two forms of design argument in natural theology. We focused in on some of the new developments in the study of complex outcomes, particularly chaos and self-organizing criticality, which reveal how complex systems are more than the sum of their parts. Finally, we looked more closely at the unpredictability of chaotic systems, stressing the importance of considering whether long-term stable average behaviour is present in the system. Many essential stable systems in nature are at root chaotic systems, yet there average behaviour changes slowly and very predictably.

References

BAILIN, D. 1989. 'Why Superstrings', *Contemporary Physics* 30, 237.

BAK, P. 1991. 'Self-organizing criticality', *Scientific American* 264, 46–53.

——. 1996. *How Nature Works?*, New York: Copernicus.

BARROW, J. D. 1988. *The World Within the World*, Oxford: Oxford University Press.

——. 1991. *Theories of Everything: the Quest for Ultimate Explanation*, Oxford: Oxford University Press.

——. 1992. *Pi in Sky: Counting, Thinking and Being*, Oxford: Oxford University Press.

——. 1995. *The Artful Universe*, Oxford: Oxford University Press.

——. 1998. *Impossibility: the Limits of Science and the Science of Limits*, Oxford: Oxford University Press.

BARROW, J. D. and TIPLER, F. J. 1986. *The Anthropic Cosmological Principle*, Oxford: Clarendon Press.

BENTLEY, R. 1693. *A Confutation of Atheism from the Origin and Frame of the World*, London.

CHAITIN, G. 1980. 'Randomness in Arithmetic', *Scientific American*, 253, 80.

——. 1987. *Algorithmic Information Theory*, Cambridge: Cambridge University Press.

DAVIES, P. C. W. 1987. *The Cosmic Blueprint*, London: Heinemann.

DAVIES, P. C. W. and BROWN, J. R. (eds). 1988. *Superstrings: A Theory of Everything*, Cambridge: Cambridge University Press.

GLEICK, J. 1987. *Chaos: Making a New Science*, New York: Viking.

GOUGH, C. 1991. 'Challenges of High Tc', *Physics World*, 259, 26.

GREEN, M. 1986. 'Superstrings', *Scientific American*, 259, 48.

GREEN, M., SCHWARZ, J. and WITTEN, E. 1987. *Superstring Theory* (2 vols), Cambridge: Cambridge University Press.

GREENE, B. 1999. *The Elegant Universe*, London: Jonathan Cape.

JANET, P. 1878. *Final Causes*, trans. W. Affleck, Edinburgh: T&T Clark.

LLOYD, S. and PAGELS, H. 1988. 'Complexity as Thermodynamics Depth', *Annals of Physics*, 188, 186.

MORAVEC, H. 1988. *Mind Children*, Harvard, Mass.: Harvard University Press.

PAGELS, H. 1985. *Perfect Symmetry*, London: Michael Joseph.

PALEY, W. 1802. *Natural Theology*, London.

POLKINGHORNE, J. 1995. 'The Metaphysics of Divine Action', in R. J. Russell, N. Murphy and A. R. Peacocke (eds), *Chaos and Complexity: Scientific Perspectives on Divine Action*, Vatican City: Vatican Observatory, and Berkeley, Cal.: CTNS.

STEWART, I. 1989. *Does God Play Dice: the Mathematics of Chaos*, Oxford: Blackwell.

WEINBERG, S. 1983. *The Discovery of Sub-Atomic Particles*, Basingstoke: W. H. Freeman.

ZEE, A. 1986. *Fearful Symmetry: The Search for Beauty in Modern Physics*, Basingstoke: Macmillan.

3

Revisiting Darwin on Order and Design

JOHN HEDLEY BROOKE

Introduction: The Invocation of Darwin

During his Cambridge days, when Darwin preferred beetles to books, he was preparing to become a priest in the Anglican Church. Late in life he looked back on his intentions and saw the irony: 'Considering how fiercely I have been attacked by the orthodox it seems ludicrous that I once intended to be a clergyman' (Barlow 1958, 57). The reasons why he was attacked by the orthodox have never been difficult to chart. By providing a naturalistic explanation for the emergence of human beings from ape-like ancestors, Darwin trod on religious sensibilities as well as common sentiment (Ellegard 1958). His theory of evolution by natural selection impinged on the question of biblical authority at a particularly sensitive time, when the even greater challenge of German historical criticism was being felt (Chadwick 1975). Among secular thinkers it became a common saying that Darwin had shown how man had risen not fallen. A related issue concerned the nature of divine activity in the world. Even among Darwin's scientific peers there were some who believed that the origin of living things, and especially of human beings, would remain beyond the limits of science (Gillespie 1979, 19–40). Darwin's demonstration that this need not be the case altered the picture, familiar from Milton's *Paradise Lost*, of a Creator who miraculously conjured new species into existence by divine fiat. Much of the mystery was removed from what Darwin once described as the 'mystery of mysteries', the origin of new organic forms.

But there is another reason why Darwin has become an icon of modern secular culture. This was his challenge to the argument for design (Dawkins 1986). In the English-speaking world organic structures and their marvellous adaptive functions had often been compared with the work of human craftsmanship, as in the design of a clock or delicate watch. Using such analogies it had seemed appropriate to speak of the wisdom and power of God, whose creatures far transcended anything we mortals could make. They had a beauty and complexity that could be deeply impressive (Brooke and Cantor 1998, 207–35). In earlier periods, and even in Darwin's own day, this argument for design had incorporated the latest science and had even been strengthened by it. In the second half of the seventeenth century the microscope had disclosed a new world of great beauty and wonderful precision in the minutest organic structures (Hooke 1665, 2, 4 and 162). Human art compared with nature's art was defective and inferior. Because the sciences had so often been seen as supportive of religious belief, the Darwinian challenge was especially poignant. Darwin never denied the appearance of design in the wonderful adaptations he studied; but his mechanism of natural selection enabled one to see, almost as in a conversion experience, how nature could counterfeit design. Was not the appearance of design an illusion?

To compound the problem yet again, the challenge was not only to William Paley's 'Watchmaker God'. Darwin's emphasis on divergent lines of evolution from common ancestors was represented by the image of a branching tree or branching coral. This made it more difficult to believe in the unfolding of a divine plan. The only diagram in the *Origin of Species* depicted this repeated forking and branching, enabling Darwinists with atheistic leanings to say that humans are the product of a process that did not have them in mind.

This is such a familiar story that it is not difficult to see why Darwin is so often invoked in contemporary discussions of order and design. The naive objection to evolutionary theory that a developing organ is only of any use when fully developed was answered by Darwin himself. Taking the most difficult case – the human eye – Darwin showed how our reason must conquer our imagination (Darwin [1859] 1950, 161). He admitted to a shiver up his spine every time he thought of the eye; yet he had an answer for his critics. It has been quoted many times, and recently by Kenneth Miller in his book *Finding Darwin's God* (Miller 1999, 135):

> . . . reason tells me, that if numerous gradations from a perfect and complex eye to one very imperfect and simple, each grade being useful to its possessor, can be shown to exist; if further, the eye does vary ever so slightly, and the variations be inherited, which is certainly the case; and if any variation or modification in the organ be ever useful to an animal under changing conditions of life, then the difficulty of believing that a perfect and complex eye could be formed by natural selection, though insuperable by our imagination, can hardly be considered real.

From that passage we learn something of Darwin's skill in the art of rhetoric. With honesty and candour he freely admits the difficulties that his theory has to face. He admits that there are phenomena, such as the caste system among neuter ants, that he once considered 'fatal' to his theory (Darwin [1859] 1950, 202–7). He then cleverly shows how every difficulty can be overcome. It is a brilliant strategy for pre-empting criticism. But his very honesty means that modern critics can invoke his name for their destructive purposes. A recent example would be Michael Behe who builds on Darwin's statement that 'if it could be demonstrated that any complex organ existed, which could not possibly have been formed by numerous, successive, slight modifications, my theory would absolutely break down'. Behe's argument is that the theory does break down because there is an irreducible complexity in the biochemistry of the cell (Behe 1996; Miller 1999, 140–7). Darwin can be invoked to make the historical point that when he advanced his theory, he was completely ignorant of the workings of the cell. And Darwin can be invoked again to make the philosophical point that his argument concerning gradations in the eye cannot work at the cellular level. The reason it cannot work, according to Behe, is that where there is irreducible complexity, there can be no continuum of functional precursors on which natural selection could work. Hence his readmission of design.

Because the name of Darwin is invoked in these current debates, it seems especially important to clarify what Darwin himself had to say about order and design. It may even be that there are certain (and instructive) respects in which Darwin failed to achieve clarity. He once told Asa Gray that on the question of design he was in a 'hopeless muddle' (F. Darwin 1887, ii, 353). He could not think that this wonderful universe was the product of chance alone; but nor could he believe with William Paley that the details of living structures had been purposely designed. There may even be something to learn from the fact that so great a scientific mind was pulled in both directions. In his maturity Darwin was inclined to think that the universe was the result of designed laws, but with the details left to chance. In a typical nuance he added that not even that idea really satisfied him (F. Darwin 1887, ii, 312). So let us revisit Darwin on order and design.

Darwin's Critique of Natural Theology

Superficially it may seem that there is nothing to add to conventional accounts. The Darwinian challenge to natural theology was perfectly expressed by Darwin himself in his *Autobiography*: 'the old argument from design in nature, as given by Paley, which formerly seemed to me so conclusive, fails, now that the law of natural selection has been discovered' (F. Darwin 1887, i, 309). Note that Darwin describes natural selection as a *law*, which, as we shall see, could itself have theological meanings. For many of the founders of modern science, the very existence of laws of nature presupposed a divine Legislator. But let us for the moment stay with the threat to Paley. The triumph of the Darwinian theory is so taken for granted in the modern world that we may forget how it can still be a profound existential experience when, as a child or adolescent, we suddenly see the world not as Paley saw it but through the eyes of Darwin. What we might have seen as God's well-adapted creatures suddenly become nature's products that happen to be the survivors of a long, tortuous, bloodstained process.

For Darwin himself the extent of the extinction was staggering; and if one had not been staggered one had not understood the theory (Brooke 1974, 88–9; F. Darwin 1887, ii, 218). The Princeton theologian Charles Hodge did understand the theory and in his book *What is Darwinism?* concluded that it was effectively atheistic, even if Darwin himself was not an atheist (Gregory 1986, 375–8). The theory of natural selection evacuated the concept of design as traditionally understood.

This transformation can be symbolized in many ways. One symbol might be the alteration Darwin made to his copy of William Whewell's *History of the Inductive Sciences*. Whewell had written that 'the use of every organ has been discovered by starting from the assumption that it must have some use'. As early as 1838, Darwin deleted the word 'use' and replaced it with the word 'relation' (Manier 1978). It was as if he was already wishing to block any inferences to design.

But I want to suggest now that this was neither the end nor the beginning of the story. If we focus exclusively on Darwin's critique of Paley we certainly miss the beginning. This is because Darwin's original fascination with adaptive structures derived in part from their high profile in works of natural theology. There is a sense in which Darwin was deeply indebted to the very literature that he later subverted (Ospovat 1980 and 1981). If we are to believe his later testimony, Paley was the one and only author he read in Cambridge who was of any real use to him (Barlow 1958, 59).

Darwin's Debt to Natural Theology

For some years there has existed a revisionist literature in which Darwin's debt to natural theology is explored (Brooke 1985). Through reading Paley he became fascinated by those intricate adaptations that he would eventually ascribe to natural selection. He also shared with Paley an aversion to any inherent vital force within nature that might be used, as it had been by the sceptical philosopher David Hume, as a possible explanation for natural order. It has therefore been claimed that the only universe in which natural selection could work was a universe that Darwin inherited and then stole from the natural theologians (Cannon 1961). Darwin acknowledged his debt to the argument of Malthus that, in the absence of checks, population growth would tend to outstrip food supply (Browne [1995] 1996, 385–90; La Vergata 1985). But this was also a debt to a work of natural theology. In his *Essay on Population* Malthus had been defending a God-given natural order against secular hopes of a social utopia which he considered purely visionary.

This revised view of Darwin's debt to natural theology was already in place forty years ago (Cannon 1961). There are, however, certain problems with it as the Darwin scholar David Kohn has indicated (Kohn 1989). Even to ask the question whether Darwin's science was indebted to natural theology can have the effect of polarizing opinion around extreme views: that the natural theology was of primary importance or that it was of no consequence whatever. In turn this can lead to a situation in which Darwin's other, more radical, cultural resources are neglected. There is now a newer form of revisionism, in which the young Darwin is revisited as a Romantic naturalist, entranced not so much by Paley's mechanistic anatomy as by an emotive response to the beauties of nature, enticed by the vision of tropical rain forests, intoxicated by what he read of Humboldt's travels, desolated when his ship could not land on Tenerife (Sloan 2001). This was the young man who would eventually respond so poetically when finally experiencing the Brazilian jungle for himself: 'Twiners entwining twiners, tresses like hair – beautiful lepidoptera – Silence, hosannah' (Desmond and Moore 1991, 122).

On this interpretation there was a sense in which the young Darwin found God *in* nature rather than deduced God's existence *from* it. This would be consistent with the view that he set out to reform natural theology rather than destroy it. Is this a defensible view?

Darwin and the Reform of Natural Theology

The reform that Darwin appears to have adopted had been suggested by the astronomer John Herschel and adopted in part by

William Whewell. The emphasis was to fall on beneficent laws of nature rather than on evidence for divine intervention. In Whewell's account design was to be seen in the propitious *combination* of laws that made life on earth possible. It was also to be seen in the very fact that the human mind could make scientific progress (Yeo 1979 and 1993; Fisch and Schaffer 1991). In Darwin's case, his earliest notebooks on the transmutation of species, compiled in the late 1830s, reveal him as a reformer rather than a destroyer of natural theology. In his first notebook he wrote that 'the Creator creates by laws'. In his second, he supposed that the end, the purpose, of the formation of species and genera is 'probably to add to [the] quantum of life possible with certain pre-existing laws'. When filling his third notebook he was still thinking that there were 'laws of harmony' in the system (Brooke 1985, 46–7).

Darwin's explicit reference to purposes, to ends in creation, suggests that at the time his theory took shape he did not consider that he was removing divine purposes. In the *Sketch* of his theory that he had prepared by 1842 he implied that the divine laws leading to 'death, famine, rapine, and the concealed war of nature' were justified. This was because they produced 'the highest good, which we can conceive, the creation of the higher animals' (Darwin 1842, 87). There were even the intimations of a theodicy – an attempt to rationalize the existence of pain, suffering and the uglier features of creation. Perhaps there was something to be gained by having the Creator create through intermediate processes? The deity did not then have to be directly responsible for what Darwin called a 'long succession of vile molluscous animals' (Brooke 1985, 47).

We should not dispense, then, with the notion of Darwin as a reformer of natural theology. It may help us to understand some of the early constraints on the theory of natural selection that have been noted in the literature. It turns out that there were at least two respects in which a legacy from natural theology shaped the content of Darwin's theory.

If the laws of nature were of divine origin, one might expect the perfecting of organic forms to reach levels of perfection that would preclude the continuing action of natural selection until environmental changes produced new pressures when (and only then) natural selection would cut in again. According to the Darwin scholar Dov Ospovat, this belief in perfect adaptation, which Darwin took from natural theology, constrained his theory for several years after its first formulation (Ospovat 1981). When Darwin later thought in terms of competition between relatively adapted forms rather than focusing on perfectly adapted forms the action of natural selection could be made continuous. It is an interesting example of how theological ideas, or their legacy, may shape scientific content.

Darwin freely admitted that another legacy from natural theology had shaped his thinking. In his *Descent of Man* there was a frank confession: 'I did not formerly consider sufficiently the existence of structures, which . . . are neither beneficial nor injurious; and this I believe to be one of the greatest oversights yet detected in my work.' And the reason for this oversight? 'I was not able to annul the influence of my former belief, then almost universal, that each species had been purposely created; and this led to my tacit assumption that every detail of structure, excepting rudiments, was of some special, though unrecognised service' (Darwin [1871] 1906, 92). In this passage Darwin corrects his former self and both Darwins have their disciples in current evolutionary debates. Darwin was recognizing a kind of homology between the utility of a structure required by natural theology and the utility required by natural selection. But by 1871 he had clearly had a change of mind. By then he had also had a change of heart on matters of faith. The loss of his Christian faith, probably completed in the early 1850s, had removed much of the motivation to seek evidence of design in nature. How do we account for this loss of faith?

Darwin's Loss of Faith in Design

What were Darwin's private religious beliefs and how did they change over time? One of the endings of the story is contained in a letter from Julia Wedgwood to Darwin's son Frank, where we come close to a genuinely private insight: 'Everyone who feels Religion infinitely the most important subject of human attention would be aware of a certain hostility towards it in [your father's] attitude, so far as it was revealed in private life.' She continued with the telling remark that he felt that 'he was confronting some influence that *adulterated the evidence of fact'* (Brooke 1985, 41). This makes it difficult to deny that some stages in Darwin's spiritual trajectory had been irreversible.

The standard view is one of an almost linear progression: from an early, if largely nominal, Christianity in which he would astonish members of the *Beagle* crew by quoting the Bible to settle a point of morality, to a deistic position when he wrote the *Origin*, to his later agnosticism (Mandelbaum 1958; Burch Brown 1986). This is a seductive formula because of another seemingly irreversible process at work: the loss of an aesthetic sensibility which Darwin, strikingly, declared had been 'intimately connected' with his belief in a deity (F. Darwin 1887, i, 311–12). Such a neat progression also chimes well with standard models of secularization. It has, however, become less clear that Darwin can be pigeonholed at each stage of his intellectual development. On reflection it would be surprising if the man who showed us that we cannot pigeonhole pigeons could be pigeonholed himself. Darwin would speak of fluctuations of belief (F. Darwin 1887, i, 304). He had flirted with a kind of materialism in 1838 when reflecting on the workings of the mind; but there is evidence that he drew back from the abyss (Kohn 1989, 224–9). If he became a monist there were precedents for that within Unitarian Christianity, notably in Joseph Priestley (Desmond and Moore 1991, 7–9; Brooke 1990). Late in life when he preferred to think of himself as an agnostic, he still insisted that there were moments of reflection when he deserved to be called a theist (F. Darwin 1887, i, 312–13). Even his atrophied sensibilities, according to a recent study, were perhaps not as deadened in later life as he made out (Sloan 2001).

Consequently we may need to revise our understanding of Darwin's loss of faith and the withering of his confidence in a designed universe. There were many cultural resources on which Darwin could draw for his eventual agnosticism (Manier 1978). These included the scepticism of Hume and the positivism of Comte. We have long known of his early doubts about sacred texts and how on the *Beagle* voyage he had come to doubt whether an intuitive sense of God was a universal human characteristic. His cousin, Hensleigh Wedgwood, had tried to persuade him that this sense of God differentiated us from the animals. But in a notebook entry Darwin differed. It was not so in a Fuegian or Australian (de Beer 1960, 111; Darwin [1871] 1906, 142–5).

A radical claim would be that Darwin's loss of faith had little or nothing to do with his science at all. It has even been proposed that the theory of natural selection was a working out in Darwin's science of a moral revolt against Christianity that had already occurred (Moore 1982). But it is difficult to make such a radical hypothesis stick. Darwin emphatically did make connections between scientific and extra-scientific reasons for his religious doubts. An extension of the domain of natural law did make miracles more incredible (Barlow 1958, 86). The extent of human suffering was what one might expect on the basis of natural selection but was deeply destructive of belief in a beneficent God (F. Darwin 1887, i, 311). There was an element of randomness in the appearance and distribution of variation that was difficult to square with divine control (Moore 1979, 273–6). And on top of this was the consideration that his wife Emma had expressed with concern just before their marriage – that the critical, questioning mentality appropriate to a life in science might encourage incredulity with regard to the simple verities of a Christian faith.

Having said that, the newest and most sensitive accounts of Darwin's doubts have stressed their extra-scientific origins: there was the death of his father in 1849 which forced him to confront once again that 'damnable doctrine' of eternal damnation. 'I can hardly see how anyone ought to wish Christianity to be true,' he would later write in a passage that his wife considered 'raw' and wished to have excised (Barlow 1958, 87). And excised because in her opinion Charles's characterization of Christian doctrine had become a caricature. On top of this, early in 1851, was the tragedy of his daughter Annie's death, which affected Darwin so deeply. How could a beneficent God allow so innocent a child to die? He spoke of the crucifixion of all his hopes (Desmond and Moore 1991, 375–87).

The crucial point is that many of the ingredients of Darwin's agnosticism sprang from incidents and insights that can easily be overlooked if the focus rests only on the content of his science. It would be easy to miss the impact of a revelation that came to him during his London years when he mixed with the circle of Harriet Martineau, who translated Comte into English. This was the realization that his friends could lead an exemplary moral life without embracing the Christian religion (Erskine 1987). In other words, Darwin's doubts about design should not be deduced directly from his science. Indeed when he tried to explain what he meant by natural selection he had sometimes described its action as analogous to the work of a Being who had foreseen the results of selective processes (Darwin 1842, 45; Darwin 1844, 114). On this analogy the details of evolution may not have been micro-managed but the main contours of its course could have been foreseen by a deity. If we ask why Darwin did not believe that the evolutionary process had been micro-managed, one answer would be that he had rejected a doctrine of Providence on other grounds. In his private correspondence with the American botanist Asa Gray, he pointed to fortuitous events in nature that he could not believe had been designed. When a particular man was struck by lightning under a particular tree he could not believe this particular event was the result of design. He conceded that many did believe it, but he could not (F. Darwin 1887, i, 315). We catch a glimpse here of another crucial point: whether one perceived design in nature or not largely depended on whether one had a prior faith.

Design as an Article of Faith

Darwin's correspondence with Asa Gray is the classic source for his ideas on design. Gray tried to argue that the variations on which natural selection worked were in some sense led in propitious directions. But Darwin could see no directionality in the process. He flattened Gray with a powerful analogy. Nature provides rocks and stones with which a man may build a house; but no one would argue that the rocks had been deposited to enable that particular house to be built. Darwin considered it was the same with respect to naturally occurring variations. They were random in their appearance and could not be said to arise with a prospective use in mind. The interesting point is that Gray was deflated. He conceded that he had no answer – except that the perception of design had to rest on faith (Moore 1979, 276). This was surely a decisive moment in the cultural history of the West. Darwin rejoiced in having won the argument (F. Darwin 1887, i, 314); yet for those with the eye of faith the very possibility that such wonderful structures could evolve was still testimony to a higher-level design.

At times, amid the fluctuations of his unbelief, a residual faith would surface in Darwin himself. 'I may say', he once wrote, 'that the impossibility of conceiving that this grand and wondrous universe, with our conscious selves, arose through chance, seems to me the chief argument for the existence of God.' But again he would add his agnostic qualification: whether this is an argument of real value, 'I have never been able to decide' (F. Darwin 1887, i, 306).

It was sometimes said by his contemporaries that Darwin was distinctive among the agnostics. He appeared to hold convictions; for example, that the universe could not be the result of chance alone. And agnostics were not supposed to have such convictions. What is distinctive in Darwin is that he would not trust his own convictions; and for a reason which did stem from his science: 'Can the mind of man, which has, as I fully believe, been developed from a mind as low as that possessed by the lowest animals, be trusted when it draws such grand conclusions?' (F. Darwin 1887, i, 313). Our minds, as products of evolution, were no longer so obviously designed for the resolution of metaphysical and theological questions – such questions as whether there might be intelligent design.

There is a topical question here. In a recent essay on epistemology, Alvin Plantinga has borrowed these Darwinian doubts and transferred them from the domain of metaphysics and theology where they belong to epistemological issues in general. He then seems to imply that Darwin's account of the evolution of the human mind should call into question its potency in the scientific sphere itself. Should the human mind place confidence in its scientific conclusions? Perhaps Darwin's confidence in his own scientific theory was misplaced? (Plantinga 1993, 219). I am unhappy with Plantinga's move because it seems to blur crucial distinctions that Darwin himself drew. Plantinga quotes a particular letter written late in life in order to justify his move. But in that same letter, written in July 1881, Darwin makes it perfectly clear that there is no warrant for doubting robust scientific achievements. He refers to 'laws as we now know them' – established laws such as the law of gravitation, the law of the conservation of energy and the laws associated with the atomic theory (F. Darwin 1887, i, 315–17). Darwin had such confidence in them that he supposed they must also apply to the moon. And he mentioned the moon because he wanted to dissociate laws from purpose: 'Would there be purpose', he asked, 'if the lowest organisms alone, destitute of consciousness existed in the moon?'

It is possible, as Neal Gillespie once suggested, that Darwin's confidence in his own science was underpinned by his residual theism (Gillespie 1979, 144–5). However, one of the interesting features of the letter that Plantinga quotes is that, if anything, it points away from that possibility. It also shows that in old age Darwin was happy with the idea that one could have order without design.

Order Without Design

Darwin writes that he can no longer digest the claim that the existence of natural laws implies purpose: 'I cannot see this. Not to mention that many expect that the several great laws will some day be found to follow inevitably from some one single law' (F. Darwin 1887, i, 315). I find this statement interesting in several respects. He has clearly moved away from the position we saw earlier in the transmutation notebooks. There he had written that the Creator creates through laws. In this letter to William Graham, the Creator has disappeared. Even more interesting perhaps is the argument he uses to question the inference to design. If the laws of nature can be shown to follow inevitably from some higher-level law, then their very inevitability destroys any reference to divine choice. In making this move Darwin seems to anticipate the similar move made by critics today who refuse to allow the anthropic coincidences to speak of design. Surely, it is often said, the coincidence between the parameters necessary for human life and their instantiation in our universe would cease to be remarkable if they could be subsumed under a higher law that made their appearance inevitable?

Darwin's argument is not of course proof against theism. The single higher-level law to which he refers could still be the product of a divine Will. Historically, the quest for unification to which he refers has often been grounded in a monotheism. For example, Newton's confidence in the universality of his gravitation law was linked in his own mind to the omnipresence of a single deity whose very omnipresence constituted space (Westfall 1971, 397). This raises the question whether the unity of the evolutionary process itself might still be made the basis of a design argument. Even Darwin's most assertive disciple, Thomas Henry Huxley, saw no reason why design should not have been incorporated in the primordial state of the universe (F. Darwin 1887, ii, 201–2).

Unification and Design

Darwin's great achievement was to bring unification and coherence to the explanation of disparate phenomena: the fossil record, the geographical distribution of species, and problems in taxonomy. If life had evolved from a few or just one original organism, could the evolutionary process be said to have a unity? I think this is an interesting question because religious thinkers who have been sympathetic to Darwin's theory have usually, and perhaps even unconsciously, spoken of a single unified process (Ward 1996, 92–3). Secular scientists with no theological investment have usually been more comfortable with references to evolutionary processes – in the plural.

Could Darwinism be reconciled with design through an appeal to unity in the natural order? Asa Gray certainly thought so. For Gray, evolutionary relationships show how biological species 'are all part of one system, realizations in nature . . . of the conception of

One Mind' (Larson 1998, 23). Another of Darwin's converts, Frederick Temple, who eventually became Archbishop of Canterbury, even suggested that the unity of the Darwinian process constituted a better argument for design than the concept of separate creation. The point was that Paley's argument from adaptation to design was vulnerable to Hume's objection that one might as well infer that several designers had been at work. However, as long as Darwinian evolution could be construed as a unified process in which potential was actualized in higher organic forms, the inference, Temple suggested, had to be to a single designer (Elder 1996, 158; Greene 1963, 66). In the eighteenth century Kant had indicated that the idea of the unity of nature was fundamental to physico-theology. In the nineteenth century, the idea of unity became embedded in affirmations of evolutionary progress and in substitute religions that promised human perfectibility. Darwin himself clung to that vision of perfectibility while recognizing that the forces of nature would one day operate against human interests:

> Believing as I do that man in the distant future will be a far more perfect creature than he now is, it is an intolerable thought that he and all other sentient beings are doomed to complete annihilation after such long-continued slow progress. (F. Darwin 1887, i, 312)

He was staring at the eventual exhaustion of the sun.

I believe there is more work to be done on concepts of unity among Darwinian thinkers. In Britain popular advocates of theistic evolution, such as the Duke of Argyll, wrote large books on the *Unity of Nature*. Participating in the post-Darwinian debates, Argyll observed that a separation of the sciences from theology had certainly occurred; but he added that an almost mystical sense of unity had become prevalent even among 'men over whom the idea of the personal agency of a living God has a much weaker hold' (Argyll [1866] 1884, 3–4). Argyll's argument for a designing Mind was premised on a unity discernible in nature. His evidence was drawn from what was known in all the physical sciences, and especially from the fact that the same forces appeared to operate through all space. The main issue, of course, was whether it was legitimate to privilege one main line of advancement in the evolutionary story – the line that led towards human personality (Lloyd Morgan, 1922–3).

It should be noted that there have been contexts in which theologians have been willing to reject the image of an overarching single, divine purpose behind the universe. This has usually been in response to human and natural disasters when the theodicy problem has proved particularly acute. To absorb such disasters within a single unified purpose can seem impossible. In his Gifford Lectures, William Temple had proclaimed a single process of progressive development, but writing in 1942, during the war, he found it impossible to be so optimistic. He conceded in his private correspondence that the world at that time was not a rational whole and, like a drama, its order would only become manifest at the end (Bowler 2001). Earlier in the twentieth century the Catholic modernist George Tyrrell tried to find words that made sense in the light of a terrible earthquake that had just shaken Italy. He could only make sense of such events by abandoning belief in a single divine purpose. His solution was to explore new metaphors for God's relation to the world. Nature became the canvas of a divine artist who was not tied to a single goal but whose work reflected a profusion of different purposes. As he put it himself:

> [The universe] teems with aims and meanings, although it has no one aim or meaning. It is like a great tree, that pushes out its branches, however and wherever it can, seeking to realize its whole nature . . . in every one of them, but aiming at no collective effort. This is its play, this its life, this is, if you will, its end. (Tyrrell 1914, 252–73)

It is striking that he chose the same tree metaphor that Darwin had used to depict his evolutionary process.

I have mentioned these two examples of Temple and Tyrell because they show the power of metaphors when trying to get a grip on the question of design. Temple redraws the world as a drama, Tyrrell redraws the world as an artist might. In conclusion, I should like to pause for a moment to consider the rhetorical force that such metaphors may carry.

Metaphors by Design?

When we speak of design in nature we are already using metaphorical language. In the popularization of science, other metaphors have become potent symbols of secular values: selfish genes would be one example; the 'blind watchmaker' another (Dawkins 1986 and 1989). I think we may need to become more sensitive both to the potency and the limitations of language in such cases. When Richard Dawkins describes human beings as 'robots' seemingly at the mercy of their selfish genes, the metaphors begin to take on a life of their own, over which an author may soon lose control (Brown 2000, 39–40). The metaphor of the blind watchmaker may be a convenient way of expressing Darwin's riposte to Paley, but as Holmes Rolston has argued in his recent Gifford Lectures the watchmaker analogy is itself inappropriate when considering the evolutionary pathways by which information content has increased. As he puts it:

> It is not that there is no 'watchmaker'; there is no 'watch'. Looking for one frames the problem the wrong way. There are species well adapted for problem solving, ever more informed in their self-actualizing. The watchmaker metaphor seems blind to the problem that here needs to be solved: that informationless matter-energy is a splendid information maker. (Rolston 1999, 370)

Rolston points out that the word 'design' nowhere occurs in Genesis and he mischievously adds that it rarely appears in his book, by design! (Rolston 1999, 369). But other metaphors do appear, and they too make an interesting study. Believing that there is a God at work in the world, he speaks of the way of nature as a *via dolorosa*; that the secret of life is that it is a 'passion play' (Rolston 1999, 369–70). Ultimately there may be no neutral language when it comes to the cultural meanings of science. In *Genes, Genesis and God*, Rolston declares that: 'Humans are *made* godward, to turn toward God, but shrink back and act like beasts.' There looks to be an importation of the Fall narrative here even in its redescription. The rhetorical force of metaphor is even more conspicuous in an example that has had much publicity: Darwin's 'black box'.

Back to the Black Box

When I was kindly invited to give this lecture, the hope was expressed that I might relate what we find in Darwin to the recent debate over Michael Behe's book. Here are four points that one might make, some of which Darwin might have made to Behe.

The 'black box' metaphor could be said to have had a short life because, in the very year that Behe published, an account was given in the *Journal of Molecular Evolution* of how the different components of the Krebs cycle could have evolved (Miller 1999, 150–2). In his recent book, *Finding Darwin's God*, Kenneth Miller also shows how Behe's prize example, the delicately balanced system that controls blood clotting, can also be explained by the selection of precursors. Conceptually, the crucial point is that the parts of what may appear to be an irreducibly complex system can be selected separately, adapted first to different biochemical functions that had nothing to do with the eventual chemistry of the complete cycle or system. With reference to the evolution of the Krebs cycle, Miller writes that 'just like the evolution of the cytochrome c oxidase protein pump, the individual parts of the complex machine appear first as functional units, which are then borrowed, loaned or stolen for other purposes' (Miller 1999, 151). I think one could show that Darwin fully recognized that integrated systems could have functions that had superseded the functions of precursors. In considering the transitions of organs, Darwin wrote, 'it is so important to bear in mind the probability of conversion from one function to another' (Darwin [1859] 1950, 164). In chapter six of the *Origin of Species* he discussed the swim bladder in fishes because it showed the 'highly important fact' that 'an organ originally constructed for one purpose, namely flotation, may be converted into one for a wholly different purpose, namely respiration' (Darwin [1859] 1950, 163–5).

Representatives of the new 'intelligent design' movement have also exposed themselves to the criticism that they are reluctant to say at which points there has to be some kind of divine injection to supplement otherwise natural processes (Van Till 1999, 667–82). In his critique, Miller asks Behe, 'When would his intelligent agent go to work, and what exactly would he do?' If Behe's answer is that his designer did all his work on the first ancient cell, not only is it hard to make sense of this in scientific terms (Miller 1999, 162–3) but it would also violate the sensibility we can see in Darwin and even in his clerical sympathizers. Was there not more wisdom in a God who could make all things make themselves?

Following on from this one might put another question to Behe: does he believe that it would *not* be within God's power to construct a mechanism by which seemingly irreducible systems could emerge from precursors? This is a question, surprisingly perhaps, that Darwin might have asked in the same theological terms. To deny that God was capable of producing 'every effect of every kind' through 'his most magnificent laws' was once described by Darwin as an act of profanity (Ospovat 1980, 183).

For Darwin the mistake would have involved more than a lapse into a god-of-the-gaps. There was also the theodicy problem on which he had reflected. The more closely the details of organic systems were ascribed to meticulous design, the greater the theological difficulty in explaining away the vile, the monstrous and the ugly. We must not forget there were works of nature that Darwin found horridly cruel and wasteful. What a book, he famously exclaimed, a devil's chaplain might write about them! (Desmond and Moore 1991, 441–50).

References

ARGYLL, DUKE OF. [1866] 1884. *The Unity of Nature*, London: Strahan.

BARLOW, NORA. 1958. *The Autobiography of Charles Darwin*, London: Collins.

BEHE, MICHAEL J. 1996. *Darwin's Black Box*, New York: Simon & Schuster.

BOWLER, PETER J. 2001. *Reconciliation Denied*, Chicago: University of Chicago Press.

BROOKE, JOHN. 1974. *Darwin in the Crisis of Evolution*, Milton Keynes: Open University Press.

BROOKE, JOHN. 1985. 'The Relations between Darwin's Science and his Religion', in John Durant (ed.), *Darwinism and Divinity*, Oxford: Blackwell, 40–75.

——. 1990. '"A Sower Went Forth": Joseph Priestley and the Ministry of Reform', in A. Truman Schwarz and John E. McEvoy (eds), *Motion Toward Perfection*, Boston: Skinner, 21–56.

——. 1991. *Science and Religion: Some Historical Perspectives*, Cambridge: Cambridge University Press.

BROOKE, JOHN and CANTOR, GEOFFREY. 1998. *Reconstructing Nature: The Engagement of Science and Religion*, Edinburgh: T&T Clark.

BROWN, ANDREW. 2000. *The Darwin Wars*, London: Simon & Schuster.

BROWNE, JANET. [1995] 1996. *Charles Darwin: Voyaging*. London: Pimlico.

BURCH BROWN, FRANK. 1986. 'The Evolution of Darwin's Theism', *Journal of the History of Biology* 19, 1–45.

CANNON, SUSAN F. 1961. 'The Bases of Darwin's Achievement: A Revaluation', *Victorian Studies* 5, 109–34.

CHADWICK, OWEN. 1975. *The Secularization of the European Mind in the Nineteenth Century*, Cambridge: Cambridge University Press.

DARWIN, CHARLES. 1842. *Sketch*, in Gavin de Beer (ed.), *Evolution by Natural Selection*, Cambridge: Cambridge University Press, 1958.

——. 1844. *Essay*, in Gavin de Beer (ed.), *Evolution by Natural Selection*, Cambridge: Cambridge University Press, 1958.

——. [1859] 1950. *On the Origin of Species*, London: Watts.

——. [1871] 1906. *The Descent of Man*, London: Murray.

DARWIN, FRANCIS. 1887. *The Life and Letters of Charles Darwin*, 3 vols, London: Murray.

DAWKINS, RICHARD. 1986. *The Blind Watchmaker*, Harmondsworth: Penguin.

——. 1989. *The Selfish Gene*, Harmondsworth: Penguin.

DE BEER, GAVIN. 1960. 'Darwin's Notebooks on Transmutation of Species', *Bulletin of the British Museum (Natural History)*, Historical Series, 2, parts 2–5.

Desmond, Adrian and Moore, James. 1991. *Darwin*, London: Michael Joseph.

Elder, Gregory P. 1996. *Chronic Vigour: Darwin, Anglicans, Catholics, and the Development of a Doctrine of Providential Evolution*, Lanham: University Press of America.

Erskine, Fiona. 1987. *Darwin in Context: The London Years*, PhD thesis, Open University.

Fisch, Menachem and Schaffer, Simon. 1991. *William Whewell: A Composite Portrait*, Oxford: Oxford University Press.

Gillespie, Neal C. 1979. *Charles Darwin and the Problem of Creation*, Chicago: University of Chicago Press.

Greene, John C. 1963. *Darwin and the Modern Worldview*, New York: Mentor.

Gregory, Frederick. 1986. 'The Impact of Darwinian Evolution on Protestant Theology in the Nineteenth Century', in David C. Lindberg and Ronald L. Numbers (eds), *God and Nature: Historical Essays on the Encounter between Christianity and Science*, Berkeley: University of California Press.

Hooke, Robert. 1665. *Micrographia*, London.

Kohn, David. 1989. 'Darwin's Ambiguity: The Secularization of Biological Meaning', *British Journal for the History of Science* 22, 215–39.

Larson, Edward J. 1998. *Summer for the Gods*, Cambridge, Mass.: Harvard University Press.

La Vergata, Antonello. 1985. 'Images of Darwin: A Historiographic Overview,' in David Kohn (ed.), *The Darwinian Heritage*, Princeton: Princeton University Press.

Lloyd Morgan, Conwy. 1922–3. *Emergent Evolution*, London: Williams & Norgate.

Mandelbaum, Maurice. 1958. 'Darwin's Religious Views', *Journal of the History of Ideas* 19, 363–78.

Manier, Edward. 1978. *The Young Darwin and his Cultural Circle*, Dordrecht and Boston: Reidel.

Miller, Kenneth. 1999. *Finding Darwin's God*, New York: HarperCollins.

MOORE, JAMES R. 1979. *The Post-Darwinian Controversies*, Cambridge: Cambridge University Press.

——. 1982. '1859 and All That: Remaking the Story of Evolution-and-Religion', in R. G. Chapman and C. T. Duval (eds), *Charles Darwin: A Centennial Commemorative*, Wellington: Nova Pacifica.

OSPOVAT, DOV. 1980. 'God and Natural Selection: The Darwinian Idea of Design', *Journal of the History of Biology* 13, 169–94.

——. 1981. *The Development of Darwin's Theory*, Cambridge: Cambridge University Press.

PLANTINGA, ALVIN. 1993. *Warrant and Proper Function*, New York and Oxford: Oxford University Press.

ROLSTON, HOLMES. 1999. *Genes, Genesis and God*, Cambridge: Cambridge University Press.

SLOAN, PHILLIP. 2001. Unpublished paper on Darwin's intellectual formation, to appear in *Osiris* 16.

TYRRELL, GEORGE. 1914. 'Divine Fecundity' in *Essays on Faith and Immortality*, London.

VAN TILL, HOWARD. 1999. 'Does "Intelligent Design" Have a Chance?', *Zygon* 34, 667–75.

WARD, KEITH. 1996. *God, Chance and Necessity*, Oxford: One World.

WESTFALL, RICHARD S. 1971. *Force in Newton's Physics*, London: Macdonald.

YEO, RICHARD R. 1979. 'William Whewell, Natural Theology and the Philosophy of Science in Mid Nineteenth Century Britain', *Annals of Science* 36, 493–516.

——. 1993. *Defining Science: William Whewell, Natural Knowledge and Public Debate in Early Victorian Britain*, Cambridge: Cambridge University Press.

4

Beyond the Balance: Theology in a Self-Organizing World

NIELS HENRIK GREGERSEN

Introduction

The question about how to relate fundamental physics and evolutionary theory has been a major issue of discussion since Darwin in 1859 introduced his theory of natural selection. With the so-called Neo-Darwinian Synthesis from the 1930s onwards, a working division was achieved whereby chemistry provided the background conditions for evolutionary processes, while the principles of variation and selection were supposed to provide a sufficient explanation of macroevolutionary processes (Mayr 1988, 8–23). In more recent years, however, insights from both applied mathematics and complexity theory seem to suggest that we need more than variation and selection to explain the intricate world of biology.

In what follows, I want first to discuss the reasons for thinking that the Neo-Darwinian Synthesis needs to be supplemented (though not replaced) by theories of chemical pathways and self-organization. In a second step, I lay out some reasons for believing that there is, after all, some directionality to evolution – propelled by universal chemical constraints on selection and the likewise universal tendency for collective behaviour. I shall here focus on

Per Bak's theory of self-organized complexity (SOC), on Gell-Mann's idea of complex adaptive systems (CAS), and on the theory of autopoietic (or self-producing) systems (APS). In the third and final part, I will then discuss how this grander picture of evolution might be appropriated from a theological perspective. How can we speak about a divine purpose in relation to a world which in some respects is fixed and balanced, regulated by natural law, yet in other aspects fluid and beyond the balance, poised at the critical boundaries between order and disorder?

Beyond the Balance: Complexity

Recently Edward O. Wilson, in *Consilience: The Unity of Knowledge*, wrote a sort of personal confession which shows the extent to which the so-called 'anthropic principle' (Barrow and Tipler [1986] 1996) has impressed also the mind of an agnostic. Wilson restates the assumption that Darwinian theory bluntly contradicts belief in a God who is genuinely concerned about the well-being of the creatures, but he adds that physics may in fact provide space for divine activity:

> On religion I lean toward deism but consider its proof largely a problem in astrophysics. The existence of a cosmological God who created the universe (as envisioned by deism) is possible and may eventually be settled, perhaps by forms of material evidence not yet imagined. Or the matter may be forever beyond human reach. In contrast, and of far greater importance to humanity, the existence of a biological God, one who directs organic evolution and intervenes in human affairs (as envisioned by theism) is increasingly contravened by biology and the brain sciences. (Wilson 1998, 263)

Even though biology, according to Wilson, renders unintelligible the notion of a God working *within* this world, we might still be in need of an explanation of the fundamental *framework* of cosmos. In a world governed by natural selection, however, there remains nothing for God to do, and given the merciless character of natural selection we could not even wish God to be its designer. In the view of Wilson and many others, the amount of evolutionary suffering constitutes a strong counter-argument against traditional belief in a loving and merciful God.

Wilson's argument thus comes down to a kind of reverse natural theology. Observe here the stunning continuity between pre-Darwinian and post-Darwinian modes of thought. According to William Paley's *Natural Theology*, what calls for a religious explanation is the delicate congruence between highly specified parts of bodies. 'Some degree therefore of complexity is necessary to render a subject fit for this species of argument,' he argued (Paley [1802] 1828, II, 147). Similarly Maynard Smith: '[t]he main task of any theory of evolution is to explain adaptive complexity, i.e. to explain the same facts which Paley used as evidence of a creator' (Maynard Smith 1969). Natural selection is here perceived as the scientific explanation that replaces obscure religious explanations, but the *explanandum*, the feature of complex adaptation, remains the same. No wonder, therefore, that Richard Dawkins can label himself a 'neo-Paleyist' (Dawkins 1983, 404).

But not only do Paley and the neo-Paleyists focus on the feature of adaptive complexity as their common point of reference; they also share the same sort of inferential thinking from world to God, albeit with different premises and thus with diverging conclusions. Since there exists a well-balanced order in the universe, God exists. So the natural theologies of Isaac Newton or William Paley. Since there exists a painful disorder in the world of biology, there exists no benevolent God. So Dawkins and Wilson.[1]

None of these inferences, however, are self-evident. It is indeed possible to affirm the orderliness of physical processes without invoking God as the ultimate source of natural laws. Likewise it is possible to acknowledge the relentlessness of natural selection in biological evolution without reaching negative religious conclusions

---

[1] In her analysis of the sociobiology debate Ullica Segerstråle points to the curious fact that Dawkins primarily understands religion as a misguided form of rational world-explanation: 'For Dawkins, religion occupies exactly the same slots as science in people's minds – a world-view slot – which is why they are in direct competition' (2000, 399f.). Science itself is supposed to be beyond myth. Wilson, by contrast, knows that religion is deeply and ineradicably rooted in our emotional structure: 'faith is in our bones'. Accordingly, the first construes science and religion as explanatory rivals, whereas the latter seeks to establish evolutionary theory as 'the best myth that we will ever have' (quotations in Segerstråle 2000, 402–3).

(Ruse 2001; Gregersen 2001a). More importantly, the world defies global characterizations such as cosmic Harmony or Struggle. Rather purposiveness and dysteleology seem to wander together. The forms of complexity characteristic for life processes tend to appear in regimes between states that are totally ordered, governed by regularity, and states devoid of any stable patterns (Solé and Goodwin 2000, 33). Pure repetition leads to trivial orders not capable of further evolution, whereas pure randomness leads nowhere since no self-sustaining structures can be built up. It is in the delicate balance between order and disorder that those structures begin to emerge that are capable of further development. Local fluctuations are attuned to one another and form into semi-stable orders at the more global level. We thus need both variability (disorder) and regularities (order) to enable complex patterns to emerge, to propagate and further evolve.

Complexity research is the attempt to describe the general formative principles at work on the critical boundaries between physics and biology. The combined insights from the thermo-dynamical school of evolutionary theory (Prigogine and Stengers 1984; Wicken 1987) and the new paradigm of complexity theory (Kauffman 1993; 2000, chs 3–4) might suggest that Darwinism will have to be supplemented. Life seems to organize itself beyond the balance, and the principle of selection is not quite as 'omnipotent' as claimed by the champion of neo-Darwinian theory, August Weissmann, at the turn of the twentieth century.[2] Rather the processes of variation and selection seem more and more to be embedded in a chemical world that heavily constrains what is viable in the game of life. After all, evolution presupposes laws and constants of nature that historically precede biological evolution

---

[2] David J. Depew and Bruce H. Weber trace neo-Darwinism back to the rejection of Lamarckism by the German biologist Weismann, a follower of Ernst Haechel's materialistic monism. By denying the inheritance of acquired traits ('Weismann's barrier') and by professing the 'omnipotence' (*Allmacht*) of selection in explaining both ontogeny and phylogeny, neo-Darwinism departed from Darwin's own causal pluralism and broke with the developmental tradition within English and particularly American Darwinism (Depew and Weber 1996, 187f.; 516–17).

by some 10 billion years. Certainly, one secret of biology resides in the intricate structure of the DNA, but another secret is found in the mathematical principles of economy that has guided evolution and channelled the organization of chemical compounds long before the emergence of DNA-based reproduction (Stewart [1998] 1999). If we cannot explain evolutionary processes with variation and selection alone, a grander picture of evolution emerges, which also offers new possibilities for a theological understanding of evolution.

I. Maxwell's Intuition and the Limits of a Universal Darwinism

In 1873, in his address to the British Association, James Clerk Maxwell made the following uncompromising statement:

> No theory of evolution can be formed to account for the similarity of molecules, for evolution necessarily implies continuous change, and the molecule is incapable of growth or decay, of generation or destruction. (1890, II, 376, quoted from Barrow/Tipler 1998, 88)

Like many other physicists of his time (including an authority such as Lord Kelvin), Maxwell thereby pointed to the physico-chemical basis of evolutionary processes – a basis which cannot be accounted for in terms of Darwinian evolution. Despite its reactionary undertone, there is an almost prophetic intuition in Maxwell's opposition to a universalization of evolutionary thinking. Still today we can provide a fully satisfying picture of, say, the regularities of the periodic system without even mentioning the Darwinian principles of selection, variation and reproduction. While the kingdom of life is evolutionary, the world of chemistry is a 'periodic Kingdom', as phrased by P. W. Atkins (1995).

Clearly the boundary between chemistry and macroevolutionary theory no longer appears as strong as in the days of Maxwell and Kelvin. With the inclusion of Mendel's genetic theory into Darwin's theory of natural selection, the evolutionary synthesis (developed between 1930 and 1950) was able to provide a general statistical framework for explaining how minor variations, arising at random in the biochemical genome of a living organism, gradually, through selection processes, lead to significant changes at the population level.[3]

But still today the relation between the physical and biological is far from settled. As early as 1990 Peter Schuster (one of the close collaborators of Manfred Eigen) pointed this out in his general address to the ESSSAT conference in Geneva:

> How much natural selection dominates biological evolution is still a matter of debate among biologists. The neo-Darwinian or functionalist's view considers external or environmental influences as the relevant driving force for biological evolution, whereas the structuralists assign more weight to internal evolutionary forces and constraints. (Schuster 1992, 55)

This discussion between structuralists and functionalists revolves around the question of whether evolution is guided by internal propensities or is a result of external events, be they a matter of historical contingencies or the results of selection processes. Not least the emergence of the field of complexity research within the last ten years has further strengthened the structuralist position by studying how specific pathways are preferred in evolution and constrain the array of evolutionary possibilities. The point is not that the functional constraints of selection do not play a significant role in evolution but that the principle of selection is not able to explain *all* relevant data about evolution and all types of evolution. Darwinism, with its emphasis on 'functional constraints', would have to be supplemented by the acknowledgement of 'structural constraints'.

---

[3] As defined in note 2, the term 'neo-Darwinism' has a wider scope than the term 'evolutionary synthesis'. But also this latter term has several shades of meaning (Depew and Weber 299–303). It generally designates the synthesis between Medelianism and Darwinism achieved in the 1930s by Ronald Fisher, Sewall Wright and others, but the term has also (especially in Julian Huxley's *Evolution: The Modern Synthesis* from 1942) been used to refer to the unification of all the biological disciplines in the framework of population genetics. Finally the term can be defined not so much via the method of statistical population genetics as through its conclusions, especially the revolutionary 'population thinking' (so Ernst Mayr). For our subsequent discussion it is important to note Depew and Weber's point that modern Darwinism, as a historic and probabilistic science, 'does not fit well with models of scientific method, or criteria for successful science, devised for physics' (302).

If this is so, the explanatory monism of a globalized selection theory should perhaps give way to an *explanatory pluralism*. The term 'universal Darwinism' has been coined by Richard Dawkins for the position that Darwinism (defined as natural selection working on random variation) is 'the only theory that *can* adequately account for the phenomena that we associate with life', namely the 'adaptive complexity' so characteristic for the presence of life. According to Dawkins, Darwinism is *not* a local theory confined to explaining life on planet Earth; it is a *universal* theory explaining the evolution of adaptive life wherever and whenever. Let us call this the postulate of universality. Furthermore Dawkins claims that gradual variation plus selection is the *only naturalistic* way to explain adaptive complexity (1983, 403f.; 412; 430–3). Let us call this the postulate of explanatory exclusivity. Ruled out thereby is Lamarckism (which actually might apply to the level of cultural evolution where learning processes are crucial carriers of evolution). Likewise Dawkins also a priori dismisses ideas of 'built-in capacity for, or drive toward, increasing perfection' as 'obviously mystical' (1983, 406).

The problem with Dawkins' 'universal Darwinism' is in my view not so much his postulate of universality, but his postulate of explanatory monism. Theoretical biology is indeed open to adopt an explanatory pluralism which is sensitive to the *different levels of explanation* (genes, organisms, groups, and ecosystems).[4] Further-more, an explanatory pluralism is open to the possibility that the structuring causes behind evolution might be *different in kind*: some traits of biological organism may be accounted for in terms of contingent events (such as the extinction of the dinosaurs by meteors), other traits in terms of selection (such as the extinction of the Neanderthals), and yet other events in terms of chemical information (such as the symmetry of the building plates of organisms). I believe it is fair to say that in the ten years since Peter Schuster referred to the internal debate among biologists between functionalism and structuralism, the universalization of selection

---

[4] For a pluralist conception of Darwinism, see the advocacy of Eliot Sober and David Sloan Wilson (1998, 329–37).

has been challenged from several quarters. From the side of physical chemistry it is argued that the limits within which selection can work are more narrow than hitherto acknowledged (a viewpoint that reminds of Maxwell's intuition). From the side of the complexity sciences, however, it is claimed that there is a greater richness to evolution than allowed for in the standard version of Darwinism (Kauffman 1995; 2000). Let us begin by focusing on the chemical constraints on natural selection, before we, in section II, focus on complexity studies.

Constraints on Evolution by the Mathematical Economy of Physics

The basic idea that the processes of selection take place within a narrow range of chemically viable routes is far from new. At the turn of the twentieth century we find a strong school within German morphology which argued that certain development lineages were imprinted on matter (perhaps endowed by God). At the end of the nineteenth century, when Darwinism had not yet adopted Gregor Mendel's genetic theory, this theory was strong, and Darwinism was in the defence as a declining paradigm (Bowler [1983] 1999).

The Scottish biologist D'Arcy Wentworth Thompson renewed this school of morphology while divesting it from its idealistic underpinnings. He wanted to give the study of morphology a firm mathematical basis. His major work, *On Growth and Form* from 1916 has therefore experienced a true renaissance over the last years (see, e.g. Kauffman 1993, 557f.; Ian Stewart 1999; Ball 1999). According to D'Arcy Thompson, zoologists have been much too reluctant in invoking the aid of physics and mathematics in biological explanation:

> Cell and tissue, shell and bone, leaf and flower, are so many portions of matter, and it is in obedience to the laws of physics that their particles have been moved, moulded and conformed. They are no exceptions to the rule that theos aei geometrei [God always geometrises]. ([1916] 1942, 10)

Without at all questioning the fact of gradual evolution, D'Arcy Thompson pointed out that Darwin often invoked selection pressures to account for biological phenomena which simply result from the mathematical properties of matter. The hexagonal structure of the bee's cells, for instance, should not be seen as caused by a selection in which the original circular shape of bee cells are becoming hexagonal as a result of the antagonistic pressures of the other cells. There has never been anything like a 'struggle for space' between bee cells. Rather, hexagonal configurations are spontaneously formed when semi-fluid stuff is warmed up, whatever the source of warmth may be ([1916] 1942, 537–43). Similarly, the spiral shape of horns among sheep and goats is to be seen as the simple result of the torsion of elastic bodies where the growth rate is not exactly homogenous on all sides. The shape of the horns here follows the general rules of logarithmic spirals; only when the growth rate is identical on all sides will the horns be straight. Again the point is that the spirals of the horns should not be seen as a response to external stimuli, nor to the selectionist advantages of spiral horns, but to the internal 'formal' causes of matter: 'the point at issue being no other than whether direct physical causation, or the Darwinian concept of fitness or adaptation, should be invoked as an "explanation" of biological phenomena' ([1916] 1942, 888).

Since D'Arcy Thompson many others have followed in his footsteps. Especially, the theoretical biologist Brian C. Goodwin has extended D'Arcy Thompson's vision to include not only the morphology of individual organisms, but also the evolution of distinct species. There may be 'generative laws' of a mathematical nature that pervade the living world of biology. As stated by Goodwin:

> A possible consequence of this is that the hierarchical taxonomies of organisms arise not from dichotomous branching due to the historical winnowing process of natural selection, producing a discrete spectrum from an initial continuum, but from the intrinsic discontinuities that separate natural kinds generated by dynamical laws. If this is the case, then biological taxonomy has a basis not in the contingencies of history, but in the rational [mathematical, NHG] dynamics of biological organization. (1992, 213)

If there is only the slightest truth in this view, the universal features of biochemistry (e.g. symmetry of bodies, the general shape of cells and tissues) depend on thermodynamics plus basic chemistry. Only the specifics of gene sequences, etc. are rooted in the tinkering of microevolutionary processes. Many features of living systems do not happen as a result of selection, but in spite of selection!

In *Life's Other Secret*, the mathematician Ian Stewart has also reminded us of the obvious fact that the genes presuppose quite a few ready-made inorganic patterns, including the geometry of the molecules and their interaction. The genetic code may be one secret of life, but the other is the built-in mathematics of nature. One example is the the six-fold structure that we see in snowflakes, and in many other organic structures (including the aforementioned bees-wax). This structure has not been selected as a result of an evolutionary arms race; it is simply given by nature's general preference for economic arrangements. Mathematics thus places stringent limits on the architectural building plates of living systems (Stewart 1999, 30–4; 66). In the same vein, Philip Ball (a former editor of *Nature*) refers to numerous pattern formations that depend on the physical structure of the molecular world, such as bubbles, waves, spirals and branchings. According to Ball, form does not always follow function, for the palette of nature is not infinite:

> Once you start to ask the 'how?' of mechanism, you are up against the rules of physics, chemistry and mechanics, and the question becomes not just 'is the form successful?' but 'is it physically possible?' (Ball 1999, 6)

Nature's *Self-Made Tapestry* (the title of Ball's book) allows for some forms, not for others. Nature favours some patterns, whereas other demand very specific conditions. Also the principle of varia-tion is constrained by mathematics.

It should be noted that these findings neither question a gradualist view of evolution nor dispute that variation and natural selection play a key role in evolution. The point is *not* that the evolutionary synthesis is fundamentally wrong (as it has been claimed by Michael Behe, and other proponents of the anti-naturalist design theory). The point is much more modest, namely that the principles of variation and selection are not omnipotent, since evolution is also driven by internal generative principles. From the perspective of chemistry there seems to be less contingency and more rigidity to evolution than allowed for by the received view of the neo-Darwinian paradigm. The principles of variation, selection and differential reproduction depend on a pre-established framework. However, the scientific jury is still out concerning the question of how much necessity, and how much contingency there is in biological evolution.

Chance or Convergence: Gould versus Morris

The explanatory monism of selectionism is also questioned from the side of palaeontologists within the camp of evolutionary biology. Stephen Jay Gould thus argues that the 'modern synthesis is incomplete' though 'not incorrect' (1982, 382). According to Gould, microevolutionary genetics cannot account for the highly contingent evolutionary lineages at the macroevolutionary level. If we were able to rerun the tape of evolution (as Gould argues in his famous analogy), we would see in front of us quite another world filled out by other creatures than present-day arthropods and vertebrates; most likely we would not be here to watch the video tape since the evolution of humans is overwhelmingly improbable (Gould 1989, ch. 1). In Gould's view, the world we see around us is thus a large-scale result of historical contingencies.

Other palaeontologists, however, point to the *convergence* of the evolutionary trajectories. The Cambridge palaeontologist Conway Morris (ironically an authority on the very fossil records of the Burgess Shale on which Gould builds his argument) argues that even though contingency does play a role in determining the origin and survival of specific lineages, there is an overall trend towards the emergence of general properties such as feeling and consciousness. After all, intelligence has dawned both among mammals and among molluscs (in the octopus). We also find the same camera-like eye in the octopus and mammals, even though their lines departed from each other some half-billion years ago, long before eyes had developed. Similarly, the compound eyes (well-known from the insects) have developed independently at least three times (Morris 2003, forthcoming). In this light, not every evolutionary option is also chemically achievable:

> Put simply, contingency is inevitable, but unremarkable. It need not provoke discussion, because it matters not. There are not an unlimited ways of doing something. For all its exuberance, the forms of life are restricted and channelled. (Morris 1999, 13)

Morris' argument for the ubiquity of evolutionary convergence is not only provided by the fact that, for example, movability, feeling, perception and consciousness are advantageous in the game of selection. Morris also points to the fact that a common genetic structure underlies very different building plates and phenotypical expressions among animals. Much research has been done on the class of genes called the Hox genes which control the embryological development. In this case there is a direct match between front and back of both the genotype and its phenotypical expression in the body plan of the animal. A fruit fly and a mouse are indeed different creatures, but both the symmetry of their body plans and the sequence of their body parts from front to end seem to be uniquely determined by the sequence of the Hox gene (Morris 1999, 147–53).

No doubt both Gould and Morris are working within the broad paradigm of the evolutionary synthesis (as defined in note 3). However, they are both challenging the standard Darwinian assumption that microevolutionary processes of selection and adaption provide a sufficient explanation of macroevolutionary processes. The omnipotence of selection is thus under pressure from two sides, from the 'historical' side of macroevolution (Gould) and from the side of 'law-like' biochemistry (Morris). None of these positions denies the central explanatory role of selection, but they do question the postulate of explanatory monism that we find in standard, neo-Darwinism accounts.[5] What are at stake in the debate between Gould and Morris, however, are not only rival explanatory models of evolution but also different world-views – the meta-

---

[5] Francisco J. Ayala (1983, 392–400) has offered a clear neo-Darwinian response to the critique of S.J. Gould. Ayala admits that macroevolutionary theories (like punctuated equilibrium, or gradualism) cannot be *derived* from micro-evolutionary knowledge. Thus, there is a certain autonomy of macro-evolutionary *theory*. However, he also points out that (a) the natural *entities and processes* of population genetics and macroevolutionary theory are identical so that the living organisms in which mutation and natural selection operate are

physics of ultimate chance in Gould versus a potentially theistic interpretation of evolution in Morris. A clash of world-views seems to energize not only the 'Darwin industry' of popular literature, but also divergent theoretical research programmes.[6] But since the scientific jury about the weighting of historical accidents, selection pressures and underlying chemistry is far from settled, theology would be wise in suspending judgement. Theology should neither buy into a universalized selectionism, nor fight against selection and contingency as if these features were in principle devastating for a theological interpretation of evolution.[7] As will become evident below, I think that the strongest theological position will consist in a combinatory approach in which chance and selection are seen as processes that are always teamed within a wider framework of nature. The world is a hospitable place, because matter is ready-made for life and sentience. On the other hand, life and sentience develop under the condition of learning processes instigated by coincidences and memorized via natural selection.

II. How Evolution is Enriched by the Complex World of Co-evolution

Unlike traditional biochemistry, complexity theory deals with natural systems of such size, variability, and fuzziness that one cannot hope to use an analytical method that singles out very specific features and causal routes. Only a general model of the

---

the same, which make up the higher taxa studied in macroevolution. Against this background, he further argues that (b) population genetics can *account for* the macroevolutionary events since the latter are consistent with the former. While this latter 'consistency claim' as I would call it, is uncontroversial (and so also the claim that population genetics has important explanatory power with respect to macroevolution), Ayala occasionally also raises a 'sufficiency claim' of popula-tion genetics: 'the microevolutionary processes identified by population geneticists (mutation, random drift, natural selection) are sufficient [!] to account for the morphological changes and other macroevolutionary phenomena observed in higher taxa' (1983, 392, cf. 393–6). This sufficiency claim epitomizes the standard neo-Darwinian position which is under attack today.

6 See also Sterelny 2001 (on Dawkins versus Gould).

7 On God and chance, see Bartholomew (1984), and my own stance in Gregersen (1997). On theodicy and selection, see Haught (2000) and Gregersen (2001a).

systems as wholes is attainable. Accordingly, the vision of complexity theory is not to represent, or mirror, particular objects of the world.[8] The vision is to model *possible worlds*. A complexity theory of evolution, for example, will not rest content with a historical account of the long and detailed route of evolution 'from molecule to man' (as it has been phrased). Complexity theories would ask about possible evolutionary scenarios, and aim to model different ways that might have lead from molecules to highly organized organisms – on planet Earth or elsewhere in the world.

The Theory of Self-Organized Criticality (SOC)

A groundbreaking example of complexity studies is the theory of self-organized criticality by Per Bak and colleagues at the Brookhaven National Laboratory, Long Island, and at the Niels Bohr Institute in Copenhagen.[9] Interestingly, SOC combines standard metaphysical assumptions of a *constitutive materialism* (that is, there exist no other constituents in the world of nature than material particles) with a *holism*, since global properties emerge in nature as a consequence of the concerted co-operativity of many elements within large systems (Bak 1997, 2, 155f.). Nonetheless, SOC demonstrates that complexity should not be defined as something which escapes law-like formulations. On the contrary, the lesson to be learnt is that even extremely simple physical laws can be responsible for the production of highly complex structures. Complexity is not without laws, nor without data.

In his book *How Nature Works: The Science of Self-Organized Criticality* (1997), Per Bak takes his point of departure in the observation of simple and empirically confirmed regularities (such as the Gutenberg–Richter law of earthquakes). Likewise, he has been able to find fairly good correlations between computer models and available empirical data. Thus many physical systems display the phenomenon of '1/f noise', that is a catastrophic variability over

---

[8] On the general nature of complexity studies, see for example, Waldrop (1996); Bak (1997, 9ff.); or (ed.) Gregersen (2002).

[9] Bak 1997. See also P. Bak, C. Tang and K. Wiesenfeld (1987); P. Bak, K. Chen and M. Creutz (1989); and P. Bak and K. Chen (1991).

short time (such as minutes or hours) and only very slow variation over long time (years or epochs). Light from quasars, the flow of the river of the Nile, the frequency of earthquakes, the formation of sand-piles (and maybe even stock-rates) are of this kind. Systems in equilibrium do not display these features, nor do systems in non-stable forms such as clouds. Even chaotic systems display the '1/f noise' only on the critical points where the transition to chaos occurs.

The basic model for the theory of self-organized criticality is a sand-pile, a very simple example of self-organized complexity (see Bak 1997, ch. 3). Imagine a flat table onto which sand is added, one grain at a time. The flat state exemplifies the equilibrium state, the adding of sand the kinetic energy input. In the beginning, the grains of sand will be placed more or less where they landed. However, as more grains are continuously added, the sand-pile gets steeper, and small sandslides as well as bigger avalanches begin to occur. At this stage, the addition of single grains may produce local disturbances in the pile, but nothing dramatic happens. At this point, there is not yet any global communication between the many individual grains of sand.

However, as the pile builds up, it comes into a state where single grains are more likely to cause other grains to topple further down the pyramid and produce major avalanches. The pile is now in a *critical state* where the shape of the pile may dramatically change its form. Later on again, the slope reaches a more stable energetic state, because the grains of sand added to the top of the pile are balanced on average by the grains that are falling off the edges. This is called a *stationary state*. At this point, one can speak of a 'communication throughout the whole system' – between sand added to the pile at the top and the grains falling off along the edges (Bak 1997, 51). The emergent dynamic of the sand-pile begins to acquire global features. Thus the dynamic of the pile can no longer be understood from the perspective of the properties of the individual grains. However, from time to time, the system will relapse into the previous critical state with system-wide avalanches which evidently also impact the sand-pile system as a whole. This is the *catastrophic state* of the system.

The sand-pile is an example of a self-organized criticality in the following meanings:

(1) SOC is *self*-organized in so far as it is not tuned by an external designer. The model is robust, because the same dynamics can be triggered by many different ways of adding the grains. Thus, the sand-pile is not a mere result of external environmental influences. The system has 'many degrees of freedom' (Bak 1997, 51), but what happens with the pile at t1908 is of course co-determined by what has happened in the period between t1 and t1907. The slow building up of the 'identity' of the system is pivotal to the emergence of these sorts of systems.

(2) SOC is self-*organized* in so far as the system displays a global dynamic in its recurrent flow between stationary and critical states. The same dynamic is responsible both for the stationary and for the critical states of the system.

(3) *Critical* is the state, because the sand-pile (which is an open system dissipated by energy) recurrently (but not periodically) makes transitions between states of rest and states of catastrophe. Also systems like these sometimes reach an upper limit beyond which they cannot develop.

Some of the most interesting features of SOC are as follows:

• The pile shows an *un-periodic behaviour* though with *recurrent* features. A sand-pile likens punctuated equilibrium, where states of stasis are interrupted by major domino effects.

• The pile behaves as one ever-changing system, whose physical appearance looks dramatically different from one situation to another, but the states are always spurred by a *comprehensive, underlying dynamics*.

• This dynamics can only be understood as an *emergent property* of the sand-pile as a whole. It is not possible to give a detailed account of the moves of the individual grains. 'In a critical state, the sand-pile is the functional unit, not the single grains of sand. No reductionist approach makes sense' (Bak 1997, 60).

- Most importantly, however, the dynamics of the complex system of the sand-pile can be shown to follow a general pattern which can be formulated as a 'power law' as simple as follows:

$$N(s) = s^{-t}$$

where N stands for the number of avalanches, (s) for their sizes, and t is the exponent which for the sand-pile is 1.1, but differs from one system to another.

- The exponential law explains the *overall distribution* of stationary and catastrophic states, but the law does not permit any precise prediction about the where and when of the avalanches.

The sand-pile model is of course extremely simple.[10] However the achievement of the sand-pile model is that it is paradigmatic for other cases of self-organized criticality. The exponential 'power laws' of SOC have proven their applicability to many other non-equilibrium and non-periodic systems such as earthquakes, the extinction of species, forest fires, measles epidemics, neuronal states of the human brain, cotton prices and even traffic jams. Indeed, the logarithmic function (t) differs from case to case, but the general algorithmic relations remain the same.

SOC illuminates the interrelation between order and disorder. Earthquakes are one example that we touched upon. Earthquakes are usually taken to be signs of the arbitrariness, and the whole genre of Early Modern theodicies, beginning with Leibniz' *Essais de Théodicé* of 1710, were instigated by the great earthquakes in Lisboa in 1531 and 1755. We know today that earthquakes are caused by movements of the continental plates. But why are some earthquakes enormous while other ones are small? Seen from a phenomenological perspective, earthquakes happen at random. No pattern emerges to the natural eye. However, we have the Gutenberg–Richter law, a statistical scaling law that states the

[10] The sand-pile, as described above, is a physical model of SOC. Bak and colleagues have also made simpler computer models based on individual agents ('grains') moving in a two- or three-dimensional lattices. This will not be discussed here.

relation between small and major earthquakes: if there are fifty earthquakes each year of magnitude 2 on the Richter scale, there are only five of magnitude 3 (which are ten times bigger than magnitude 2), 0.5 of magnitude 4, etc. In other words, a pattern that cannot be immediately discerned appears as soon as one puts the number and sizes on a logarithmic plot. In the case of earthquakes, there seems to be a simple 'power law' or exponential law (which is particularly beautiful here because the exponential function is very close to 1). Thus earthquakes are self-organizing, following the same pattern everywhere. However, SOC does not help us predicting when and where the big earthquakes are going to take place. Here one should rather consult the geologists who analyse the concrete conditions at the given place and time.

SOC also explains the general properties of mass extinctions during evolution. On this issue there has been a debate between those who believe that the so-called K–T extinction around 70 million years ago was caused by meteors, that is, an external, environmental disturbance, and those who believe that the dinosaurs died out naturally, for internal reasons (Raup 1992, 64–88). This is still an open question. But how can we scientifically 'understand' mass extinctions? They happen rarely, and the so-called 'Big Five' (that themselves differ in size from 3 per cent to 52 per cent killings of families, roughly equating up to 96 per cent of species) happened within the last 600 million years. Nonetheless, the occurrence of extinctions follows a similar power law (in this case close to 1.1). If this is so, there seems to be an internal drive towards extinctions that can be plotted on a Kill Curve. This shows that extinctions are not exceptions, but part of a more general pattern in which many smaller extinctions are coupled with a few big ones. Also ecosystems are, after all, living beyond the balance: if some populations die out, they might inaugurate an avalanche process, whereby many other populations, even genera and species, die out in a domino effect.

Thus there seems here to be a *natural cycle of order and disorder built into the very structure of self-organizing systems*. As pointed out by Per Bak, '[t]he self-organized critical state with all its fluctuations is not the best possible state, but it is the best state that is dynamically achievable' (Bak 1997, 198). Whether we see this interface of order and disorder as something good or bad can only be clarified on a new interpretative level, in this case by an ethical re-description of an already scientifically described world. However, it is at least relevant for a moral evaluation to notice that with the downfall of one species or genus, there is room for developing new species and genera that inhabit the same ecological niches, yet also create new forms of interaction between species and environment. The general tendency of mass extinction may even pave the way for more complex life forms. The emergence of *homo sapiens* in the wake of the extinction of the big reptiles serves as an outstanding example.

Now, how far can the theory of SOC explain the trend towards complexity that we see in evolution? As we have seen SOC does not pretend to be able to explain the particulars of evolution (why *this* extinction?), nor does it pretend to sort out the efficient causes behind the general outcomes. SOC is more a 'formal' than a 'material' understanding of evolution. As such, however, self-organized criticality has the advantage of been universal. Thus, SOC provides us with a clue for understanding the mathematical basis of more developed forms of biological complexity. For example, Per Bak argues that if SOC is applicable on macroevolutionary processes, the theory would 'represent the link between Darwin's view of continuous evolutions and the punctuations representing sudden quantitative and qualitative changes' (Bak 1997, 131). That is, SOC might be able to provide a general mathematical framework for Gould's theory of 'punctuated equilibrium'. In this case Gould's reference to contingent occurrences as the 'cause' of macroevolution would itself be framed in by a mathematical theory. Contingencies, after all, are placed within a mathematical order.

The wide applicability of SOC is a sign of the *robustness* of self-organized processes, that is, self-organization does not depend on specific external conditions and does not demand fine-tuning. Observe here the difference to a highly-tuned system such as the famous Zhabotinsky–Belousov reaction, a chemical clock which beautifully oscillates between several states, or Benard's convection cells spontaneously formed in water under the right conditions.

Such 'dissipative structures', well known from the work of Ilya Prigogine, are after all relatively rare phenomena in nature. We could hardly build a general theory of self-organization on such rather isolated cases.

Because of its general applicability, the theory of SOC is more closely related to the so-called *chaos theory*. Both chaotic systems and SOC systems are non-linear systems; both display a transition back and forth between chaotic and ordered states, and both systems are governed by mathematical laws. However, according to Per Bak, SOC differs from chaotic systems on two interesting points. First, the complexity of chaotic systems is not robust, since the critical state only occurs in the ephemeral interface between ordered and disordered states. The Lyaponov-coefficient of chaotic systems is therefore not able to explain the universality of self-organized systems. Secondly, chaotic systems tend to oscillate back and forth due to the strange attractor and cannot build up unique systems slowly over time. The dictum of Per Bak is un-compromising: 'In short, chaos theory cannot explain complexity' (1997, 31).

However, there are important barriers to the explanatory power of SOC as well. For all, SOC does not cover the specific functions of programme- or information-based systems such as genetic organisms. Though there is a kind of 'memory' distributed in the SOC system as a whole, there are no clear feedback channels from the environment into the system itself. After all, a volcano is more easily understood than an amoeba, even if the former is larger and has more variegated elements than the latter. However, the amoeba, despite its smallness, has a considerably higher degree of autonomy vis-à-vis its environment than the volcano. Volcanoes don't move away from dangers, and are not attracted to some environments rather than other. They just come to pass. So, the question is whether one can proceed one step further into the complexity of living systems.

From SOC to Complex Adaptive Systems (CAS)

What is missing from Bak's model of complexity is the function of learning that is characteristic for *Complex Adaptive Systems* (CAS), as they have been named by another physicist Murray Gell-Mann (1994a; 1994b). As Nobel Prize winner in quantum physics, Gell-

Mann has devoted most of his senior work time to develop the Santa Fe Institute for complexity studies.

Many systems have an internal programme which controls the system–environment exchanges. Think of a thermostat, which directly adapts to the environment by controlling the input–output relations of temperature. A thermostat is certainly an example of organized adaptive complexity, however, it is not an example of *self*-organized complexity. A thermostat has something that the sand-pile does not have, namely an internal programme, but this programme does not develop itself under the influence of the environment. It connects directly, in a prefigured way, to the relevant aspects of its environment ('now too hot, now too cold'). In short, there is no learning involved in the process.

In the case of CAS, by contrast, a self-selective process takes place within the system. Inside the organism, an internal schema of the environment is carved out which is then – by trial and error processes – adjusted to the subsequent experiences of that system.

Wouldn't this idea of complex adaptive systems be a confirmation of Darwinian selection processes? Yes and no. Yes, because a mechanism of selection is certainly at work in these quasi-cognitive processes. One could here argue (with Popper and other proponents of evolutionary epistemology) that if an organism's schema of reality is fundamentally misleading, it will soon begin to starve, have difficulties in finding a mate – and soon it will be outselected. However, the interesting claim of complexity theory is that adaptation is something that happens at *all* levels of reality: at the level of the ecosystem (think of the emergence of the earth atmosphere of oxygen, etc.), at population level (think of foxes surviving in cities), at the level of the individual organism (learning processes), at the cell level (think of the neurons in the human brain), and at the gene level (the unit of selection and reproduction in the received view of neo-Darwinism). According to the standard view of adaptation, however, '[a]n adaptation is a property of an individual organism, not of an ecosystem', as Maynard Smith pointed out in his critique of Gell-Mann's theory of CAS (in Pines 1994, 580).

Thus it seems that the idea of complexity may enlarge our standard picture of adaptation significantly. If learning processes take place at many levels, there are also many 'agents' of evolution, for whom the enviromental influence 'makes a difference'. We are here approaching a biosemiotic view of evolution, according to which something (the environmental influences at large) means something specific ('light', 'food', 'mating') for somebody (an organism with internal, preferential schemas for orientation). Thus the idea of complex self-adaptation is structurally in accordance with Charles Sanders Peirce's definition of a sign: a sign means something (reference) to somebody (the interpreter) in a certain respect (the context).

From CAS to the Theory of Autopoietic Systems (APS)

With the concept of complex adaptive systems involving self-selective behaviour, we are approaching the notion of *autopoietic systems*, or self-productive systems. Often (also in otherwise good literature) the more general idea of self-organizing systems is mixed up with the notion of autopoietic systems. The difference is, however, that while self-organizing systems combine great variability with internally regulated mechanisms or programmes, autopoietic systems produce new internal components and thus continuously create new system environment-interactions. While the concept of *self-organization* still retains the idea that systems are organized out of pre-established elements, the concept of *autopoiesis* more radically contends that the components themselves may be created only inside organized superstructures. Self-transformation extends not only to the organization of the system but also to the elements specific for that system.[11] It is only in a cell, for instance, that we meet the special arrangements of molecules that make up its membrane. The membrane is not only a demarcation line between the inside and the outside of the cell: its elements also participate in the internal life of that cell and cannot exist independently from the cell system as a whole. Or consider the

---

[11] By 'elements', I am not here referring to the physical elements of matter like quarks and atoms but to the components of specified higher-ordered systems (think of neurons in the brain, lymphocytes in the immune system). All such system-specific elements are of course themselves constituted by the elements of fundamental physics.

procedures of the immune system: when an organism is under attack, the specialized cells called lymphocytes respond by producing antibodies to the molecules that invade and threaten the organism; but out of the lymphocyte repertoire for producing antibodies, only those antibodies are cloned that match the invader (Edelmann 1992, 73–80). Or, again, consider, how the carvings of the brain (like physically engraved schemata) are produced in a kind of 'topobiological competition' (Edelman 1992, 83), that recurrently reshapes the neurons and their interacting networks. Selection processes thus take place also in the brain, to the benefit of the brain's overall plasticity.

In autopoietic systems, therefore, there is no separation between producer and produced. A cell's being is given only by virtue of its internal dynamical operations and the system is not a substance definable prior to its operation (immune systems therefore vary significantly in genetically identical twins). It is the internal functioning of the system that both determines *whether* or not the cell should build up new elements, and *how* the cell picks up (or ignores) specific elements of the external world (Maturana/Varela 1992 (1987), 43–52).

Taking the feature of complex adaptability seriously means taking seriously the pluralistic order-and-disorder of nature. The world has many centres of control, and to each is assigned a certain *process autonomy*. Like other types of complexity theory, the theory of autopoietic systems presupposes a *constitutive materialism* ('there exist no other elementary particles than those known by the physical sciences – or in principle knowable by them'). However, what are important are not the singular objects (e.g. atoms or molecules), but the work cycles they perform within holistic, yet highly specialized networks. What matters is not the generic amount of matter's physical energy, but the specific physical organization of matter.[12]

---

[12] Against this background, our very concept of matter has to be reflected so as to include both the physical substrate, the physical energy *and* matter's physical organization. Cf. Davies and Gribbin (1992, 15): 'matter as such has been demoted from its central role, to be replaced by concepts such as organization, complexity and information'.

The pluralistic order-and-disorder has its ontological basis in the *operational closure* of the different systems themselves. That is, a system is not acting at the mercy of the environment, but is itself determining what is relevant, and what is not relevant in the surroundings. Accordingly, there does not exist one objective environment, common to all systems, but there exist as many environments as you have adaptive systems. Autopoietic systems may react to their environments on all grades from negative feedback (balancing each other) to positive feedback (mutual enhancement). Eventually we face a continuous *criss-cross interpenetration* of different kinds of operational systems. Evolution seems to be driven by type-different autopoietic systems, sometimes competitive, sometimes symbiotic, sometimes in synergetic resonance, then in dissonance with each other.

Elsewhere I have tried to formulate some of the basic principles of autopoietic systems as follows (Gregersen 1998, 338):

(1) Autopoietic systems are *energetically open systems*, dependent on external supplies.

(2) While autopoietic systems are energetically open, they are *operationally closed*. The closure of the system is even a precondition for the way in which the given system handles its openness vis-à-vis its environment. The cell, for instance, is open for energy supply only so long as the energy input does not break down its own membrane and internal structures.

(3) The self-reproduction of autopoietic systems is *not necessarily tied to specific physical structures*, since the structures may change as the dynamical system operates. The immune system, for instance, does not always protect the frontiers which are under attack but may, rather, reproduce the system by forming new strategies of survival through structural self-transformations. Self-*re*production often happens through self-*production*.

(4) The *elements* of the autopoietic system are constituted by the system itself, by way of (selective) inclusion or exclusion.

The membrane, for instance, only lasts as long as the cell-system lasts.

(5) *Interpenetration* between differently structured systems always takes place on the basis of the given system itself. In one system, the intrusion of a new chemical element makes no difference; in yet another, the consequences can be enormous. The causal effect is always co-determined by the system itself.

Against this background I have earlier argued (following the common opinion of autopoietic theory), that the idea of auto-poietic systems implies a farewell to any idea of pre-established blueprints of creation (Gregersen 1998, 338). This sentence still holds true in so far as biological self-productivity is laying down its own pathways in the process of walking, and often takes advantage of the breakdown of previous structures (as we saw in the case of the mass extinctions). However, I would now add that self-productive rhythms nonetheless take place in an environment which in general is hospitable to the emergence and sustenance of such types processes. Physical law and chemical structures may well undergird autopoietic processes. I therefore think that we should not be pitting against each other the idea of pre-established design(s) and the notion of the local, context-dependent creativity of autopoietic systems. In fact I am going to argue that even though the classical notions of design may not work with respect to self-organizational processes (which take place *within* the framework of the world), they might nonetheless apply well to the basic framework *of* the world (cf. Gregersen 2002).

III. Seeing God in a Waterdrop: A Theology of Complex Adaptive Systems

Now what are the theological perspectives in supplementing standard neo-Darwinian theory? On the one hand we see a renewed reflection on the chemical constraints that constitute the framework and channels of evolutionary processes; on the other hand we see mathematical models of complexity that insist on the openness of co-evolution and learning processes. Evidently variation and selection are not the only driving forces of evolution. What are the lessons to be learnt for theology?

Combining Anthropic Principle and Autopoiesis

Elsewhere I have proposed a theology of autopoiesis which I claim is both consistent with the Judeo-Christian idea of God as creator and congenial with the thought models provided by the complexity sciences (without the former being derivable from the latter). Provided (a) that God is the creator of all-that-is, and provided (b) that the capacity for self-productivity and self-selectivity is an innate property of complex adaptive systems, God (c) can be seen as supporting nature's self-creativity and perhaps even stimulating the overall process of evolution in certain directions (Gregersen 1998; 1999).

This theological hypothesis rests on a specific co-ordination of concerns expressed in the classic Christian doctrines of creation and providence (Gregersen 1997). A distinction is made between God's power of ontological origination, as expressed in the notion of God's creation 'out of nothing' (*ex nihilo*), and the many ways in which God may have chosen to sustain and further develop God's world of creation (*creatio continua*). The idea of God's creation *ex nihilo* is here taken to mean that God is the ultimate source of-all-that-is. As such the term was used by the anti-Gnostic church fathers from *c.* AD 180 in order to clarify (against Platonic thought) that God is not only the creator of form and information, but also of the material world itself.[13] In particular, this doctrine had the anti-Gnostic thrust that since the material world is created by God (and

---

[13] See the important monograph by Gerhard May (1978, 151–82) who points out that the doctrine of *ex nihilo* was developed as a Christian doctrine in the period between AD 170 and 250 in writers such as, first, Tatian (Or. 5,3), then Theophil. (Aut. I, 4; I, 8) and Irenaeus (Adv. Haer. II, 1,1; II, 10, 4). It is not found in the creation narrative of Genesis which depicts the emergence of the world out of chaos; also the occasional reference to God's creation 'out of nothing' in 2 Macc 7:28 and Rom 4:17 does not seem to have any clear cosmological intention (May 1978, 7). Before this time, Hellenistic Jews and Christians understood divine creation after the model of forming an intelligible world out of formless matter (e.g. Sap. 11, 17; Athenagoras: Suppl. 22, 2).

does not constitute a second principle besides God), the material world should be appreciated as 'indeed very good' (Gen 1:31). Positively speaking, the world is created because God freely wants the world to be, and the divine will to create flows out of God's love. Thus, the *ex nihilo* is a negative way of stating that the world comes into being by the benevolent love of God, *ex amore dei* (Fiddes 2001).

Now if we by autopoiesis refer to a self-creativity from scratch, we would presuppose a competition between God's self-originating power and nature's power of self-organization. But this is not what Varela and Maturana claim. Both the concept of complex adaptive systems (Murray Gell-Mann) and the idea of autopoietic systems (in the tradition of Varela and Maturana) deal with the self-production of systems that are already in the flow, dissipated by energy and thus beyond the balance of thermodynamical equilibrium. Theological reasons do not forbid us to see the energizing presence of God 'in, with and under' the fertile self-productivity of the creatures. On the contrary, this is what sacramental theology has always done (Peacocke 2000), and a 'divine blessing' can be discerned in the very mundane processes of growth (Gregersen 1998, 351–3).

What I want to do now is to propose a combination of a *theology of the anthropic principle* (which addresses the constitution of the initial conditions and constants of the universe as we know it) and a *theology of self-organization and autopoiesis* (which concerns the highly delicate structures that emerge through the processes of self-organization in the course of evolution).[14] This combined approach is guided by the intuition that *we are living in a world which is so designed that we are enabled to live beyond design*. The world is graciously designed for the freedom of self-development and co-evolution.

Before laying out this proposal let me face some of the objections that might be made against the attempt to re-describe autopoiesis in terms of God's inner-worldly activity. Indeed, at first glance the concept of self-organization may seem to make superfluous any talk of God's transformative presence in the history of evolution. Both

---

[14] The following argument is presented in more detail in Gregersen 2002.

Per Bak (1997, 48) and his Santa Fe colleague Stuart Kauffman (1995, ch. 4) argue that an increasingly complex order 'can and will emerge "for free" without any watchmaker tuning the world'. Indeed, the *robustness* of self-organizing systems implies that they develop rather independently from specific boundary conditions, and thus are not in need of an especially designed fine-tuning.

Compare here the idea of autopoiesis with the anthropic principle. According to the anthropic principle, the fundamental constants of nature (for example, the relation between matter and anti-matter in the universe, or the expansion rate of the universe) and the initial conditions of our universe (for all, its size) need to be delicately fine-tuned in order to create the material conditions for life. In this case, the hypothesis of a divine designer could well be said to explain the highly delicate co-ordination of the many cosmic parameters (at least, theism offers an economical explanation of these features). By comparison, there is no such extraordinariness about the dynamics of self-organizational systems. Not the delicacy of the narrow co-ordination of the many parameters is awe-inspiring here, but the fact that the processes of diversification are driven forth by relatively simple laws. They seem to guarantee, 'for free', that we attain increasingly complex orders.

Re-describing Autopoiesis Theologically

Provided that my analysis so far is essentially correct, theology faces a curious dilemma. On the one hand, a traditional design hypothesis is a viable option in the context of the anthropic principle, where its religious significance is faint. On the other hand, design arguments appear as an intrusion in the context of self-organizing systems where its religious importance would be more obvious. After all, religious life is more interested in the active presence of a provident God in the midst of the world, than in a designer God at the edge of the world.

Are there any ways out of this dilemma? I see two viable and complementary options for theology. One is to follow up upon the *explanatory approach* and revise the inherited idea of design so as to combine a more general notion of a divine 'meta-design' with the temporal dimension of a 'process design'. How to think of an efficacious divine interaction with the world is an important task for a philosophical theology, but not one to be pursued here. Here I shall confine myself to exemplifying the other option for theology, a *descriptive approach* which is more in line with the tasks of constructive theology. While the first approach argues for God's causal impact on self-organizing processes, the latter focuses on the qualitative aspects of nature that are open for a religious interpretation which seeks to discern a divine presence in the details of nature.[15] As I see it, one of the most congenial theological engagements with complexity theory consists in elaborating the prior theological assumption that *a creative Logos is at work in the mathematical order of the universe*. Logos is here the Christian term for the wellspring of intelligibility and creativity (John 1:1–14) whose character is assumed to be revealed in the life-story of Jesus.

The lead question here is not, 'What difference does God make in evolution?', but rather, 'How do natural processes *express* the characteristics of the God who is at the centre of religious worship'? Whereas the causal approach attempts to make an *inference* to God from the structures and processes of the world in the mode of a 'natural theology' (or at least wants to locate a reasonable place for a divine action in the context of modern science), the qualitative approach *presupposes* the reality of God on pre-scientific grounds and aims then to *re-cognize* the works of God in the world of nature. The perspective on nature is here internal to religion.

However, when re-describing a reality which is already partially described in terms of the sciences, we should not expect a full

---

[15] Each of the two approaches (the causal and the qualitative) have their limits. The causal-explanatory approach performs an apologetics which tries to argue for the reality of God within a scientific context. The danger is here the self-alienation of faith, which is so well analysed by Michael Buckley in his important book *At the Origins of Atheism* (1987). The qualitative or re-descriptive approach (which I want to pursue here) risks the danger of preaching for the already converted. However, there is also strong commitment to rationality in this approach, in so far as a theology working in a transdisciplinary field will have to show the illuminating force of religion with respect to the world as already described by the sciences. The type of rationality present here is one of systematic coherence more than of causal explanation.

translatability between science and theology. Similar to the way in which ethics provides a new perspective on reality that does not merely reduplicate factual statements, so does religion provide a new language in order to catch important differences in reality, namely qualities that are conformal with God's identity (such as generosity, humility, faith, hope, and love), and features that run contrary to God's identity (such as small-mindedness, compulsory repetition, pride, aggressiveness, despair). There is, in other words, a semantic surplus, a *lingua nova*, of religion which transcends that of science.[16] And yet, as we shall see, the theological perspective is by no means unrelated to the world of nature, as it is actually described by the sciences.

The Kingdom of God amongst us

According to the notion of self-organization, natural processes, given enough time, *guarantee* that the world of creation attains increasingly complex orders – 'for free'. Do we in religion find a similar awareness of orders that emerge 'for free'?

We do. One example is the notion of *divine blessing*, common to the three Abrahamic faiths. God's blessing is perceived as spreading into the networks of creation, so that the blessed person is enabled to pass on the power of blessing to others; at the same time, human agents are enabled to 'bless' God by thanksgiving. Hereby a divine–human economy of superabundance is slowly built up. This economy is both forceful and fragile: the blessing never reaches a state of natural equilibrium. At any time, it can be irrupted by non-reciprocation which may initiate avalanches of catastrophic processes. The blessing, however, is abundant as long as it lasts. The blessing of God thus at work is a structuring principle, at once transcendent in its origination and immanent in its efficiency. God is not perceived as a remote, a-cosmic designer of a world, but as creatively present in the midst of life by eliciting processes of fruitful albeit risky self-developments. Exactly the unfathomable richness

---

[16] Observe that the Judeo-Christian perspective that I want to draw on in the following, is more than evaluative, since it perceives differences and qualities in the world that could not be perceived apart from a religious perspective.

of pattern formation *within* the world reveals the *transcendence* of divine creativity.[17]

In the present context, however, I want to draw attention to the New Testament concept of the *kingdom of God*. It is generally acknowledged that the kingdom of God is not conceived of as a place nor as a separate realm, but is simply the exercise of God's reign in the world of creation in such a manner that God is revealed in these very mundane occurrences. For even if God is omnipresent in the world of creation, God is not manifest everywhere.

Now, what are the similarities between the idea of the kingdom of God and the theory of self-organizing processes? First, there is a common awareness of the self-creative powers of nature. In the teaching of Jesus, the kingdom of God is likened to the scattering of a mustard seed on the ground which grows and sprouts while you are at sleep, you don't know how (Mark 4:26–8). And the text continues, 'The earth produces of itself' (Mark 4:29, *automatikē*). According to the New Testament scholar John D. Crossan (1992), the kingdom of God is compared with the mustard seed which in antiquity was considered a weed. If this is so, it is the relentless will to existence that is compared with the kingdom – the same inconsiderate insistence that we see in beggars, or in the woman who lost a penny and went on searching until she finally found what she wanted (Luke 15:8–10).

Second, the kingdom of God is related to open-ended possibilities. In Matthew, the kingdom of God is also called the kingdom of the heavens, whereby heaven is a symbol of those aspects of creation that are beyond our control, and yet determine our existence. Speaking of the heavens as belonging to the kingdom of God articulates the trust that even the powers of irruption and irregularity ultimately belong to God. The powers of disorder are not free-floating powers of an animistic sort (Welker 1999, 36–40). Thus, the notion of the kingdom of heaven both encapsulates the unity of the world of possibilities (heaven not being divine, but an integral part of God's reign) and the multiplicity of new relevant

---

[17] A more detailed examination of the idea of blessing, with references, is found in Gregersen (2001b).

possibilities (what Stuart Kauffman refers to as 'adjacent possibilities').

Third, the idea of God's reign addresses the fact that the world is construed as a series of openings, or invitations. However, an invitation has to be received in order to reach the goal aimed for. The symbolic world of the parables is full of people who either accept the invitation, or do not. Accordingly, New Testament scholar Dan Otto Via (1967) has proposed that the parables can be seen as falling into two main categories, the comic parables of odd people who are opening up to the invitations, and the tragic parables of self-enclosure. Think of the parable of the king who invites his friends to a wedding banquet, but they refuse to come, and the king then extends the invitation to the destitute on the street (Matt 22:1–10). Or think of those who bury their talents rather than using them (Matt 25:14–30). The choice of accepting or not accepting (or using the options or not using the options) exemplifies the formal features of autopoietic systems in so far as these are bound to adapt to their environments. To adapt, or not to adapt, that is the question. But the point is that *one has to adapt to oneself in order to adapt appropriately to the environment.*

As we know from the theory of autopoietic systems, operational closure precedes openness. Self-adaptation precedes adaptation. Accordingly, the one who is addressed by the parables will have to change his or her mental framework in order to catch the novel adjacent possibilities of the kingdom of God. For the same reason, the ontological status of God's reign is not, and cannot be, easy to determine. We hear that the kingdom is not a reality which can be observed, and yet it is said to be amongst us (Luke 17:21). The reason is simply that the adjacent possibilities of the kingdom of God have to be caught, taken up. If taken up, however, the internal structure of the human person is necessarily changed. The kingdom of God is an objective-relational reality, in so far as it only becomes real at the moment when one enters into the relational networks elicited by the approaching kingdom. Accordingly, when Christians pray, 'Thy kingdom come', they presuppose that the reign of God is not already here. There is not a ready-made design, a fulfilled reality imprinted on the structures of reality; rather, the reign of God is in the process of coming to us. The kingdom is not of this world, and yet its efficacious presence can be depicted in scenes from everyday existence. As argued by the German theologian Michael Welker, 'the reign of God is in a process of emergence'. As such it is similar to a surprise: 'a surprising change of configuration is delineated that . . . requires new powers of self-organization' (Welker 1992, 509).

However, something important about the kingdom cannot be appropriately expressed in the formal language of systems theory. After all, the kingdom of God is an emergent phenomenon of a very specific sort. First, the parables of the kingdom highlight the ambivalence of affirming the vitality of self-productivity as such. Recurrently, Jesus ascribes the kingdom of God to those who do *not* have: the children, the poor, the destitute. The kingdom of God is so inclusive that it even seems to exclude those that are in possession of power and richness. Blessed are the poor, for theirs is the kingdom of God. Blessed are those that mourn and have lost, for they will inherit the kingdom of God (Luke 6:20–6).

Thus the semantic complexity of the parables tackles a problem that inevitably results from autopoietic systems but cannot be addressed from the perspective of science. From a theological viewpoint, not all self-organizing processes can be described as a blessing. Quite a few self-organizing systems operate in a way that indeed inhibit the operation of other systems. The distinction between blessing and curse is a distinction between: (1) self-organizing processes that create a field of resonance with other highly specified systems, and (2) self-organizing systems that produce themselves at the expense of other life forms. Cancer cells reproduce themselves to such an extent that they destroy other functions of the human body; the AIDS virus hijacks the immune system and deprives it of its flexibility. A purely scientific description cannot sufficiently grasp this difference, since the so-called defect of the immune system could as well be described as the efficiency of the AIDS invader.[18]

---

[18] This is also the reason why it is difficult to speak about complexity within the neo-Darwinian paradigm. Adaptive complexity is here measured as reproductive success, which does not in itself guarantee any upwards trend in cosmic evolution

Nor can the ethical difference between that which is morally good and that which is morally evil catch the difference, since cancer cells and vira are not moral agents. It seems that a language is needed, which is capable of noticing how natural and moral conditions are intertwined. It is distinctive for religious language that the world as known by everyday language and by the specialized languages of the sciences are re-described under the aspects of God's good creation and sinful distortion. For even though God is present everywhere in the cosmos – 'in, with, and under' natural events of any sort – the purpose of God is not revealed everywhere. The role of theology is thus not only to explain the world as it is. In re-describing a reality, theology should be able to both account for what *is*, and to account for what the world should be like, but *is not*. Accordingly, the parables of Jesus consistently intertwine the awareness of the goodness of creation and the need for readjustment and redemption. The grace of God is graspable only in the creative zones between that-which-is (creation) and that-which-is-not-yet (the kingdom of God) by the exclusion of that-which-destroys creaturely coexistence (sin). The kingdom of God therefore presents itself in the fragile yet potentially fertile regimes between order and disorder. We thus find cross-fertilizations and co-adaptations on every scale:

(1) We have the interrelation of *nature and culture* (on the spatial axis). Nature is not perceived as enslaved by laws but as consisting of autonomous agents in a constant process of co-ordination. Neither are human beings exercising freedom at its fullest scale. Human beings are blind, unless they adjust their mental frameworks to the new possibilities of the kingdom.

(2) We also have the interrelation of the *world of actualities* and the *world of possibilities* (on the temporal axis). Unexpected chances for self-development emerge in the always critical

(McShea 1998). Nonetheless, as argued by Conway Morris (1998), the trend towards complexification (however measured) seems an unnegotiable fact of the some 15 billion years history of our universe.

system–environment interactions in which novel ways of structuring oneself are opened up.

(3) Finally, we have the interrelation between the *finite realizations of order* and the *divine wellspring of unprecedented novelties* (on the vertical axis). The notion of divine blessing, but even more so the idea of the kingdom of heaven specify, within a highly complex network of images, the difference between self-productive processes that are resonant with God's will and those who are not. A divine–humane economy of superabundance is articulated where more comes out of less in the highly ordered yet fragile zones of collaboration between human beings and their natural environments. Here the freedom of autopoietic systems coincides with the grace of God.

The sudden emergences of the kingdom of God is like seeing God in the fluids of a waterdrop. You need both to have the curved structure of the fluid drop 'out there', and to adjust yourself 'internally' to seeing God in that fragment of reality. Nothing goes without the other. For in the world of autopoiesis, no adaptation happens without self-adaptation.

References

ATKINS, P. W. 1995. *The Periodic Kingdom*, New York: BasicBooks.

AYALA, FRANCISCO J. 1983. 'Microevolution and Macroevolution', in D. S. Bendall (ed.), *Evolution from Molecules to Men*, Cambridge: Cambridge University Press, 387–402.

BALL, PHILIP. 1999. *The Self-Made Tapestry: Pattern Formation in Nature*, Oxford: Oxford University Press.

BAK, PER. 1997. *How Nature Works: The Science of Self-Organized Criticality*, Oxford: Oxford University Press.

BAK, P., CHEN, K. and CREUTZ, M. 1989. 'Self-Organized Criticality in the Game of Life', *Nature* 342, 1989, 780ff.

BAK, P. and CHEN, K. 1991. 'Self-Organized Criticality', *Scientific American* 264, 46ff.

BAK, P., TANG, C. and WIESENFELD, K. 1987. 'Self-Organized Criticality: An Explanation of 1/f Noise', *Physics Review Letters* 59, 381ff.

BARROW, JOHN D. and TIPLER, FRANK J. [1986] 1996. *The Anthropic Principle*, Oxford: Oxford University Press.

BARTHOLOMEW, DAVID J. 1984. *God of Chance*, London: SCM Press.

BOWLER, PETER J. [1983] 1999. *The Decline of Darwinism*, New York: John Hopkins.

CROSSAN, JOHN DOMINIC. 1992. *The Historical Jesus: The Life of a Mediterranean Jewish Peasant*, Edinburgh: T&T Clark.

DAVIES, PAUL and GRIBBIN, JOHN. 1992. *The Matter Myth: Dramatic Discoveries that Challenge our Understanding of Physical Reality*, New York: Simon & Schuster.

DAWKINS, RICHARD. 1983. 'Universal Darwinism', in D. S. Bendall (ed.), *Evolution from Molecules to Men*, Cambridge: Cambridge University Press, 403–25.

DEPEW, DAVID J. and WEBER, BRUCE H. 1995. *Darwinism Evolving: Systems Dynamics and the Genealogy of Natural Selection*, Cambridge, Mass.: MIT Press.

EDELMANN, GERALD. 1992. *Bright Air, Brilliant Fire: On the Matter of the Mind*, New York: BasicBooks.

FIDDES, PAUL. 2001. 'Creation out of Love', in John Polkinghorne (ed.), *The World of Love: Creation as Kenosis*, Grand Rapids: Eerdmans.

GELL-MANN, MURRAY. 1994a. *The Quark and the Jaguar: Adventures in the Simple and the Complex*, New York: W. H. Freeman.

—— 1994b. 'Complex Adaptive Systems', in George A. Cowan, David Pines and David Meltzer (eds), *Complexity: Metaphors, Models and Reality*, Cambridge, Mass.: Perseus, 17–47.

GOODWIN, BRIAN. 1992. 'The Evolution of Generic Forms', in Fransisco J. Varela and Jean-Pierre Dupuy (eds), *Understanding Origins. Contemporary Views on the Origin of Life, Mind and Society* (Boston Studies in the Philosophy of Science vol. 130), Dordrecht: Kluwer Academic Publishers.

GOULD, STEPHEN J. 1982. 'Darwinism and the Expansion of Evolutionary Theory', *Science* 216, 380–7.

GOULD, STEPHEN J. 1989. *Wonderful Life: The Burgess Shale and the Nature of History*, Harmondsworth: Penguin.

GREGERSEN, NIELS HENRIK. 1997. 'Three Types of Indeterminacy: On the Difference between God's Action as Creator and as Providence', in *Studies in Science and Theology* 3, 165–86.

GREGERSEN, NIELS HENRIK. 1998. 'The Idea of Creation and the Theory of Autopoietic Processes', *Zygon: Journal of Religion and Science*, 33:3, 333–67.

——. 1999. 'Autopoiesis: Less than Self-Constitution, More than Self-Organization. Reply to Gilkey, McClelland and Deltete, and Brun', *Zygon: Journal of Religion and Science*, 34:1, 117–38.

——. 2001a. 'The Cross of Christ in an Evolutionary World', *Dialog: A Journal of Theology*, 40:3, 192–207.

——. 2001b. 'The Creation of Creativity and the Flourishing of Creation', in Philip Hefner, *Created Co-Creator* (*Currents in Theology and Mission* 28:3–4), 400–10.

——. 2002. 'From Anthropic Design to Self-Organization', in Niels Henrik Gregersen (ed.), *From Complexity to Life: On the Emergence of Life and Meaning*, New York: Oxford University Press (forthcoming)

HAUGHT, JOHN F. 2000. *God After Darwin: A Theology of Evolution*, Boulder, Col.: Westview Press.

KAUFFMAN, STUART. 1993. *The Origin of Order: Self-Organization and Selection in Evolution*, New York: Oxford University Press.

——. 1995. *At Home in the Universe: The Search for Laws of Self-Organization and Complexity*, New York: Oxford University Press.

——. 2000. *Investigations*, New York: Oxford University Press.

MATURANA, HUMBERTO R. and VARELA, FRANSISCO. [1987] 1992. *The Tree of Knowledge: The Biological Roots of Human Understanding*, rev. edn, Boston: Shambala.

MAY, GERHARD. 1978. *Schöpfung aus dem Nichts. Die Entstehung der Lehre von der creatio ex nihilo*, Berlin: De Gruyter.

MAYNARD SMITH, J. 1969. 'The Status of Neo-Darwinism', in C. H. Waddington (ed.), *Towards a Theoretical Biology*, Edinburgh: Edinburgh University Press.

MCSHEA, DANIEL W. 1998. 'Complexity and Evolution: What Everybody Knows' [1991], in David L. Hull and Michael Ruse (eds), *The Philosophy of Biology* (Oxford Readings in Philosophy), Oxford: Oxford University Press, 625–49.

MAXWELL, CLERK. 1890. 'Address of the British Association' (1873), in *Scientific Papers*, Cambridge: Cambridge University Press, vol. II.

MAYR, ERNST. 1988. *Toward a New Philosophy of Biology: Observations of an Evolutionist*, Cambridge, Mass.: Harvard University Press.

MORRIS, SIMON CONWAY. 1998. *The Crucible of Creation: The Burgess Shale and the Rise of Animals*, Oxford: Oxford University Press.

——. 2003 (forthcoming). 'Convergence', in J. Wentzel van Huyssten, et al. (eds), *Encyclopedia of Science and Religion*, New York: Macmillan Reference.

PALEY, WILLIAM. [1802] 1828. *Natural Theology*, 2nd edn, Oxford: J. Vincent.

PEACOCKE, ARTHUR. 2000. 'Nature as Sacrament', in Jeremy Morris (ed), *Vision or Revision: Seeing Through the Sacraments* (Third Millennium 2), London: Affirming Catholicism.

PINES, DAVID. 1994. 'Search for Consensual Views', in George A. Cowan, David Pines and David Meltzer (eds), *Complexity: Metaphors, Models and Reality*, Cambridge, Mass.: Perseus, 577–87.

PRIGOGINE, ILYA and STENGERS, ISABELLE. 1984. *Order out of Chaos: Man's New Dialogue with Nature*, New York: Bantam.

RAUP, DAVID M. 1992. *Extinctions. Bad Genes or Bad Luck?*, New York: W. W. Norton.

RUSE, MICHAEL. 2001. *Can a Darwinian be a Christian? The Relationship between Science and Religion*, Cambridge: Cambridge University Press.

SCHUSTER, PETER. 1992. 'Biological Information: Its Origin and Processing', in C. Wassermann, R. Kirby and B. Rordorff (eds), *The Science and Theology of Information*, Geneva: Labor et Fides, 45–57.

SEGERSTRÅLE, ULLICA. 2000. *Defenders of the Truth. The Sociobiology Debate*, Oxford: Oxford University Press.

SOBER, ELIOT and WILSON, DAVID SLOAN. 1998. *Unto Others: The Evolution and Psychology of Unselfish Behavior*, Cambridge, Mass.: Harvard University Press.

SOLÉ, RICHARD and GOODWIN, BRIAN. 2000. *Signs of Life. How Complexity Pervades Biology*, New York: BasicBooks.

STERELNY, KIM. 2001. *Dawkins vs. Gould: Survival of the Fittest*, Cambridge: Icon Books.

STEWART, IAN. [1998] 1999. *Life's Other Secret: The New Mathematics of the Living World*, Harmondsworth: Penguin.

THOMPSON, D'ARCY W. [1916] 1942. *On Growth and Form*, Cambridge: Cambridge University Press.

VIA, DAN OTTO, JR. 1967. *The Parables. Their Literary and Existential Dimension*, Philadelphia: Fortress Press.

WELKER, MICHAEL. 1999. *Creation and Reality*, Minneapolis: Fortress Press.

——. 1992. 'The Reign of God', *Theology Today* 49:4, 500–15.

WICKEN, J. S. 1987. *Evolution, Information and Thermodynamics: Extending the Darwinian Paradigm*, New York: Oxford University Press.

WILSON, EDWARD O. [1998] 1999. *Consilience: The Unity of Knowledge*, New York: Random House.

5

Landscapes of
Human Discourse

JOHN C. PUDDEFOOT

Introduction

It is the purpose of this paper to try to initiate a process that will extend the application of our ability to classify dynamical systems to realms beyond the usual range of science by asking whether and to what extent it is possible to classify human discourse using similar concepts. The structure of human discourse is compared with the four-fold classification of dynamical systems in terms of simple attractors, multiple attractors and complex and chaotic systems. Discussion is related to issues in realism. Human discourse creates its own dynamical space, but there may be underlying laws embedded in that space. Implications for religious institutions and their doctrinal formulations are suggested. The processes are linked to the disturbances of systems envisaged in simulated annealing.

In his address to the Lyon conference, John Barrow[1] depicted variations in types of human understanding in a two-dimensional diagram where the horizontal axis represents increasing uncertainty

---

[1] I have taken the liberty of modifying John Barrow's original diagram for my own purposes. The final printed version of the diagram in his lecture reproduced in this volume was not available at the time of writing.

and the vertical axis represents increasing complexity. A modified version of that diagram is shown.

FIGURE 1

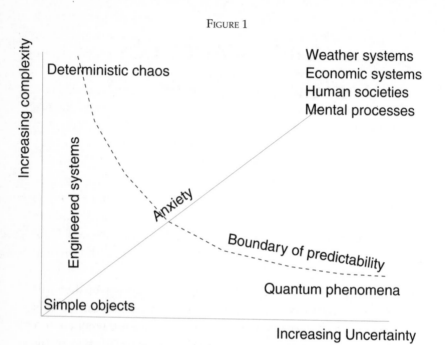

On such a diagram, the most reliable and predictable of human artefacts and discourses – those we employ in our engineering, for example, where we wish to minimize variation or deviation from an intended course – occur close to the intersection of the axes; human discourse itself, social interaction, weather patterns, and our economic systems, occur towards the top-right: here both complexity and uncertainty are at their greatest. A suitably vague curved dotted line divides the realm of science from a realm currently beyond science.

The debate about theology and science, which is at the core of ESSSAT's interests, has much to learn from Barrow's picture. For example, to what extent are we guilty of locating both theology and science at 'fixed points' of this diagram? It is easy tacitly to assume that science occupies the bottom-left corner, and theology the top-right. Theology is undoubtedly complex and filled with different kinds of uncertainty, but so is science. So neither can be located unequivocally in one place or another, even though there are those who strive to make both into caricatures of themselves in such extremes as textual literalism and classical determinism. We begin to suspect that the shapes of these and other discourses are influenced by more than their subject matter.

The modified diagram suggests the possibility of a reclassification of the discourses that we habitually assess using concepts such as truth, knowledge and reason because the distribution of discourses on the diagram does not correlate at all with their interest or importance. We find ourselves wondering whether, in the pursuit of the kind of certainty and predictability required for engineering safety, or the particular kind of repeatability required for empirical science, we 'paint ourselves into a corner' somewhere in the bottom left-hand part of the diagram by requiring the same criteria of truth to be applied everywhere while many other really interesting, important and humanly worthwhile things are going on elsewhere. The added diagonal line from the bottom-left corner up towards the areas concerned with complex and chaotic systems, seems to indicate a spectrum of decreasing certainty and increasing anxiety without suggesting any diminution of the worthwhileness of the associated discourses.

Neither are the certainty and predictability we commonly seek in our theories unequivocally beneficial. Even *stability* is not in itself always beneficial. For example, were DNA 'stable', evolution would be impossible, and we would not exist. Similarly, the dependence of religions upon established and fixed ancient texts affords them a certain stability at the expense of some degree of built-in obsolescence and inflexibility.

Somewhere behind the complexities of human discourse there may lie laws of discourse to whose existence that discourse bears witness. Such laws, if they exist, may suggest that the substance of human discourse configures the landscape of our conversation less than the type of discourse itself. This possibility suggests the need for an important clarification and distinction: is human discourse configured by the topics it addresses, or does it configure them?

Such a question has an intrinsic connection with realism. It also bears directly upon the question of what it is that configures a person, and whether and to what extent each person configures his or her discourse space and/or is configured by it. And that distinction is itself illuminated by the parallel transition in modern cosmology between Newton's 'container' view of space and the intimate interconnectedness of Einstein's space-time-mass-energy manifold. We can start to see that the 'geometry' of the human space we occupy is constituted by the living dynamic of those who constitute it. It is a living reality.

Human discourse is composed of a large number of interconnected and interdependent *voices*, each of which originates in a *speaker*. The collective dynamic influences are influenced by each of those voices and speakers, and its overall shape – what I am calling its landscape – will arise from a rich and subtle combination of voices: some that reiterate the discourse they hear and others that change it. If the space of human discourse operates according to non-linear laws, as seems highly probable, then under certain circumstances it will prove susceptible to tiny influences that it will magnify and propagate while at other times large-scale movements of discourse may dissipate and disappear. There may be some kind of 'mean' behaviour in addition to the chaotic trajectories that emanate from particular voices that ensures that human discourse itself remains reasonably coherent and stable; but there may also be occasions when individual voices precipitate wholesale changes in the whole space over long periods of time.[2]

All these ideas suggest that there may be benefit in considering the configuration of our intellectual space – the landscapes of human discourse – in terms of our classification of dynamical systems, whether or not we have any short-term expectation of being able to specify what their underlying laws might be.

Why should we suppose that the landscapes of human discourse might be modelled by the dynamics of complex systems? When

---

[2] I am thinking here of things like the 'Baker' transformation in non-linear spaces that eventually make the final position of an initial point ubiquitous. Readers may also hear echoes of the so-called 'Butterfly Effect'.

we witness complex phenomena in the natural world, we are seeing how molecules with no intrinsic connection beyond such forces as gravity and viscosity behave when moving in large numbers according to certain constraints and under certain external influences such as heating. That these essentially independent molecules generate complex systems should lead us to ask whether even more intimately connected systems of apparently disconnected entities – specifically human individuals connected by language and socially embodied practices and laws – will exhibit less or more complex behaviour. It seems, prima facie, that more complex behaviour is to be expected. The behaviour of the Lorenz attractor is generated by three simultaneous linked differential equations in three variables. How much more complex a structure should we expect when hundreds, thousands and millions of variables are connected, as in human societies? And, if the Lorenz attractor is content-neutral in that it is not specific to any particular physical situation, despite having been first recognized in Lorenz's attempt to model weather patterns, why should the landscapes of human discourse and social interaction be any more content-specific? It seems perfectly reasonable to suppose that human discourse and human society operate according to deeply embedded laws that will give rise to complex phenomena, including structures that entail, other things being equal, 'differential equations' far more intricate than those Lorenz studied.

Isaac Asimov once speculated about this possibility. His *Foundation* novels, that achieved cult status in the 1960s, were built around the notion of 'psychohistory', a fictional mathematical science invented by Harry Seldon that enabled him to write down and solve the complex equations governing human history. Seldon's predictions about the eventual downfall of the current civilization led him to establish a secret 'Foundation' given over to the study of his laws and charged with the task of salvaging something from the collapse of an intergalactic empire. Asimov's creative mind added to this fictional scenario the notion of a singular event – the rise of a mutant called 'The Mule' – so unlikely that it would throw the course of history off that predicted by

Seldon's equations. Asimov anticipated, in other words, in his fiction, the idea that no amount of mathematical equations can altogether grasp the entirety of a system. The rise of a dissident individual or minority can always change things completely.

Asimov's 'Mule' is a kind of 'butterfly' as envisaged in the familiar 'Butterfly Effect', but Asimov does not allow his new influence to be negated by statistical phenomena such as would usually neutralize the effect of any given butterfly. He makes his singularity genuinely singular. After 'The Mule' nothing will ever be the same again.

Wolfram's Classification of Cellular Automata

Stephen Wolfram has identified four classes of cellular automata that variously:

I   Evolve to a homogeneous state.

II Evolve to simple separated periodic structures.

III Yield chaotic aperiodic patterns.

IV Yield complex patterns of localized structures.

This classification has proved seminal in the development of the study of complexity, although category IV, which arose last historically, lies more obviously between classes II and III in dynamic terms. Chris Langton of the Santa Fe Institute discovered a remarkable parallelism between Wolfram's classes and numerous other physical processes loosely categorizable as transition phenomena (Waldrop 1992, 234).

Cellular Automata Class	I and II	IV	III
Dynamical Systems	Order	Complexity	Chaos
Matter	Solid	Phase Transition	Fluid
Computation	Halting	Undecidable	Nonhalting
Life	Sterile	Life/Intelligence	Noise

Continuous dynamical systems provide analogues for the classes of behaviour seen in cellular automata. Class I cellular automata show limit points, while class II cellular automata may be considered to evolve to limit cycles. Class III cellular automata exhibit chaotic behaviour analogous to that found with strange attractors. Class IV cellular automata effectively have very long transients, and no direct analogue for them has been identified among continuous dynamical systems (Wolfram 1986, 172).

Yet the emergence of life forms seems to involve an immensely rich complex system exhibiting long transients which evolve within niches in a turbulent world, and it is this arena which Langton felt to be close to 'Life and Intelligence'. As we approach a phase transition, structures emerge with more unpredictable periods; Langton speculates that 'life' arises in some of the stable patterns that emerge there, and some of the imponderable features of life therefore reflect the fundamental undecidability of certain kinds of algorithms.

Landscapes

I propose a taxonomy of attitudes to religious truth based upon the four-fold classification given above. This taxonomy itself implies that human discourse can be compared to landscapes that generate their own contours and geometries, and so exhibit certain dynamics depending upon the fundamental natures of the modes of discourse that we enter upon.

Single-point attractors (Figure 2) correspond, on this suggested classifi-cation, to the view that ultimately there is one absolute truth and that any sufficiently rational system will converge upon it regardless of starting point.

FIGURE 2

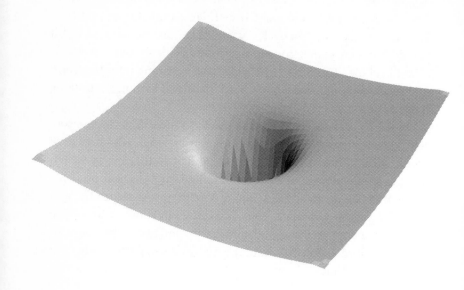

Multiple-point attractors (Figure 3) correspond to the dynamics of discourses that allow for a multiplicity of end-points towards which we can move. Religious pluralism would exemplify such a view. Moreover, the stability of the convergence under even rather large disturbances of the initial conditions might be thought to correspond with the fact that our religious attitudes are substantially influenced by our cultural and familial nurture: those born Christian, Moslem, Hindu, or, within Christianity, Catholic or Protestant, tend to stay with the faiths and denominations to which they are born and in which they are raised. (The discussion of simulated annealing below nevertheless suggests that the configuration of the discourse and its tolerance of dissent are good measures of the degree to which a system can be perturbed while remaining stable, and points towards a further taxonomy of religious conversion.) Something along the lines of a tolerant relativism seems indicated by such cases, but they can also give rise to conflict and even war.

FIGURE 3

FIGURE 3

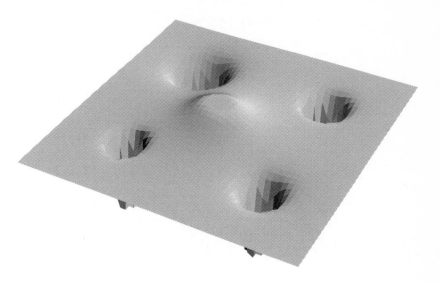

Chaotic systems correspond to a shapeless social dynamic in which we wander aimlessly from one point of reference to another. Neither starting point nor the configuration of the landscape seems to suggest any permanent resting place. Here we find not just relativism but a kind of anarchic nihilism: nowhere holds us; we believe in nothing; we sense that there is nowhere to go and that nothing is permanent.

Complex systems suggest a more subtle dynamic (Figure 4). First of all, they exhibit transient stability: our notion of truth changes with time and we find ourselves borne along to new ideas and concepts. Second, they show a marked susceptibility to arbitrarily small fluctuations in starting conditions. This is an important phenomenon: that apparently insignificant alterations to minor elements in our understanding, reflected for example in small changes in phraseology, nuance or emphasis, may contribute to major alterations in our eventual trajectory, as may apparently insignificant and even undetectable fluctuations in the circumstances in which we encounter new ideas.

FIGURE 4

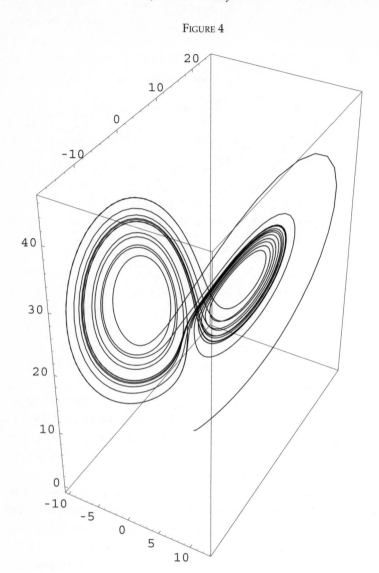

Both these characteristics of complex systems are strongly suggestive of ways in which human discourse, and especially religious discourse, may be considered. The contrasts are especially clear in relation to the first two kinds of classification, where the single or multiple-point attractors are largely determined in advance and the dynamical system moves towards them. As I am conceiving of a complex system, its landscape is largely unknown in advance, and the nature of the attractors – strange or otherwise – is created by the discourse which it models.

Realist and Non-Realist Discourses

There are thus two fundamentally different ways in which we might conceive of the landscapes of human discourse. In one, the landscape itself is already fixed, and human discourse accommodates it by following trajectories imposed by externally-determined contours and potential fields. Models of human discourse that envisage such a state of affairs are predominantly *realist*. In the other, the landscape does not exist except as configured by human discourse, and its shape is consequently as variable and variegated as that discourse, emerging as the dynamics of the discourse develops. Such a model is predominantly *constructivist* and not necessarily realist – or representationalist – in the usual sense. But neither is it anti-realist or anti-representationalist; it should rather be conceived as *creative*.

Ugo Amaldi, describing his concept of the sub-atomic world to us at CERN (Conseil Européen pour la Recherche Nucléaire) during the Geneva ESSSAT conference in 1992, spoke of a similar distinction. According to the more conventional atomic theory as conceived by the man in the street, the world is as it is, and the CERN accelerator speeds particles around causing them to collide with one another. According to Amaldi, the accelerator is in the process of setting up conditions that cause particles to be created out of the raw energy it organizes.

Just such a distinction distinguishes between pre-existing landscapes of human discourse, landscapes that such discourse in some sense *follows* – corresponding to the older, more conventional view – and landscapes that are brought into existence by human discourse, and which that discourse therefore *creates*. Parallels will be apparent between classical and quantum mechanics, especially in its Copenhagen interpretation.

Varieties of Human Discourse

Once we appreciate the distinctions between different kinds of attractors, it is far easier to understand the importance of the Langton classification, for some kinds of human discourse can then be seen to generate single, simple fixed attractors; others generate multiple fixed attractors; others behave chaotically; and in between there lies a rich region of complexity where the minutest changes in that discourse can send the ensuing conversation off on wildly different trajectories with wildly different degrees of stability and longevity. Discourses that begin in one small locality of the world can spread globally. The nexus of discourses that shapes the human world can be thought of rather like weather systems that compete with one another for ascendancy.

On the other hand, conferences and human communication, by throwing together participants in many different discourse-systems, combine strands that might not otherwise interact – and would not were they entirely like weather systems – to generate even more complex patterns of perturbations which generate their own new conceptual spaces. They occasion the creation of new centres of interest; they stimulate us; they send some of us off on hitherto unknown paths in pursuit of new goals and new kinds of understanding.

More to the point, whenever a new strand of discourse enters the human arena – even as a variation on an existing theme, and from whatever source – it reconfigures the conceptual spaces of those who come into contact with it. Different kinds of discourse give rise to different patterns of response, and it is here that the four-fold classification of dynamical systems is so suggestive.

A Remark about Non-Realist Discourse

As is the case with debates about the laws that underlie chaotic and complex behaviour, there is a question mark about the extent to which the self-generating landscapes of discourse associated with a non-realist reading are subject to deeper structural controls and laws. Is there, for example, some kind of deep grammar to the dynamics of social discourse akin to Chomsky's deep linguistic grammar, that governs the way in which our discourse-space develops?

Parallels can be seen here with the way in which W. V. O. Quine treated language in 'Two Dogmas of Empiricism' (Quine 1961): if the landscape of discourse is being generated by the dynamics of the social conversations that constitute it, there is little reason to doubt that each landscape can be reconfigured by radical changes of meaning. But rather than view these changes of meaning in a classical dynamical sense, as Quine implicitly does – the fabric of the language is structurally and dynamically simple and changes here or there occasion sympathetic changes akin to the stretching of a rubber sheet – we can now see changes of meaning in terms of disturbances to a super-sensitive system that can occasion massive fluctuations in the ensuing landscape.

Specifically, in theological language, we should not easily be persuaded that apparently minor alterations to the way we write and speak theologically will have correspondingly minor consequences. If minor changes happen to occur close to regions that are super-sensitive, we may find that they occasion massive alterations in the resulting discourse.

Such super-sensitivity could be taken as a call to a deep conservatism, but the structure of complex systems allows no such inference. As I pointed out in 'Complexity and Western Thought' (Puddefoot 1993), whichever trajectory we are on – apparently stable and 'conservative' as it may be – may lead us to the vicinity of a strange attractor, at which point even the most conservative decision, or no decision at all, may still allow us to be thrown into a radically different part of the dynamical space. Non-linearity offers no more encouragement or comfort to conservatism than it does to radicalism.

Single, Monolithic, Exclusivist Discourse

'No one comes to the Father but by me' (John 14:7) can be understood as a rallying-cry through which the churches reflect upon and engage with the singular nature of the Christ event. The Church conceives of itself and structures its proclamation as a simple-point attractor: the one way to salvation through the one Saviour. In its extreme form, not only is there only one Saviour; there is only one Church, one Religion, one Truth.

Multiple, Pluriform, Competitive Discourse

Here there are many roads to salvation, many churches, even many saviours and many religions. Different churches and sects, religions and denominations, will exhibit different degrees of stability, and group members will exhibit different tendencies to move from group to group according to the local landscape.

Chaotic Systems

Here the notion of salvation through an institutional allegiance or adherence to a particular church, sect or dogmatic formulation gives place to a radical unstructured anarchistic individualism. New Age mysticism might be thought of as such a trend.

Complex Adaptive Systems

Here the internal dynamic of the discourse encourages debate and there is a persistent open-structured interaction with the secular world. Little attempt is made to constrain the interaction or to determine whether the 'correct' views originate within or without. Reliance upon pre-designated dogmatic statements is minimized, and there is a freedom to explore areas of interest and concern that lead far from the 'centre' because there are trajectories that lead away and back again and because it is appreciated that stable configurations are in any case likely to be transient, albeit with longer periods, as we move through the dynamical discourse space.

Safety and Complexity

Some dynamical systems (landscapes) behave *ergodically*, which is to say that they eventually pass through every point in their phase-space. It is inconceivable that human landscapes of discourse exhibit such properties, but it is perfectly possible that they are *quasi-ergodic*, which is to say pass arbitrarily close to any given point given sufficient time.

The phenomenon of sudden conversion, which can also be modelled using catastrophe theory, mentioned elsewhere, in which behaviour apparently converging steadily upon one attractor is suddenly projected elsewhere to orbit another – illustrated by the Lorenz attractor – points in the direction of an interesting parallel with quasi-ergodic systems: that no matter where we may be in such a system, we cannot be sure that we will not subsequently pass arbitrarily close to any other point of the system. Positions once thought unthinkable and anathema may, on such a construction, prove accessible and attractive (no pun intended).

Measures of Complexity

One way to measure the behaviour of non-linear systems is to ask how quickly initial errors propagate. This can be done for dynamic systems using the Ljapunov exponents, which calculate the way successive orbits or cycles diverge from their initial cycles under certain error conditions (Peitgen, Jürgens and Saupe 1992, 715ff.).

Another way is to calculate the fractal dimension, and more usually the 'Natural' dimension of the dynamical system. One of the things this shows, again speaking generally, is that the dynamical systems spend significantly different amounts of time in different states. This is not surprising, but it is important when we think of parallels with landscapes of discourse. Systems that seem to be in particular places most of the time cannot be assumed to be stable, or incapable of exhibiting wild fluctuations in discursive trajectories at other times.

Moreover, before the dynamics of non-linear systems was understood as well as it is today, seemingly regular behaviour was described as, even if not strictly thought to be, 'periodic' or 'cyclic' which we now know to be neither strictly periodic nor cyclic. Our ability to conceptualize and to calculate the trajectories of non-linear systems using computers has enabled us to realize that the world is not as regular as we used to like to think. In particular, so-called economic 'cycles' are almost certainly far more complex than we suppose, and we can easily be led to imagine that we are merely in a part of a cycle when in reality we are moving towards a point where our trajectory will suddenly diverge from all anticipated patterns.

It is a sobering thought that the wars that recently convulsed former Yugoslavia, the near-anarchy in Zimbabwe in 2000, and the history of Europe over the past thousand years, may be no more than transient phenomena in a dynamical process that is impossibly complex and whose future stability is difficult or impossible to predict, still less take for granted. The extremisms that we think dead today may rule or destroy us tomorrow. Fortunately, provided I am right to suggest that we are *creating* these dynamics rather than merely *following* them, 'the future' is not 'written' in a way that makes such predictions altogether coherent. But relatively small-scale perturbations in socio-political dynamics due to unforeseen consequences of little-understood present creations can still swallow whole nations in economic catastrophe as surely as a typhoon can overturn a boat. The socio-political power of creative human discourse can be unexpectedly great, and at present we have no idea of its dynamics.

Theology in the Domain of Complexity

In the vicinity of a strange attractor such as the Lorenz attractor, tiny changes in spatial orientation can have unpredictable consequences. For example, the trajectories followed by two very close points in the vicinity of the attractor can diverge markedly soon afterwards. This super-sensitive behaviour is typical of non-linear systems.

An exciting theological analogue presents itself. It is commonly supposed, particularly by those who spend their religious lives in the discourse-spaces defined by single- and multiple-point attractors with their consequent predictability and order, that preservation of truth depends upon remaining within the vicinity of what is taken to be the centre of the attractor. Some religious systems work hard to make their precepts seem linear, for example, even to the point of claiming that there are clear-cut connections between earthly (religious) conduct and heavenly reward. Violent deviations from those points are supposed always to threaten the disintegration of the discourse-space, and perhaps also of the church whose space it defines. Consequently, high priority is placed upon doctrinal, liturgical and moral conformity.

However, I propose that a fertile and strong discourse-space worthy of a discipline that merits the name 'theology' is far more likely to have the dynamics of a complex space, and to be populated with strange attractors that defy linear models. Specific conformity to any given central location cannot have predictable results for exactly the reason that trajectories are super-sensitive to initial conditions. For example, it is commonly found that the most fervent devotees of a frame of thought, an 'orthodoxy', become the most fervent opponents of that same framework as a result of what we sometimes call a 'conversion' experience. Could it be that conversion experiences are themselves in many cases the result of inhabiting super-sensitive localities where tiny alterations in the prevailing conditions – the points in discourse-space – can have huge implications for the subsequent trajectories followed by those who experience them. And it may also be that those who are most determined to reduce their religious convictions to simple, linear relationships, are subconsciously aware of the potential disruptions to the harmony of their discourse-spaces occasioned by even minor divergences from those simple laws. To put it another way, it is often those who are most tempted by sin who insist most fervently upon morality, like Odysseus and his crew rowing valiantly but in vain to escape Charybdis having just evaded the Scylla.

Moreover, the long-term stability of a church may be greater if it is a strange attractor, for there are natural trajectories that take members of the church far away, apparently into error, immorality and unbelief, that yet bring them back to points close to those from which they began. All this is consistent with my long-standing insistence on the notion of theology as a discipline conducted in the strength and freedom of a 'faith beyond faith', that it is God's faith in us, rather than our faith in him, that sets us free. Single- and multiple-point attractors encourage belief in the stability, predictability and order of systems whose dynamical structure is defined by us; complex systems, because of their intrinsic unpredictability, suggest a richer understanding of the nature of inquiry into the being of God. Despite the fact that deterministic chaos still leads us to an inappropriate sense of the pre-defined nature of the future, we can combine the complex system with open interactive structures to produce an even better model.

Breaking the Dynamical Analogy

As has already been pointed out, human discourse, by virtue of the intricate nature of language and society, exhibits a degree of dependence and relatedness far beyond anything usually encountered in the natural world. Molecules are governed by essentially simple laws that give rise to complex behaviour when large numbers of molecules are present in situations that are non-linear.

However, it is important not to be overwhelmed by this impersonal dynamical analogy, for human societies are not composed of molecule-like entities at all. Each individual human being is unique. More to the point, human beings are singularities within the dynamical systems under question, even if their behaviour in large numbers exhibits some statistical regularities. It is the collectivity of our singularity that makes the creative dynamics of human discourse possible.

A particular reason why human beings must be regarded as singularities arises from the fact that human beings require more than a merely scientific story to be told of them: they have inside as well as outside stories.[3] Attempts to model human discourse using only outside, mathematical stories or theories, fail to take account of the importance of the two-vector nature of living beings. In particular, they fail to allow for the singular nature of *qualia*, which are in linguistic terms the features of voices that generate their singularity.

---

[3] Cf. my *God and the Mind Machine* (1996, *passim* and especially ch. 3). My first published version of this idea occurs as 'Information and Creation' in C. Wassermann, R. Kirby and B. Rordorff (eds), *The Science and Theology of Information*, Geneva: Labor et Fides, 1992.

Qualia Cannot be Disqualified

Daniel C. Dennett, in *Consciousness Explained*, argues that qualia are to be disqualified as counter-arguments to his strictly monist thesis. But qualia cannot be so disqualified, for without qualia there could be no language. When we use language, we employ terms whose meanings are to be understood as the *qualia* of language. Those qualia adhere to language in ways that make it a means of communication. But inasmuch as everything we know has at some stage been learned from a conversation, the uniqueness of these qualia must be qualified: this particular inside-looking-out is intrinsically common to other language-users. That is not to say that any two usages of a term are identical, but that for communication to be possible at all, some common usage and hence some common qualia are to be expected and required.

Quantum Theory

Quantum theory renders all electrons essentially the same but for place and motion. The mathematics of quantum theory is therefore in essence wonderfully simple: all the things it deals with are the same.

But suppose that we were able to write down the wave function of a living organism, even of a human being. That wave function would remain a part of the outside story, a description of only one of the two vectored worlds that make up a human being. So the wave function description must be incomplete. Accordingly, quantum theory cannot be a complete description of the world. It fails to take account of what it may be like to *be* a complex wave function.

Breaking Out: Simulated Annealing

Simulated annealing affords a further example of the way a system can be enriched in ways that produce more dynamic and open-ended understandings of the nature of the theological enterprise. *Mutatis mutandis*, it indicates that the most robust systems are often those that arise from and survive the most ferocious treatment. The way churches, the sciences and political systems deal with dissent may offer a measure of their long-term stability and vitality, and act as a pointer to their discourse-dynamic classification. In particular, the deliberate disturbance of a system can be seen by analogy with simulated annealing to be one means by which to escape the sterile tyranny of mechanistic systems. Voices utter what their minds conceive in their imagination of worlds as-yet unborn.

In both scientific and religious structures we can identify dynamical phenomena that are strongly reminiscent of the kinds of dynamic described by the Wolfram–Langton classification. Moreover, some of those structures exhibit an ambivalence towards dissent and disorder. They would like to be single- or, at worst, multiple-point attractors, stable under all reconfigurations, draining all basins regardless of starting point – the rationalist Enlightenment dream; but they are dependent upon the preservation of open structures and tolerance of dissent for their rejuvenation and adaptation. Those for whom science is modelled by a single-point attractor – one truth now and forever revealed by the empirical method and objectivity, for example – reveal ignorance of the history of science, yet such a model is almost single-handedly responsible for the misconstrual of the relationship between theology and science.

If we reconceptualize our sciences and our theologies and religions in terms of complex dynamical systems with open structures, and therefore see them in terms of an endless emergence and dissolution of stable configurations under the influence of external factors and internal constraints, they become recognizable as but two enterprises within the field of the fallible human quest for human knowledge, and the differences between them become much less significant.

Single- and multiple-point attractors are the idols of a cognition that would be independent of, and closed to, the creative input of God and world; they are symbols for the archetypal objectivity, truth and permanence of epistemological hubris. A complex cognitive structure forever open to new influences from God and world and thoughtful beings suggests a new paradigm that will alter the way in which we conceive of the relationship between theology and science.

In particular – briefly – the notion of a simple dynamic structure of the universe that would have brought about the purposes of God in creation without all the trouble of suffering, pain and death, dissent, argument and conflict, in other words, a universe such as human beings so often think a benevolent, wise and loving God would have created, starts to look like the unrealistic fantasy it is. And we can begin to understand why a God who recommended life for us in this universe would also feel willing to share it with us.

Conclusion

This brief excursion is not much more than an intuitive stab at an indication of further work that could be undertaken in this richly suggestive field. It is worth asking what happens if we combine the notion of simulated annealing with that of complexity, for the effect of the annealing process would not then be to guarantee a gradual convergence upon an absolute minimum, but to force transitions between widely divergent trajectories.

What does all this amount to? Have I described some form of ultra-postmodern dissolution of all human discourse into meaningless babble? Are the trajectories of human conversation no more than the empty irruptions of conversational ephemera?

No doubt there are those who will draw this conclusion and rejoice in it for their own reasons. But I envisage an altogether more positive and hopeful interpretation.

Human despair is built upon the architecture of an essentially linear model of the human mind. Even when despair acknowledges the cyclical nature of human experience, its cycles are well defined and predictable. But a non-linear world and a linear mind are strange bedfellows, and a creature that had evolved with a linear mind – or a mind capable of little more than linear thought – in a non-linear world would have poor survival-characteristics.

So my message is very much more ambitious and up-beat than the postmodern nihilists would think proper. I am working my way towards the suggestion that the human mind is only superficially linear, that the overlay of a set of linear acculturations has persuaded us to believe that we are linear beings, and that the reality lies elsewhere. If, as I suspect, the human mind is least 'at home' when it conceives of a linear world, despite believing the opposite, then the suggestions I have made in this brief paper will point towards an entirely different way of conceiving of things, living our lives, and approaching the throne of grace. I do not know what may come of it. But, then, that is the point: super-sensitive systems are non-computable, even where they are deterministic. And determinism itself may be no more than a misleading by-product of the conceptual systems naturally generated by and compatible with human minds that mistakenly conceive of themselves as linear. Attractors may be stranger than we think.

References

QUINE, W. V. O. 1961. 'Two Dogmas of Empiricism' in *From a Logical Point of View*, New York: Harper & Row.

PEITGEN, H.-O., JÜRGENS, H. and SAUPE, D. 1992. *Chaos and Fractals: New Frontiers in Science*, New York: Springer-Verlag.

PUDDEFOOT, J. C. 1992. 'Information and Creation', in C. Wassermann, R. Kirby and B. Rordorff (eds), *The Science and Theology of Information*, Geneva: Labor et Fides, 7–25.

——. 1993. 'Complexity and Western Thought', in George V. Coyne, SJ and Karl Schmitz-Moormann (eds), *Studies in Science and Theology*, Vol. 1: *Origins, Time and Complexity*, Geneva: Labor et Fides, 133–40.

——. 1996. *God and the Mind Machine*, London: SPCK.

WALDROP, M. M. 1992. *Complexity*, Harmondsworth: Penguin.

WOLFRAM, S. 1986. 'Twenty Problems in the Theory of Cellular Automata', in *Theory and Applications of Cellular Automata*, Singapore: World Scientific.

6

Science and Religion: Beyond Complementarity?

ISABELLE STENGERS

Introduction

Starting from Whitehead's proposition which reads: 'Religion will not regain its old power until it can face change in the same spirit as does science', I endeavour to approach the sciences and religion as complementary practices, which is to say as practices committed in a manner and according to values that mutually exclude each other. The assertion of complementarity thus permits the recognition of the singular, creative character of each practice and puts an end to all rivalry among them. The 'same spirit', then, can mean trust, and implies the abandonment by these two practices of all appeal to a legitimacy which guarantees their power. I conclude by showing that this trust is what we need in order to make ourselves vulnerable to risk, beyond complementarity, in the concrete situations which require of us that we think from the vantage point not of what we know but of what we do not know.

It is important, in the context of a concourse of theologians and scientists, that I introduce myself, since I am neither the one nor the other but a philosopher and, moreover, not a philosopher describing herself as Christian. This is not to say that in what concerns my education and my philosophical practice I am not, in part, defined by Christianity: after all, over the centuries philosophers have been Christian by definition and the education I have received certainly drew its values and its blindspots from a tradition which secular thought has in large part adopted even while distancing itself from it.

Qua philosopher and qua a woman participating in a history which was initially and primarily one of men, I want to be the inheritor of a tradition, but of a tradition which today is challenged by a double-barrelled question: What happened to us? How can we contribute to a common future? As I see it, these two questions are linked. For better or for worse, knowledge and technologies but also judgements about what is real, about mankind, its origins, its history (figuring under the rubric 'progress') which were produced through our own history are now playing a crucial role in the unification of the planet. We have a responsibility, then, those of us whose chief occupation is thought, to reflect on this situation and to concern ourselves with its consequences. My commitment can be summed up as follows: to endeavour to think of our history as singular, which is to say, to resist the temptation to identify some general model to which we might have been the first to subscribe but which could be offered to all. This also means trying to represent ourselves 'to others' in civilized mode, which is to say, in a way that is not an affront to them. I regard any way of saying who 'we' are which puts into play what we have come to know and what others do 'not yet' know as an affront. Put differently, the way in which we have defined progress, whether in philosophy (reason/ beliefs) or in theology (monotheism/idolatry) or in science (objective knowledge/anthropocentric illusions) is not civilized. It constitutes a declaration of war even, since, for their greater good, we mean to destroy the others by detaching them from what is their own inheritance.

I am not unaware of the fact that the threat of destruction does not come primarily from thinkers, be they philosophers, theologians or scientists, but from what today is called 'economic globalization'. This does not prevent our predominant way of representing our-selves from contributing to the process of destruction, for we coin words by appeal to which others can claim merely to be combating superstitious usage blocking the path of 'progress'. And when, for instance, we train doctors and psychologists coming from 'Third World' countries in such a way that they are led to scorn the ways of thinking about illness and cure practised in their own native countries, we contribute directly to a process of destruction via contempt and discredit.

Resisting the Modern Inconsistency

The orientation of my contribution may be seen as a revival of the position which was Alfred N. Whitehead's in his *Science and the Modern World*, which is to say before he became engaged in the speculative adventure which was to lead him to the notion of a cosmos placed under the sign of creativity. More precisely, my aim is to revive this position since it explains why Whitehead got caught up in the later adventure. It was a question of resisting the modern dichotomy between nature conceived of as blind, divested of all meaning, and the human subject, free and the source of all value. This is a dichotomy to which most of us submit unreflectively, of which we are sometimes proud (we have rid nature of all anthropomorphism) and whose paradoxes we confront (the mind/body problem). But this same dichotomy is one Whitehead deemed an inconsistency, something to be resisted:

> This radical inconsistency at the basis of modern thought accounts for much that is half-hearted and wavering in our civilisation. It would be going too far to say that it distracts thought. It enfeebles it, by reason of the inconsistency lurking in the background. After all, the men of the Middle Ages were in pursuit of an excellency of which we have nearly forgotten the existence. They set before themselves the ideal of the attainment of a harmony of the understanding. We are content with superficial orderings from diverse arbitrary starting points. For instance, the enterprises produced by the individualistic energy of the European peoples presuppose physical actions directed to final cause. But the science which is employed in their development is based on a philosophy which asserts that physical causation is supreme, and which disjoins the physical cause from the final end. It is not popular to dwell on the absolute contradiction here involved. It is the fact, however you glaze it over with phrases. (Whitehead 1967, 76)

It is from this inconsistency, this want of harmony in our understanding that I intend to proceed. Indeed, it is perhaps the tangle of contradictions that derive from it that make us so formidable. This is what Bruno Latour suggests when he describes the invincible character, not of one position but of an aggregate of positions, which allows everything to be affirmed, everything to be denounced, and their contraries likewise:

> You think that thunder is a divinity? The modern critique will show that it is generated by mere physical mechanisms that have no influence over the progress of human affairs. You are stuck in a traditional economy? The modern critique will show you that physical mechanisms can upset the progress of human affairs by mobilising huge productive forces. You think the spirit of the ancestors can hold you forever hostage to their laws? The modern critique will show you that you are hostage to yourselves and that the spiritual world is your own human – too human – construction. You then think you can do everything and develop your societies as you see fit? The modern critique will show you that the iron laws of society and economics are much more inflexible than those of your ancestors. You are indignant that the world is being mechanised? The modern critique will tell you about the creator God to whom everything belongs and who gave man everything. You are indignant that society is secular? The modern critique will show you that spirituality is thereby liberated, and that a wholly spiritual religion is far superior. You call yourself religious? The modern critique will have a hearty laugh at your expense! (Latour 1993, 38)

How is this to be resisted? asks Latour, when according to the particular representative of modernity that you are up against you will be confronted with a critique mobilizing either a transcendent nature, or an aggregate of productive forces produced by human effort, or a society freely created by men, or a society subjected to laws transcending human decisions, or a distant God, or an intimate God close to the heart of each person. Naturally, my aim here is not to propose a new coherent system but to emphasize the fact that the creation of such a system must call into question the manner in which our regnant points of reference are defined and presented, with each being defined in terms of progress (people used to believe, but we now know that . . .) but progress which defines itself primarily in terms of power, the power to criticize the other, denounce him or her as irrational and as comprehending nothing of (science, human history, religion, etc.). This, then, is what gives me the right to speak, in the context of an encounter between 'science and theology', of religion without being a believer, and of science without being a scientist. The manner in which both scientific practices and practices appealing to an order of meaning that goes beyond fact understand themselves and present themselves to others concerns all, since we are all of us the inheritors of the same conflictual history.

Let me return here to Whitehead's position in *Science and the Modern World*. For Whitehead, the fact that religion has lost its power in the modern era, that it has increasingly been reduced to a species of spiritual cosmetic 'veneer' for changes and innovations to which it was subjected rather than party, was, even for a non-believer like himself, a disaster. The techno-scientific dynamic characteristic of the modern era has not been matched by an innovative dynamic on the side of religion notwithstanding that it represents one of the elemental experiences of humanity. This elemental experience has not been nurtured, cultivated in a way that corresponds to the formidable and novel challenge constituted by techno-scientific innovation, and this has left the latter free to identify itself with progress.

> For over two centuries religion has been on the defensive, and on a weak defensive. The period has been one of unprecedented intellectual progress. In this way a series of novel situations have been produced for thought. Each occasion has found the religious thinkers unprepared. Something, which has been proclaimed to be vital, has finally, after struggle, distress, and anathema, been modified and otherwise interpreted. The next generation of religious apologists then congratulates the religious world on the deeper insight which has been gained. The result of the continued repetition of this undignified retreat, during many generations, has at last almost entirely destroyed the intellectual authority of religious thinkers. (Whitehead 1967, 188)

To use a simple example, I shall cite the problem of Darwinian evolution. Most theologians have now accepted it and powerlessly witness the rise of 'biblical creationism', whose proponents affirm that modern biology leaves no room for faith. And these creationists are not entirely wrong: the very fact that, in the name of scientific rationality, biologists like Richard Dawkins and many others under-

take to use selection to explain (away) the full panoply of human
values, social obligations, moral principles, etc. amply testifies to the
fact that Christian thinkers have not only accepted Darwin, they
have accepted him unconditionally; their acceptance has not been
so fashioned as to force biologists to view them as serious interlocutors, obliging the former to think, constraining them not to
define human history in terms of a bare tract laid wide open to
Darwinian conquest. That creationists today are able to define themselves as the sole opponents of a godless world, that they are able to
think that a literalist reading of the Bible is the only path opposition
can take, is not totally unjustified. It gives expression to the fact that,
in the officially Christian world, few Christian thinkers have put the
weight of their intellectual authority at the service of a radical and
informed critique of biological reductionism. The arrogance and, I
would add, the inanity of reductionist biology is also the expression
of this absence of opposition: when it incurs no risks thought always
assumes the power of the incumbent. That is why a philosopher,
'non-Christian', but belonging to a tradition marked by vexed and
interesting relations between philosophy and theology may regret,
along with Whitehead and Latour, that theology (whether of a distant
or absent God or of an intimate one) no longer figures as an
argumentative or creative force opposing the exclusive authority of
the sciences or, more precisely, assisting them in guarding against
the arrogance and stupidity to which their present-day lack of
fearless, imaginative interlocutors makes them prone.

   One of the aims of my account will be to try to attach a meaning
to the proposition with which Whitehead concludes his diagnostic:
'Religion will not regain its old power until it can face change in the
same spirit as does science' (Whitehead 1967, 189). How, then, might
we speak of the sciences so that the endeavours of thinkers concerned with religion might eventually meet change 'in the same
spirit as does science'?

Complementarity: A Too Easy Answer

I have set my account under the sign of complementarity. It is
common knowledge that the idea of complementarity was the issue

of Niels Bohr's thinking on pondering the implications of the then emerging quantum mechanics. Yet, outside quantum mechanics the idea can take on very different meanings.

At one extreme, if complementarity turns on content it can lead back to an earlier position, both mechanistic and Christian, dating back to the very beginnings of the modern conception of nature: nature as a clock. The works of the clock, subject to mechanical laws, are the domain of science: they are, in that they are works, intelligible, expressing the order of a world subject to laws. But they are mute as to the finality of the clock, as to its value. The same laws that explain a perfect clock explain a crazy clock. The clock, inasmuch as it tells the time, presupposes its creator, he for whom the many possibilities of adjustment between the parts are not of equal value. The clock thus articulates two points of view, irreducibly distinct, the one pointing to an order to be described and verified, and the other to what fulfils a finality, to be appraised. In this regard it illustrates the complementary character of the two approaches, each justified and necessary but neither sufficient.

As my title indicates, it is precisely this use of the notion of complementarity that I repudiate: the example of the clock blocks any progression beyond complementarity. Plainly, the image of the clock dovetails perfectly with a static conception of values and a hierarchical conception of scientific knowledge. The clock has one value, its purpose is to tell the time, it is designed to tell the time. And the works which mediate this value are also and primarily the object of one unique science. It thus implies the perspective of what might be called 'summit talks' between the one true science (physics, of course) and that (philosophy and theology?) which represents 'values'.

The image of the clock is still with us and will remain so for as long as the sciences are dominated by a hierarchical ordering. But its meaning has changed with the disappearance of Christianity as the authoritative source of values. Thus at the end of *A Brief History of Time* Stephen Hawking envisages the 'end of physics', the moment, which he considers imminent, when physicists will be agreed on the fundamental equation (a descendant of the laws of mechanics) explicitating the statement 'The Universe exists'. This equation, he explains will enable us to know 'the mind of God' as Creator of this universe, which is to say the 'how' of divine creation. It will then remain to discuss 'why' this universe and not another: that will be the time to bring together theologians, philosophers, indeed all and sundry. Hawking thus raises anew the ancient issue of the disjunction of the 'how' and the 'why' as illustrated by the clock, and he raises it in a manner which effectively brings out the fact that the disjunction is asymmetrical. The question of 'how' concerns that on which agreement is possible, and an agreement involving only the physicists, whereas the discussion turning on 'why' is open and brings in 'everyone'. What is more, the 'why' is subordinate to the 'how', it is the 'why' of the 'how': the open forum comes about after the physicists have reached agreement and it will focus on the 'why' of the matter of fact which they will have determined. In other words, behind the apparent symmetry there lies the opposition between rational knowledge, capable of harmonizing views, on the one hand, and on the other, the array of convictions, opinions, judgements as to values and ends, an 'open' array indeed, but one holding out no prospect of agreement since it is what is 'left over' when the questions on which agreement is possible have been resolved. Complementarity between a world order with the capacity to generate agreement among physicists (and, by implication, among all human beings) on the one hand, and those questions which are 'up for grabs' because they concern the final purposes of this world on the other, can admit of no 'beyond', for what it expresses is, at bottom, the opposition between reason and opinion.

Of course, the situation has changed and the sciences of today are able to put new questions which do not point to the unity of a lawful universe as something to be ascertained but to a qualitative and non-hierarchical multiplicity of intelligible behaviours. There exists, in fact, a tension between what might be called the science of principles (that of Hawking and the physicists of grand unification) and a science of models which nurtures a new empirical appetite for the plurality of events, the diversity of processes, the many distinctions between order and disorder. The themes of chaos, bifurcations, auto-organization, the frontier between order and chaos, etc. create new interests. The heap of sand, the cyclone, the wave in the ocean, the avalanche, the amoeba become 'beings' evincing specific, collective behaviours eluding the general laws of probability. New articulations are introduced which do away with the opposition between arbitrary and intelligible. Questions now come to nest around the contrast between stable and unstable: given a specific behaviour emerging from a multiplicity of interactions, the point now is to describe its relation to its 'milieu', and the way in which it will transform itself if this relation is modified.

This pluralist orientation at the heart of the contemporary sciences certainly permits the escape from the clock and the clock-maker mindset and inspires fresh images no longer suggesting that creation is a question of the imposition of meaning onto inert and blind matter. However, the seductive idea that we might identify these new developments with a 'good' science, finally offering among other things, support to religion, strikes me as dangerous. It is not because models are pluralist and because they confer an irreducible and positive meaning on unpredictability that they are able to give sense to the human demand for meaning. It is not because they elude determinism that they enable us to reflect on what we mean by 'liberty' or 'creativity'. So the question of comple-mentarity remains important and must be raised independently of particular scientific contents and the determinist or probabilistic conceptions that they propose. It is scientific practice itself that needs to be reconceived.

To underscore this point I want to establish a sharp contrast between 'probable' and 'possible'. All the models to which I have referred in the foregoing are probabilistic and thus depend on a description of the situation in terms of well-defined variables. That the sciences have always operated with the probable is neither a deficiency nor a limitation. It is the consequence of the approach they embody, requiring that the scientist be able to produce an objective description of the situation that is of interest, that is requiring of the situation itself that it be susceptible of description in terms of well-defined variables and their functional articulation. This is no trivial requirement and indeed only laboratory situations usually fulfil it. Furthermore, this requirement directly contradicts what we understand by 'possible' when it concerns the activity of human beings as well as the meaning we ascribe to their 'freedom'.

This question was discussed already in the seventeenth century. The philosopher Leibniz confronted the question of Buridan's ass, faced by two indistinguishable meadows, symmetrically extended on its left and on its right. This thought experiment was usually introduced in order to oppose free will and reason: the ass would choose without any good reason to elect the one or the other. However, Leibniz struggled against this opposition: was he going to accept that the ass remains immobilized, incapable of choice? Leibniz had the genius to recognize that the ass was in the situation we associate with unstable systems: somewhat like a pencil standing on end. Any slight difference, at this point as insignificant as to elude all description, a light breeze or the song of a bird, would suffice to 'break the symmetry' between left and right. He thus concluded that the supposed symmetry between the meadows was a sheer chimera. However, the inevitable character of the 'breaking of symmetry' which leads the ass to choose one meadow rather than another only allows Leibniz to slip his opponents' objection. It is not enough that I can speak of the instability of the unmoving pencil standing on its point and of the inability to predict in which direction it will fall (the symmetry may be broken with equal probability in all directions) to be able to speak of the freedom of the pencil. If the possible has a true, positive meaning, it requires that its actualization correspond to the transformation of the very way in which a situation may be described or defined, for example by the addition of a dimension that the variables did not take into account. Setting aside Buridan's ass, Buridan the philosopher confronted by two equal choices may well be unable, unlike the ass, to choose, because the question of what reasons to adduce to justify his choice would paralyse him. He might equally well burst out laughing when faced by the threat of paralysis and just toss a coin. Or again, he might ponder it until some novel 'sensitivity' to aspects which were not taken into account in the first definition of the choice emerged. As soon as we move from the ass to the philosopher the situation becomes indeterminate because we do not know what attitude the philosopher, or indeed any human person, will adopt;

how they themselves will be transformed by the difficulty and how they will finally define the situation with which they are confronted. The question is thus not one of the unforeseeable, which is an epistemological issue, but concerns, rather, the element of novelty, the event itself, in the sense in which it is the very description of the situation which is thus going to be transformed. The possible is not a question of knowledge but of production of existence, of becoming.

I can elicit, by way of example, an event at the Seattle 1999 demonstration against the World Trade Organization (WTO), as an example of events which both manifest a transformation of our relation to a situation and a new possibility. Suddenly, the way in which today's world economic order defines itself and the variables used to describe it are contested in a manner which make a difference. Even the American press resounded with it: there are now, American commentators understood, two different ways of conceiving globalization! What had seemed simply to yield to the probability calculus has become indeterminate because the commitment of demonstrators has thrown the description of the situation into question.

Such an event was not, however, 'unpredictable' like an earth tremor or the path of a cyclone. It had long been prepared for by groups of non-violent activists for whom the possible was alive, an obligation to act. Its success manifested itself in the introduction of what I would call, borrowing a term from the mathematicians, an 'unknown' in the characterization of our collective future: opposition is possible! It is possible to refuse to negotiate in the terms proposed but to stand out for a world whose future is not to be described in those terms. (I must now, just before the publication of this book, add that the 11 September 2001 attacks on the New York World Trade Center is also an 'unknown producing event'. We now know how far hatred can go, how 'abnormal' our world has become. A very dark possible has arisen which will not go away by the sheer power of bombs and the coalition of frightened states.)

Obviously nothing is guaranteed but one way or another the meaning of these events depends on how the possible they affirm will make a difference to us, obliging us to ensure it has consequences. It will depend on whether or not we succeed in becoming inheritors of the possibility that has been bequeathed us in the face of the probability that everything will go on as before.

This, then, is the meaning that I want to give complementarity: not the complementarity of two descriptions but of two species of practice and their respective requirements. When it is a question of probabilities the requirement is that the situation be well defined. It is the precondition for a model to articulate its variables. When it is a question of what may happen, of possibility and becoming, what is pivotal is the commitment of those who discern it, the way in which their action or way of life attests to it and makes it real for others. As is well known, the original meaning of the term 'martyr' was 'witness'. The possible only exists through its witnesses, and witnesses are not those who dictate how a situation should be defined but those whose own transformation calls into question the power of definitions.

Complementary Commitments

The sense that I have just given the notion of complementarity extends, in radicalizing it, the lesson of quantum mechanics. Complementarity in its original sense belongs to the sphere of the experimental sciences and insists on the fact that experimentation is never a matter of neutral 'verification'. It is always some experimental device which allows the assignment of a value to a variable, be it velocity, or position, or any other quantity (measure?) by which a phenomenon is characterized. And when it is a case of a quantum phenomenon it is important to recognize that this phenomenon is not in itself 'defined' by the variables whose terms we use to characterize it. To determine the velocity of an electron is not simply to get to know its velocity but is to address the electron experimentally in such a way that we can attribute the meaning of 'velocity' to the measure we take. The lesson of complementarity in quantum mechanics thus demands of us that we recognize that our knowledge is always an answer to the questions which we are capable of putting, that is to say, is relative to the determinate mode in which we address that which has to deliver the answers. This does not mean that what we address is unknowable but reminds us that knowledge presupposes the setting up of a link productive of meaning and that all setting up of links presupposes a practical choice.

In one sense the lesson Bohr drew from quantum mechanics has an ethical dimension: there is no conceivable knowledge independent of the establishing of a correlation and this correlation is not neutral, it aligns its object with what that mode of knowing requires. Again, this is not to say that our knowledge is arbitrary. The ethics of complementarity is precisely the rejection of the dismal disjunction which runs: either knowledge designates its object and is thus independent of our choices, or it designates us and is thus only 'subjective'. The recognition that we are committed by our questions, by what we define as 'valid answers', does not lead to scepticism, to a desperate relativism. But it questions the hegemony of those who claim to restrict themselves to describing reality 'as it is' and not 'as it responds to their questions and satisfies the requirements that these questions presuppose'.

That scientific descriptions are the results of scientists' practice no one would be able to deny. However in order to be able to speak of complementarity between practices we have to go further and characterize the practice of scientists in a way that brings out the fact that it is dependent on a choice and is not just neutral knowledge, capable, in virtue of its neutrality, of imposing itself on all in the same way.

When scientists define the knowledge that they produce as 'objective', that is to say also, when they define subjectivity as a defect, they are in fact describing a highly singular enterprise and characterizing as 'normal' or 'rational' the highly singular demands that the answers they deem valid must satisfy. They both proclaim and underestimate the highly singular values associated with their practice. It is important to emphasize that 'scientific objectivity' is not the result of a general method. It is a success, and it is a rare one: 'in this instance' we have succeeded in isolating a phenomenon and in questioning it in a way which enabled it in fact to create agreement among us, allowing us to affirm that we are constrained to assign to it the interpretation that we do; 'in this instance' we have succeeded in shedding all 'subjective freedom' in what concerns the construction of meaning. There is nothing neutral in such a success. It is by no means the negation of human freedom but is its very expression. Freedom is a precondition of being able to choose to assign value to those very situations in which one ceases to be free. It is not submission to the power of facts as against interpretation, since it springs from the recognition that, in general, the facts can be interpreted in multiple ways but aims, rather, at the highly sophisticated production of 'facts' having the peculiar feature of being able to authorize one interpretation and one only. It is not a case of researching neutral certitudes but is part of an impassioned, inventive, collective, and critical practice in which each member of the community has to put himself the question: has my colleague succeeded in producing a situation which forces me to say he/she is right? Is there no other way of interpreting his/her results which would invest the situation with a different meaning? It is a practice not indifferent to values but relative to a very particular value: only that statement has value which can survive controversy, stand up to the charge that it is only one possible interpretation and not the interpretation imposed by the facts. In brief, scientific practice is utterly singular because it depends not on a general power of facts to be part of a demonstration but on the production of facts capable of playing such a part.

Not all facts have the same value. It is possible to ascertain as much as one wants the fact that the inequalities between different regions of our world, and between the rich and the poor within one and the same society are deepening; these 'facts' do not have the power to impose their interpretation. They leave the economists free to propose models on which the free market and the 'flexibility' of employment automatically lead to the general welfare. The experimental sciences, which indeed assert that their facts have the power of proof, do not attain to a general 'objective reality'. What they call objectivity has as its primary value the capacity for 'progression', producing answers which will serve as a new starting point for new questions addressed to new experimental facts. I shall compare such progress to that of mountaineers scaling a steep rock face: each 'foothold' that bears the weight of their bodies is of importance only because it offers them support which allows them to gain access to another foothold higher up. In the same way as all the effort of the mountaineers is organized round the reliability of any foothold that would allow them, if it holds, to mount yet higher, all the dynamic of experimental science is organized around the creation of reliable new answers that will allow new risks to be taken. In both cases the primary question is: will it hold? Is it going to meet the demands that a foothold must satisfy? And in each case progress would not obtain without the trust that the success can be repeated, that progression may be pursued. This is why sciences respect the *pro tempore*. Success, for them, is not a stable conclusion but a result whose interest lies in its making further results possible.

Philosophers or theologians who take seriously scientific statements bearing upon, say, the origin of the universe and its intelligibility, should thus beware of conferring on such statements a status not conferred by the physicists. The Big Bang, for example, or the models of origin which today inform the anthropic principle, may as well be denied as upheld by the physics of tomorrow. And the fact that they may have been tied in with philosophical or religious stakes will not matter to the physicists. These theories are the exclusive province of those who have assigned to them a scientific meaning and for those so engaged they have no value beyond that of being a staging post on the way to a future where they might well be refuted.

Perhaps it is now possible to speak of 'choice' in what concerns scientific practice and to characterize that on which it depends. The precondition of the scientific dynamic that I have described is its capacity to mark out and be about those aspects of reality which can be 'objectively defined', and I hope it is now understood that it is an extremely restrictive condition, a condition which neutrinos, electrons, atoms, molecules, bacteria do indeed satisfy but one which ceases to be satisfied if we turn to something we recognize as capable of conferring a meaning on what happens to it. The problem is already there when it concerns rats in the laboratory; it is patently obvious in the case of human beings. To return to the metaphor of the mountaineers, let us imagine that the rock face which they are scaling is sensitive to their efforts, that it can choose to offer them purchase or to give way suddenly, to co-operate with their efforts, even to thrust them towards the upper reaches or to rid itself of them in one brusque convulsion. Learning to scale such rock faces would perhaps involve the patience and love with which we create bonds with shy animals but such climbers would no longer be mountaineers since the skill of the mountaineer presupposes the indifference of the rock face and not the question of what the rock face feels when it offers support. In the same way, the entire spectrum of laboratory trials presupposes that the scientists are free to manipulate a particular being's environment to explore the variables which will figure in their description, and also the way in which its behaviour articulates variables; but such variables cease to perform that role if what is being investigated is capable of interpreting what it is being subjected to.

Committed to the Possible

If Whitehead's proposition has a meaning, if religion could come to 'face change in the same spirit as does science', it cannot be a matter of 'resembling' it. Resemblance is neither possible nor desirable as the 'same spirit' must characterize a practice which, far from demanding facts able to be part in a proof, should be responding to a 'complementary' commitment. That the neutrino, the electron, the atom, the molecule, the genome, the bacterium, inasmuch as science has been able to define them, offer no support to those questions which preoccupy a practice of a religious type, enters into the very conditions of their scientific definition: this definition has as its condition the satisfaction of experimental demands which imply the pertinence (not the truth) of a description representing such beings as ones incapable of conferring a meaning on what happens to them. On the other hand, if one takes religion in the broadest sense, in the sense in which it also includes, for instance, the rites of traditional hunters who request of the spirit of the animal they intend to kill both permission and pardon, it must be said that the religious question is posed every time we feel that the manner in which we investigate a being may destroy or create something possible, may mutilate, diminish, humiliate or affirm, raise up, or amplify. The value of these practices has as its condition that what they address is not indifferent, that it may be transformed for better or for worse. When it's a matter of religion, it is a question not of proof but of possibility. It is the difference that it is possible to make to the other, and with the other, which commits and obligates. We have here a true practical complementarity since it is a condition of success that the one excludes the relevance of the other and vice versa.

How, if these practices are complementary inasmuch as the values with which they engage are mutually exclusive, can they, as Whitehead proposes, 'face change in the same spirit'? The key word here might well be 'trust'. The work of scientists has as a precondition a trust in the possibility of progress, a trust without which surprises, difficulties, would hardly constitute for them an 'opportunity' inviting an effort of creation. Scientific objectivity itself does not refer to a pre-existent 'objective reality' but to a kind of success of which trust is the condition. It is only when objectivity is defined in an abstract fashion, when 'facts' no longer purport to be the answer to a 'good' question but to represent access to an objective world, that scientists tend to forget about their own trust. They then present themselves as those who 'restrict themselves to describing' the world, a world which they then proclaim is such as can accord no meaning to trust, freedom, creative effort. Forgetting that, qua scientists, they have freely chosen to value what restricts their freedom and that they need the trust in the possibility of so doing, they disavow the very phenomena which are integral to the production of scientific description.

If science involves commitment and trust, the fact that scientific visions of a world devoid of finality, of a world inhabited by forces and particles 'hurrying . . . endlessly, meaninglessly' (Whitehead 1967, 54) successfully asserted themselves against the intelligibility of the world conceived in terms of 'design', the realization of a divine plan, is a fact which must be understood not as a confrontation between two modes of commitment but as a confrontation between two powers. Reference to a divine plan grounds the power and authority of religion just as a reference to an 'objective reality' grounds the power of science which claims to restrict itself to being its faithful mouthpiece. Complementarity, as I have proposed it, submits each of those modes of commitment that it articulates to a common trial: to renounce such justifications as would confer on either a universal and neutral legitimacy, and to present themselves as creative, each affirming in its own way a trust which lays itself open to risk and the possibility of learning. It is as creative, but through the very differences between the values and the requirements of their respective creations, that complementary enterprises, divergent constructions of truth can, not only offer mutual recognition, but mutually protect the other from the seductions of power.

So we do indeed 'miss' the 'old power' of religion, whose destruction was part of the problem presented by our 'modern world' as Whitehead interpreted it. What is missing is not, however, the authority of any particular statement of religious truth but the trusting and creative power that would oblige scientists to reflect on what they do and to represent themselves in the singularity of their own commitment and creative effort. In other words, the possibility of reviving this old power would involve its representing itself as a practice and a practice which must indeed 'face change in the same spirit as does science'. Confronted by the imaginative dynamics of science, only imaginative trust can give non-scientific thinkers (I am thinking as much of philosophers as of theologians) the boldness to accept a commitment 'to the possible', as inventive, creative and daring as that of scientists 'to proof'.

Trust, if understood 'in the same spirit' as that embraced by science, is essential to commitment, to the effort of creation which it demands. It has no guarantee in some external reference in which one can trust. This does not mean that it is necessary to renounce the religious conviction according to which reality answers to a 'design', but it signifies, perhaps, that what is understood by 'design' must be, like scientific objectivity, separated from any reference to power. If I might play with words, we would no longer proclaim that 'in God we trust' but maybe we would be committed by God's trust in us.

The metaphor of the clock systematically linked objectivity (mechanics has the power to say how the springs work) and design (the clock's function, to tell the time). The clock's design expresses the aim and volition of the clockmaker who constructed it. In this perspective the hypothesis of design implies that even if 'God's ways are unfathomable' such ways do exist, which means that religion can compete with science in delivering the best way of describing the workings (predicated on their functioning or their function) and can share with science the power of judgement, of contrasting 'truth' with illusion. Indeed a reference to the ways of God, even if unfathomable, implies that there is a difference between what conforms to them and what ignores or betrays them.

An Adventure of Hope?

Should we, then, abandon 'design'? It is worth emphasizing that while the respective meanings of the Anglo-Saxon term 'design' and the French *'designer'* (to designate, to point out) have diverged, their common etymological root returns them both to 'what is marked by a sign'. Now the sign does not give the power to adjudge, nor is it an instrument with which to discriminate truth from illusion. The sign is always, primarily, relative. This is patently so since for a sign to figure as such we need the relation between something or someone producing it and someone to whom it will make a difference. But here I propose to go beyond the routine signs which convey the impression that the relation predates the occurrence of the sign (we know how to interpret the road sign) in order to conceive the relation as an event and to appreciate the difference the sign makes in opening up a new possibility of thinking and feeling. The event at Seattle (December 1999), where the seemingly invincible power of the WTO in redefining our world was confronted is a sign for those who 'feel' the 'non probable' possibility of an alternative narrative. It is not a question of indices (which would establish the existence of a tide of opposition), it is not a question of icons (such an event gives us nothing to understand and contemplate), and it is not a question of symbols (it does not place us in the position of interpreters). Peirce's classification in terms of indices, icons and symbols belongs to a theory of knowledge. Here we have signs which do not turn on a reference to an external reality but on a production of existence. Their efficacy must be spoken of in terms of becoming and not of knowledge. Such signs only exist for those who wonder how to respond to them and have no other meaning than that which they will prove capable of assigning to them: the meaning here is a production, a creation, a process of learning, not an interpretation which attempts to go back to the intentions of whoever produced the sign.

To understand 'design' in terms of 'marked by signs' which are also questions whose meaning has to be constructed, in their lives and in their practice, by those who 'are marked' by them, implies the abandonment of a problematic of knowledge (including unverifiable knowledge if the ways of God are indeed unfathomable) in favour of a problematic of commitment 'to the possible'. If the world 'gives a sign' it is in the mode of an event, of the creation of a relation here and now between the world and he or she for whom it is a sign. And in this case religious practices would indeed 'face change in the same spirit as does science'. Their trust would be in this world qua 'designed', 'marked by signs', in the sense in which it is this world, and not a power that transcends it, which obliges us to think, create, lay open to risk what we know and what we are. It is 'this world' too, in which we are prompted to feel and think by the beings that inhabit it, which ought to equip us to oppose the reductionist arrogance of biologists for whom the sole rationale underlying the history of living things is genetic selection.

If 'design' refers to events that engage us, or adventure our lives and practices, it refers, as Whitehead proposed, to change, to the creation of possibilities where what we saw were facts. Let us take, say, changes such as those associated with women's movements but also those linked to movements opposed to the exploitation and torture to which we subject animals: in all these cases that which was once tolerated has become intolerable and the new possibilities created by those changes ought to be explored in their many implications. They should force us to question anew, with the same type of eagerness and confidence, with the same radicalism as do the sciences, all those religious and philosophical statements which imply, in one way or another, that what today is regarded as intolerable might be tolerated. And to do so, not with remorse or guilt but through a creative effort which explores the new possibilities ushered in by change. Another example is the way both Western religion and philosophy were for a long time defined by their common condemnation of what they deemed superstition, idolatrous beliefs, fetishisms: in so doing they justified the destruction of living traditions in the name of God or reason. The world has changed and it is well understood that today we all refuse to perpetuate the violence of the past to which we are the heirs. But in order to succeed in avoiding a simply 'tolerant' stance, a radical effort of creation is required from both monotheistic faith and philosophical reason. It is not only a question of renouncing ambitions of conquest and of conversion, it needs the words with which to celebrate our common world as peopled by fetishes, ancestors, strange divinities which our mores lead us to denounce. Again, any such effort requires a trust in a possibility which is contemporaneous with us and which would have seemed utter madness fifty years ago: to actually succeed in creating a human history of which all peoples, all those traditions which confer on groups the power to 'design' and be 'designed', would become the co-authors.

Only trust, then, is capable of reuniting complementary items, of envisaging going 'beyond complementarity' without an appeal to any knowledge with the power to reunite and uncover the harmony underlying divergence. As I read it Whitehead's great work, *Process and Reality*, *is* the exemplar par excellence of this double movement: the affirmation of trust and the renunciation of power. It is the very point of 'speculative philosophy' as Whitehead proposes it, whose purpose it is to define the history of the philosophy it inherits as an adventure of hope. For Whitehead, trying to construct concepts which confirm the intelligible coherence of the totality of what exists is not a normative enterprise but an adventure and the full unfolding of this adventure requires from the philosopher that he/she renounces as much the authority of scientific reasons as that of moral reasons since these two authorities plunge us into incoherence, the one referring to an 'objective' world, the other to a self-conscious subject, responsible for the meanings that direct his or her life. The concepts that Whitehead constructs in *Process and*

Reality do not appeal to any authority higher than science and morality but to what both science and morality attest through their practices: creativity. Authority, even when it seeks to assert itself in a neutral and universal fashion, attests, through its bold dis-qualification of what would not be a matter of 'neutral' or 'objective' knowledge to this ultimate fact, creativity. But speculative philosophy requires, further, that creativity not be blind, that it give a meaning to trust in the possibility that contradictions may be overcome by an experience which affirms them qua contrasts. Indeed it is not a question of going beyond this world, but one of coherence since the very existence of speculative philosophy as part of this world testifies to this trust. Whitehead's God is the conceptual answer to this speculative requirement that conflict and contradiction not be the last word. It is a strange God indeed, radically devoid of the kind of power that we associate with a creator, a judge, a father or even a designer. It is a 'creature of creativity' since it only transcends the world through everlasting urgency, through everlasting yearning, the vector of an everlasting question posed, not in general, but always to this world, this experience: what is the best way out of this impasse, can the future get beyond this disjunction, 'that . . . or else that' for a contrasted affirmation 'and . . . and'. It is the everlasting reiteration of an unknown which refers not to Its own design but to creativity of which It is itself a creature. Qua Deity it is neither a source of truth beyond this world nor the truth of this world, but what we presuppose when we affirm possibility, when we affirm that our individual singular experiences are not closed off through our sticking to what we know, but may arise in the light of what we do not know.

We have no general idea of what it means to place oneself beyond complementarity but we are able to recognize concrete situations which oblige us to learn to start from the unknown. Such is the significance I would ascribe most particularly to Gaia – that being our planet qua living thing, a creature of life and the condition of our lives of which James Lovelock has proposed that we learn to develop an awareness and respect. Gaia has been denounced by scientists as not having objective existence and by some theologians as threatening a return to idolatrous cults, transforming a scientific construct into an object of worship. And indeed Gaia does go beyond the order of 'facts' as determinable by science. More precisely, to those collective systems which scientists have shown to be responsible for the habitable nature of the earth and of whose stable or unstable character they debate, it adds a name which points up the movement from the scientific question ('now we know') to a question addressed to us all, denizens of the Earth: 'What ought we to do?' Gaia bespeaks our belonging to the Earth and does so in a way that creates a new type of 'us': we are all, henceforth, through science but beyond science, forced to conceive of ourselves as embedded in a long, gradual and vexed history, the story of our Earth which we are incapable of mastering and subjecting to our ends, but which we are now quite capable of modifying in a way that would be disastrous for us. There is indeed no common measure unifying human 'means' and the energies that bring about tornadoes, tides, monsoons, and so on. But the instability or meta-stability of Gaia as a collective tangled set of processes means it is 'ticklish', which is to say that human activities can trigger effects of a magnitude answering to no common measure with their causes, with the energy we mobilized. Gaia is that which could with a shrug of the shoulders as easily rid itself of humankind as of a gnat tickling it: the shrug of the shoulders is, quantitatively, a disproportionate reaction in relation to the contact with the gnat and implies not a reaction of controllable cause and effect but a sensitivity. Gaia thus obliges us to cease thinking of nature as wild or domesticated, to be exploited or to be preserved, but in terms of a delicate agency of ungovernable forces.

To respect Gaia does not mean making it the object of a cult or ascribing to it intentions or judgements but being obliged to think of a future in which we should learn how not to 'irritate' the sensitivity of a Being proof against our reasons and indifferent to our projects. To name Gaia is to give to a set of unknowns on which our common future depends a new kind of importance: here are not problems to which tomorrow progress will deliver solutions but ones from which we must begin learning today what we should be taking into account. Put differently, Gaia implies and demands the creation of a new type of 'us' beyond complementarity, not just a 'we, unanimously', mobilized, putting aside differences in the face of threat, but a 'we' emerging from the multiplicity of bonds that we should succeed in creating if we were to become capable of transforming the threat of Gaia into a vector of learning and creativity.

Why Don't We Miss the Absent Ones?

I want to conclude with a question which offers a more direct example of the link I am seeking to establish between the question of a 'beyond complementarity' and the challenge of thinking from the vantage point of what we do not know. The scientific committee for our conference brings together, besides theologians and philosophers, scientists from the fields of chemistry, mathematics, zoology, biology, biochemistry. Where, may I ask, are the specialists from sociology or psychology? More importantly, why do we not miss them? Why do the sciences which make human beings and their societies their object of study not constrain us, as do the natural sciences, to reinvigorate our vocabulary and our hypotheses? Make this absence your starting point and perhaps, like me, you will begin to see how much the contemporary situation, how much the relations between 'science and theology' which bring us together here, are marked by the fact that when we think of science we think of natural science . . .

Of course what we 'know' as specialists in natural science, as theologians and as philosophers is how disappointing the social and human sciences can be, and what I've said about scientific practice is able to explain this. If to be a scientist is to require that what is investigated should have the power to expose risk to its interpretations, to vindicate one over others, how can this requirement be met when it is human beings that are studied, who are themselves products of interpretation and thus capable of interpreting the question addressed to them, of conferring a meaning upon it and offering answer that is a function of this meaning? It comes as no surprise, then, that so often when it is a matter of human beings and their societies, scientific descriptions cease to be creative, become reductive, failing to assist us in thinking in terms of what human beings are – or could become – capable of, but representing them, rather, as under the sway of beliefs, interests, relations of power or domination, habits and social or cultural prejudices. Such descriptions imitate those of 'objective' science, assuming that success in defining the way an electromagnetic field determines an electron's behaviour is replicated by a definition of the way in which the sway of prejudices determines the behaviour of a human being ... and forgetting that in this latter case it amounts to no more than describing in a sophisticated manner what the expression 'sway of prejudices' already implies.

However, if we attempt to think 'from the vantage point of what we do not know' we should find ourselves wondering what the relation between the sciences and theology would be like if the human sciences had taught us things as relevant and unexpected about humans, social relationships and societies as do the natural sciences about chaos, atoms, genes and neurones. Then we might be able to assess the extent to which we miss them, the extent to which we need the knowledge which exposes to risk our ideas and prejudices about humans. And perhaps the situation that is ours, which may appear 'normal' to us, will look like a direct expression of the incoherence that Whitehead described: the human sciences are literally the victims of this incoherence, called upon to privilege what explains our histories and our behaviours in a causal, passive, probabilistic way and to eliminate what attests the possible, the capacity of humans to take a stand, to become actively involved and to go on becoming.

What the social and human sciences investigate situates itself, indeed entirely, 'beyond complementarity', at the point where all definitions become a problem or a challenge, where every explanation prompts a transformation through which it loses its power, where every new link engages a becoming. This does not mean that the social and human sciences should situate themselves 'beyond complementarity', that they should take as their object possibility or becoming. It could well mean that they ought to become as risky and selective as the experimental sciences. Indeed, that which they should be investigating, that from which they might learn, would not be general situations but the ones which have the power to put at risk our ideas and our prejudices, events through which humans generate new ways of becoming, of getting involved and being committed, new capacities for calling more things into question, new sensitivities defining as intolerable that which has been tolerated, new modes of situating themselves in the world. And, above all, new practical experiences in self-organization leading to creative, empowering modes of togetherness.

What would happen if the specialists in the human and social sciences sought not to imitate the objective sciences in terms of method or proof but, rather, with a view to placing at risk the justifications and the representations which dominate those practical domains (teaching, justice, health, political organization, production and the discussion of knowledge, modes of debate and resolution, etc.) which are their proper concern? If they were to declare themselves as dependent on what actually attests to the possible in their fields, on the actual processes of creation of new meanings and commitments as the specialists of objective sciences are dependent on the production of new experimental settings? If they were to commit themselves 'to human history' in the same spirit as do the objective sciences 'to nature', which is to say by investigating history as what constrains us to think and learn?

Were that the case, concourses like this one would be altered by the presence of those for whom it would be vital to learn what is possible, what counts as success and failure, when scientists, theologians and philosophers meet. And the effect of their attentive, questioning, interested presence would be to produce a situation 'beyond complementarity', where to our respective enquiries and knowledge is added the question that unites us and 'de-signs' us, marks us out with a sign, without belonging to any of us: how might we construct a common world where our many differences in respect of what animates us – causing us to think and feel – are not only noted and tolerated but celebrated and cultivated, recognized as multiple modes of participation in what Whitehead called the creative adventure of reality?

References

LATOUR, BRUNO. 1993. *We Have Never Been Modern,* New York: Harvester Wheatsheaf.

WHITEHEAD, ALFRED NORTH. [1925] 1967. *Science and the Modern World,* New York: The Free Press.

7

On Finality in Creation Theology: Epistemological and Theological Considerations

CHRISTOPH THEOBALD, SJ

Introduction

Seeking to conclude an alliance with recent cosmology, a sector of contemporary creation theology has allowed itself to be seduced into replacing its former Aristotelian underpinnings with the 'anthropic principle'. This contribution formulates certain reservations as to a possibly too ready alliance between faith in a creator God and an 'anthropic' cosmology which fails to take account of the internal differentiation of scientific positions, inseparable as these are from philosophical or ideological positions. The pluralism of these positions is essential to theologians themselves who, for theological reasons, reckon with the freedom of human beings to interpret their existence at the heart of the universe. It is this capacity which the 'anthropic' argument risks depriving human beings of when it naively presents itself in scientific guise. To specify the *relative* position that creation theology confers upon the notion of finality, the author briefly recalls the scientific and philosophical critiques of this concept; he then returns to the epistemological conditions of a *critical articulation* between the approaches of cosmology, even of biology, and those of theology in respect of creation, before concluding with a properly theological reflection on the messianic opening of the universe, such as it may be conceived on the basis of the biblical tradition.

It would appear that the genesis of the universe, the biosphere and the anthroposphere cannot be understood in the perspective of creation theology without introducing the concept of finality. That is clear in the most general sense where the existence of creation and the anticipation of its conclusion refer to the ideal of 'God's project' *(prothesis)*, a term coined by apocalyptic literature, then taken up and modified by Pauline theology.[1] In the same vein, and after much oscillation, Vatican Council I codified the Scholastic doctrine of the two aims of creation – the glory of God and the good of the creature – insisting on their interpenetration: the Creator seeks his glory *through* the good he procures (for) his creatures (Denzinger–Hünermann 1966). But must we infer from the global orientation implicit in the very concept of creation its legibility in a series of 'final causes' connecting the different levels of cosmic, biological and historical evolution? That is the question I shall be seeking to answer.

St Thomas appears to offer an affirmative answer in that he reverts to the Aristotelian doctrine of 'causes'.[2] But the distance separating the Angelic Doctor from Aristotle is not always taken into account: even if he makes effective use of the causal schema to conceive the *relation* between Creator and creature, the latter receiving from God his or her right to exist, St Thomas untiringly asserts that this mode of 'causality' is utterly unique and that it allows for the *autonomous* operation of secondary causes; irreducible to the first term of a series, the concept thus has a quite different acceptation than contemporary usage might lead us to suppose.

Seeking to conclude an alliance with modern science, in particular with recent cosmology, a sector of contemporary creation theology has allowed itself to be seduced into replacing its former Aristotelian

---

[1] Cf. Rom 8:28 and 9:11; Eph 1:11 and 3:11.
[2] See esp. *Summa Theologiae* Part 1, q, 44.

underpinnings by the 'anthropic principle'.[3] Now over recent years at least four versions of this principle have been distinguished: the weak anthropic principle, the enlarged weak principle, the strong principle and the enlarged strong principle (1994, 143–51). For the moment the details are unimportant; the epistemological import of these distinctions is the introduction into scientific cosmology of the concept of finality. While absent from the *most simple formulation* of the principle (Brandon Carter's of 1974) – 'What we can hope to observe must be *compatible* with the necessary conditions for our presence as observers' (1994, 143) – finality specifies the *enlarged strong principle* which postulates a necessary ordering of the properties of the universe in terms of a purpose, namely the appearance and development of living beings: 'The Universe must have those peculiar properties which allow life to develop within it at some stage in its evolution', so Barrow and Tipler's formulation (1994, 148). In another context Jacques Demaret and Dominique Lambert introduced a conception – designated by the term *strong principle* – which, as regards the concept of finality, replaces the traditional ideal of intention by that of coherence: 'The elements of the universe constitute a *coherent* totality – in the sense that they are all interdependent – whose foundation may be found in the human phenomenon.'[4] It is understandable that theologians should be interested in the progressive extension of the anthropic principle as a kind of interface between science and creation theology, highlighting the unity of the universe and exploring the limits of scientific knowledge. I want, however, to formulate certain reservations as to a possibly too ready alliance between faith in a creator God and an 'anthropic' cosmology which might not take into account the internal differentiation of scientific positions, inseparable as these are from philosophical or ideological positions.

---

[3] See, for example, Demaret and Lambert 1994, 214–17. The authors relate the Thomist doctrine of creation and the strong anthropic principle without any examination of the Angelic Doctor's modification of the Aristotelian system of causes in the light of the Scriptures.

[4] Ibid., 148. The authors also offer the following formulation: 'There exists a unified, coherent description of the entire universe founded on the existence of human beings.'

In any case it cannot be ignored that scientists themselves are far from being in agreement on the pertinence of the anthropic principle. In an over-eagerness to place reliance on it as theologians, do we not run the risk of missing the lessons, both epistemological and theological, of St Thomas' discussion of the Averroistic thesis of the eternity of the world? If he takes the trouble seven times over to show that the world's having a beginning is indemonstrable, it is to avoid conveying the idea that the believer adheres to the things of faith for flimsy reasons (Sertillanges 1945, 40f.).

This claim of the liberty of faith in respect of this or that vision of the world definitely does not mean that scientists themselves cannot undertake a comprehensive approach to interpretation of givens which oversteps the bounds of the standard model. On the contrary, the pluralism of positions is here absolutely essential to theologians themselves who above all reckon with – and for theological reasons yet to be elucidated – the freedom of human beings to interpret their existence, embedded as they are in a universe whose dimen-sions defy all imagining. This constitutive reliance of creation theology on the contingency of human freedom, which is not lawless – as the Bible and Kant knew – outweighs all teleological argument which, when represented naively in scientific guise, risks depriving human beings of the capacity to give meaning freely to their lives.

To specify somewhat the significance and position, quite relative, accorded to the idea of finality by creation theology, we can begin by briefly recalling to mind the scientific and philosophical critiques of this concept. We shall then return to the epistemological conditions of critical articulation between the approaches offered by cosmology, and even biology, and those of theology as regards creation before concluding with a properly theological reflection on the 'messianic opening' of the universe, drawing on the traces in the biblical tradition.

I. The Scientific and Philosophical Critique of the Concept of Teleology

In this first section I shall seek to show how the evolution of the modern sciences, above all biology and cosmology, have led to the systematic elimination of the concept of finality within their area of competence – this is their critical side – and how this development has, in a way, triggered a plurality of intellectual stances in relation to scientific givens which in future will need to be taken into account – this is their positive side.

Breaking the Links with Anthropomorphism

1. *In order to acquire scientific status, physics, and subsequently the life sciences, have had to combat anthropomorphism and anthropocentrism.* Let us begin with the life sciences, hallmarked from Aristotle to Kant by *finalism or teleology*: why not, in effect, avail oneself of the finality characteristic of so many human activities to use it as a universal model for explaining everything that, in nature, appears to be directed to an end, inferring from the evident purposefulness of the organs of a living being the intention of a creator? Now, Darwin shows how the combination of three simple conditions explains the semblance of pre-established design: it suffices that the fundamental structures of life vary, that they are hereditary and that the reproduction of certain variants are favoured by the environment. Thus it is that the notion of *natural selection* becomes primary. It offers, as it were, a direction for change and guides the play of variations produced by chance by configuring ever more complex wholes adapted over the course of millions of years in response to the challenges of the environment (Jacob 1981, 32f.). Already Darwin had to oppose the resurgence of the anthropomorphism that consisted in making selection a natural force. More recently, Stephen J. Gould has had to take up arms against an 'adaptationist' interpretation of evolutionary theory which assigns to natural selection the power of an optimizing agency and neglects a whole series of constraints – morphological ones for example – which do not depend at all on adaptation to the environment. The reduction of living organisms to characters or structures, each of which fulfils at best one function, results in the construction of what Gould calls a 'Panglossian universe' after Voltaire's famous

doctor who explains to his pupil Candide that it is impossible that things should not be as they are 'since everything is made for the best purpose'.

Scientific cosmology has thus had to contest the same battle against both anthropomorphism and anthropocentrism. Well before the birth of modern biology, in classical physics, and a fortiori in Einstein's cosmology governed by general relativity, the cosmological principle stated that the universe has the same appearance (not in its details but in its global aspects) *regardless of the point from which it is observed*. From this postulate, which is the foundation of all scientific physics, it follows that the earth or even our galaxy occupies a position without particular characteristics in the universe. The relativistic models of Friedman–Lemaître have been constructed on this base: they presuppose that the curvature of space is everywhere the same and that the rates of cosmic expansion and its deceleration are everywhere the same; the Big Bang models known as 'standard models' constitute a subclass, fashioned at the price of supplementary hypotheses whose consequences were verified later with great precision.

2. *Behind this gradual epistemological rapprochement of biology and physics, indeed relativistic cosmology, a mental revolution stands out whose hard core is, in effect, the critique and transformation of the concept of teleology.* The self-regulating machine – the automaton of a feedback circuit making use of the outcomes of an action to govern its subsequent course – provides the simplest model of a regulatory device which appears to be animated by the intention of a goal but which in reality proceeds through progressive adaptation and the successive registration of trials produced by chance, and which succeeds. The recent coinage of the term 'teleonomy' captures perfectly this displacement: finality is no longer the work of a *logos* or of a form originating from another source but is the work of the *nomos* itself written into matter and already at work underlying the emergence of what we call 'life'. Relying on this highly rudimentary schema, we begin by decoding

how a living individuality builds up and maintains its own organism and *through progressive enlargements* proceeds to reproduction – the elucidation of the structure of chromosomal DNA has opened up this field of research – and how at one and the same time the invariance of a specific type of living population combines with the variance due to genetic mutations and the controlling of the course of such variations through functional adaptation to the environment. Ultimately it is evolution in its entirety which lends itself to comprehensibility in virtue of a universe capable, depending on whatever material and physico-mechanical structures are appropriate, of working with its own contingencies, of recording them in its programmes and, on that basis, turning them into replicable constitutions which preside over the destinies of individuals and of living species (Dubarle 1972, 461–77; 1973, 141–67). But in this progressive enlargement toward the totality of the universe lie concealed alternatives and important epistemological determinations which must now be elucidated.

3. Classical science formulates – it will be recalled – physical laws that under the modality of necessity connect the various states of a system with what proceeds from a given contingent state of this system at a certain point (taken in time as initial, but reflecting yet earlier states going, if need be, back to infinity). In such a universe there is no room for *chance*. It is, in fact, extremely difficult to conceive it; and there is no recognition of it by the theory of general relativity. Now the transformation of teleology into teleonomy in the field of biology compels a specification of its status. Since the seventeenth century it has been linked to the distinction between the universe of possibilities made up of very great or infinite eventualities and the actual world which is constituted by a sequence of choices or determinations within possible combinations. Darwin was the first to discover that this sorting among possible eventualities does not at all require the intention of a decider but merely a situation of vital competition among populations or individuals.

This type of chance can perfectly well be linked to the 'initial conditions' of long ago which, once in place, modify irreversibly – according to the logic of a lottery – the conditions of the following draw, thus giving rise to the necessity of the course constituted by the recordings of successive sortings. The progressive integration of biology and physiology has made it possible to trace these workings right down to the elementary structures of the self-reproductive programme represented by the genetic code, thus constituting a quite exceptional 'category of initial conditions'. But – and this a fundamental point – it thus becomes impossible to reconstruct an initial state in its totality from the vantage point of the present situation since, in a universe where chance plays a preponderant part, neither the principle of causality nor a fortiori the use of a probability calculus allows us to reach back to events in the past that are now gone for ever. And should we be able, for instance, to reconstruct the parameters necessary for the emergence of life, they will not suffice for that end since we are not entitled to conflate what remains of the past – the conditions retraceable from an actual matter of fact (carbon as a condition of the existence of life) – with what is forever absent, since it consists of conjunctures, unpredictable events, contingency. Already in the nineteenth century Cournot had made the observation: 'However bizarre the assertion might appear at first glance, reason is better qualified to cognize scientifically the future than the past' (Cournot [1851] 1912, 447).

4. Here we touch the point where the epistemological switch from teleology to teleonomy and the concomitant appearance of the notion of chance at the core of biology reverberates through to the *whole* of scientific cosmology, making manifest the aporetic character of its '*initial* conditions' sometimes also called 'constraining conditions' (Lachièze-Rey 1993, 544). How can we conceive at the same time of the *cosmological principle* which postulates that the laws of physics, properties of space, time and matter have not varied over time, and of the *finite* duration of the expansion of the universe which

follows from it when we move from relativistic models to the subclass of Big Bang or standard models. The problem of the initial conditions of the universe is then transformed into the question of the *limits of the very concept of the universe.*

A number of intellectual stances present themselves at this point. There are those who argue from the fact that the 'first moments' of duration in the Big Bang model would constitute constraining conditions where density and energy are so concentrated that known physics does not apply for the adoption of an *agnostic position* which, in the name of the cosmological principle itself, refuses to overstep the absolute boundary set by contemporary physics. Others extrapolate here the *teleonomic reasoning* of biology by introducing the concept of the 'ensemble of possible universes' subject to random selection to make intelligible a posteriori the more or less probable constraints which the effective presence of the observer imposes on the initial conditions of the universe: a stance formalized in one of the versions of the weak enlarged anthropic principle. Yet others refer to these very specific and highly improbable initial conditions to reintroduce into cosmology a teleological and finalistic argument which ultimately consists in assigning to the observer a privileged position in the universe and thus *relativizing* the cosmological principle which otherwise maintains the indifference of the position of the observer in the universe.

The Sciences between Myth and Philosophy

The classical frontier between science and myth which reappears in this gamut of positions has thus become once again movable. While contending unrelentingly against anthropomorphism and anthropocentrism, today cosmology and biology must recognize (along with microphysics) that they cannot place themselves outside the relation between the observed and the observer. Already their elementary concepts such as, for instance, 'genetic programme' are *metaphors*. These are undoubtedly of considerable heuristic and operational value but they lose such value, if it is forgotten that they are indeed metaphors designating mechanisms that we do not understand (Atlan 1999, 769). Besides, as soon as one wants to bring together the vast amount of data in a 'natural history' or 'history of the universe' one needs to have recourse to the cinematographic concept of scenario. F. Jacob writes:

> It is not certain, that we shall ever come to know how living beings have emerged from an inert universe. Nor that we shall ever understand the evolution of the brain and the appearance of the ensemble of properties that we have difficulty in defining but which we call thought. Every attempt to describe the evolution of the brain and the mind can thus be no more than a simple story, a scenario. (Jacob 1981, 116)

The *theory of evolution*, which no one any longer contests in its entirety, in fact enjoys a peculiar status; less on account of its containing hidden within it mechanisms that we do not yet understand or because it lends itself to diverse interpretations (as was mentioned above) but primarily because its global status allies it with myth. Has it not been used and is it not still often used – for example in the context of sociobiology – to explain the array of cosmological, biological, cultural, even moral transformations of our world? Even if one objects to these unjustified extensions, it cannot be denied that the theory of evolution brings in the observer, his need for coherence and his desire to give meaning to his own existence in the universe.

Further, the *standard models* of cosmology are based even more on a highly specific type of theory. Jean Ladrière has offered the most precise description:

> It is a sort of encompassing theory of physics. This is not surprising since it is the aim of cosmology to study the structure of the whole, spatial and temporal, of the universe or cosmos, considered as a *sui generis* object, susceptible to analysis conducted according to the tried and tested methods of physics. But the object in question has no outside and contains all the others. It is thus both an object in itself and the totalizing principle of all objects. It is at once a phenomenon, inasmuch as it is an object effectively accessible to observation, at least in part, in what is called the horizon of the visible, and yet is concurrently nature, inasmuch as it is the universal horizon shared by all phenomena. Insofar as it is nature, it is the condition of all particular objects. Insofar as it is an object itself, it is, if one may put it thus, its own condition. This shows up its singular character and makes us expect of the theory aiming at giving an account of it, that it be both homogeneous with classical

theories inasmuch as, like them, it is concerned with a determinate object, and yet also profoundly different from classical theories inasmuch as it is concerned with a universal condition necessarily reflexive. (Ladrière 1987, 12)

This Kantian-type reasoning[5] allows us to appreciate the justification for the diversity of positions on the concept of the universe presented above. Confronted with this totalizing approach on the part of cosmology or biology, one may indeed have recourse to a radical agnosticism that may nonetheless assume various guises: materialist ('only what may be subjected to scientific scrutiny exists'); sceptical ('it is absurd to speak of a world since chaos has the last word; our splendid intellectual constructions are derisory'), etc.

Emphasis may instead be laid on the pragmatic aspect of scientific progress, pertinently where – and only where – it functions *effectively*; thus one speaks of 'local' or 'regional' coherence, excluding all processes of totalization (or all conceptions of the universe which imply a tendency towards an empirical synthesis of all phenomena). There too, this position may take on diverse attitudes: a certain methodological prudence ('we only do science; so we cannot pronounce on matters that elude its province'), a type of cynicism ('let's not ask questions: so long as it works, let's develop scientific knowledge'), etc.

It must be asked, however, whether cosmology (the standard models) and biology (the theory of evolution) do not already imply totalizing reasoning. For it is on that account that the antinomy of the concept of the universe arises, functioning simultaneously as encompassing ('the unconditioned' in Kantian terms) and as an object marked, as is every object, by the bounds of finitude. The undecidable nature of this antinomy might militate in favour of the two preceding solutions; but it might also be held that the antinomy arises from the imagination being implicated in all cognitive

---

5 Kant speaks here of *Weltbegriff*, of a 'cosmical concept': 'I entitle all transcendental ideas, in so far as they refer to absolute totality in the synthesis of appearances, *cosmical concepts*, partly because this unconditioned totality also underlies the concept – itself only an idea – of the world-whole; partly because they concern only the synthesis of appearances, therefore only empirical synthesis' (Kant 1781–1787, A 408, 409 (trans. Norman Kemp Smith [1929] 1982, 385)).

processes, its spatial and temporal structure. The imagination leads us spontaneously to *reify* the world and to situate ourselves outside of or opposite this universe. Now, the idea of the universe or of totality can never become an *object* of knowledge *facing* a subject. The antinomy thus only presents itself when the limits of knowledge are overpassed: how could one cognize that which encompasses space and time without the imagination situating it anew in a space/ time? The undecidable nature of the antinomy proves its usefulness, however, to the extent that the recognition of the proper limit of all knowledge leads us to *conceive* the idea of the universe not as an ontological affirmation but as a *regulatory* idea, as Kant put it, a condition of the possibility of cosmological or even biological reasoning, having no other function than that of sustaining a process of cognition forever incomplete.

It is here in fact that the specific position of contemporary cosmology and biology appears in relation to the concept of teleology. Whether one introduces the concept of finality – as in the enlarged strong anthropic principle – or whether one is more orientated towards a model of multiple universes, random selection and teleonomic verification, as in the case of the enlarged weak anthropic principle, it becomes impossible to discard the epistemological framework of a regulative principle once the conception of a totality or of a universe is in play, on pain of making that principle a tautology or of curtailing the process of explanation. Now, to introduce teleology or teleonomy as regulative ideas is to rely on a radical contingency which affects not only the universe and its manifestation of life in all its degrees and at every moment but also the observer and his perspective. Explanatory coherence, established by the researcher, will hence never be free from the bonds of 'historical' contingency which orient him via a retrospective reasoning, susceptible to modification, each time there is a shift in the perspective of the observer.

II. The Defence of a Model of Critical Articulation

The theologian has every interest in noting the epistemological conditions of cosmological models and of the theory of evolution and of embedding them, in critical fashion, in his theology of creation. If the readiness of the sciences of the nineteenth century simply to substitute their theories for the creationist interpretation actually provoked on the side of Christians either a reaction of denial (*Conflict model* or the denial of articulation) or, notably in Protestant theology (as for example in K. Barth and R. Bultmann), a renewed insistence on the difference in perspective between science and faith (*independence model*), the new sensitivity of sciences to the particular status – quasimythical – of cosmology or theory of evolution has led to numerous attempted syntheses of the scientific approach and a 'spiritual' interpretation of natural history and life (*convergence model*).[6] The work of Teilhard de Chardin but also *Process Theology* inspired by Whitehead, or again *God in Creation* (1985) by J. Moltmann are inspired by this integration model (which, it may be noted, the theologian from Tübingen dubs the 'perichoretic model'). On the scientific side in popularizers like P. Davies, F. Capra and other supporters of New Age, a growing interest may be observed in Asian spiritualities and their 'holistic conceptions' of the universe, barely sensitive to the battles between faith and science which have punctuated the history of European modernity. With what right should we deny Asians the integration into their own cultural context of sciences engendered, mainly, on Greco-Judaeo-Christian soil? And why not see the globalization of all interchange as favouring a radical pluralism which dovetails perfectly with a global consciousness, reckoning with the divine (void or replete, little does it matter) as origin and end of the universe with its infinite variations of life?

Science and Faith

One needs to note, however, the insufficient knowledge in scientific quarters of the religious sources to which they make reference.[7] This occasions in them, but equally (conversely) in theologians espousing

---

[6] Pierre Bühler and Clairette Karakash (1992) analyse and compare various typologies of the relation between science and faith.

[7] This is noted by Alexandre Ganoczy (1995, 178).

the convergence model, significant conceptual shifts, whether it concerns the ontological and theological use of the fundamental law of Complexity-Consciousness by Teilhard or the identification of subatomic movement and the dance of Shiva, or again, of the passage of evolutionary cyclic models to the cycles of the Upanishads in others. The metaphorical status of a certain number of basic concepts in biology runs the risk of being replaced by an extensive and mythic conception of the evolution of life, which thus eliminates any possibility of criticism. In the final analysis, it is the *conditions of writing* of a 'narrative' of the history of life and the world that the proponents of the convergence model relegate to the background, confident that their narratives are without presuppositions (e.g. Reeves, de Rosnay, Coppens and Simonnet 1996).

In any case, Christian theology is more at ease, it seems to me, in *a model of critical articulation* which simultaneously takes into account the specificity and the articulation of scientific perspectives, on the one hand, and the human postulate of a meaning, on the other. *The act of faith, as well as the conferral of meaning, are not of the order of knowledge or of representation.* When the mother in the Second Book of the Maccabees addresses her sons, who are preparing to face martyrdom, she confesses ignorance as to the origins of life: 'I do not know how you came into being in my womb. It was not I who gave you life and breath, nor I who set in order the elements in each of you. Therefore the Creator of the world, who shaped the beginning of man and the origin of all things, will in his mercy give life and breath back to you again . . .' (2 Macc 7:22f.). But it must immediately be added that *there is no act of faith without anthropomorphic representations* – as the words of this mother testify – representations that are both mutable and plural depending on cultures and traditions. But this is not to say that all representations are equally valid, that all are compatible with the act of faith, which is, so to speak, at work at the very heart of our images of the universe and life.

It is thus not difficult to show that cosmology and the life sciences have led modern exegesis and Christian theology towards the double theological realization of the unfathomable nature of the

origin of life (not to be confused with its beginning) and the necessarily anthropomorphic status of all the 'narratives of origin'. But,
conversely, the presence of the Christian faith, like that of other
traditions and meaning postulated in our societies, refers the
scientist to his own convictions, urging him not to expunge from
his cosmological model and his evolutionary narrative his own
stances, always singular and, in any case, rooted in his own liberty
of conferring meaning. This reciprocal questioning of scientists
and theologians, which presupposes in each of its interlocutors a
capacity for self-criticism, is the true strength of a model of critical
articulation.

This requires, in the final analysis, that theologians and
researchers reflect, each according to his or her perspective, on the
anthropomorphic status of the concepts of universe and life: we are
inescapably situated *in* the universe and in human life. It is this
'boundary' that constitutes us; but to recognize it as such is an act
of reflection by virtue of which one has already 'gone beyond' it:
this 'going beyond' comprises both our irrepresentable relation to
the origin ('I do not know how . . .') and – of another order – the
endeavour of science to reach, independently of our imagination,
the very mechanisms of the universe and life.

On the *theological* side, anthropomorphism is both honoured
and surpassed by the paradoxical affirmation of the creation of
life, by the Living One, *ex nihilo* (2 Macc 7:28): the *whole* of life
comes only from God; it is the trace of a free gift. Now the mark of
a gift is that it conceals the giver on pain of obligating the recipient
and thus destroying what is characteristic of gift: its utter
gratuitousness. From a theological point of view, the anthropomorphism of the narratives of the beginning of life means that it
is impossible to speak of the whole of life in an 'objective' manner
in abstraction from the human individual who freely accords
meaning to the origin of life. Indeed, how could one recognize
the creation of life without so doing through the very form of
gift, which is freedom. In *scientific* milieux this treatment of
anthropomorphism is not inadmissible provided that it is conceived
in terms of the 'postulation of meaning'. Two elementary rules seem
to apply to it.

The Regulation of the 'Postulation of Meaning'

Most scientists who reflect on the universe and the evolution of life tie together, at the end point of their mediation, various strands of reasoning – scientific, aesthetic, metaphysical and possibly religious; they tie them, which is to say, hold them together because at such crucial moments where the issue is one of meaning, it is no longer the anonymous voice of science but the scientist in person who speaks. Respecting the rights of critiques to the very end requires that the 'thresholds' between these various 'levels' of an itinerary of meaning be well marked.

The transition from one level to another is never of the order of 'necessity'. No one is obliged, for instance, to interpret the singularity of our universe (with its so precise initial conditions) as the fruit of chance or, on the contrary, as the project of a being desirous of a world capable of giving rise to human consciousness; no one is constrained to read the emergence, by chance, of human life as a genetic ruse, or as the first manifestation of the tragic in life or, again, as a promise. It is precisely here that the freedom of the researcher to give meaning to his own life in the universe enters in.

Although not necessary, the transition from one level of discourse to another is, however, neither arbitrary nor merely irrational. It proceeds, in effect, as if the level of discourse of meaning had left 'traces' (or 'limits') at the level of scientific discourse: these present themselves as 'problems' or 'aporias' or 'questions'. Again, it is necessary to know how to spot them: one thing is, in effect, to know how to vary the values of each of the physical constants necessary to describe a universe, and another to realize that this reasoning (prematurely 'comparativist') which consists in determining thus the initial conditions of our universe in the midst of a multiplicity of possible universes is already laden with the question of the contingent singularity of what exists; one thing is to analyse genetic structures with the help of the concept of information; another is to perceive that forgetting the metaphorical status of this concept means the opening up of a 'preformationist' interpretation of the entirety of a genetic and epigenetic process, a philosophical inter-pretation which is assuredly not the only candidate in the field. It is probably necessary to have reflected on science as both an individual and social human activity in order to be sensitive to this subtle overlap between scientific reasoning and philosophical enquiry. It might be said that one needs to have already passed to the level of discourse of meaning to be capable of spotting its traces at the very heart of a discourse on the history of the geo- and the biosphere.

Is there a real awareness of the extent to which this articulation of different types of reasonings obeys a complex logic? Such an articulation combines a non-necessary modality with a non-arbitrary modality in the transition from one level to another, thus conjoining an intellectual treatment which has its origin in scientific discourse to one which is based on the human fact of the postulation of meaning. There are several ways of understanding the complex status of statements which depend simultaneously on science and the human 'sciences' or philosophy: the notion of 'trace' causes us to pass from the rational mode of scientific explanation of things to that of the interpretation of texts, the two being linked by the well known 'hermeneutical circle'. Noting on the trajectory of the first arc of the circle – which starts off from the universe to explain the emergence of life – aporias or questions already presuppose the second arc of the circle which starts from the human person and his or her freedom to invest existence with meaning in interpreting the traces of meaning that the emergence of life offers (or their absence). The metaphor of the circle serves to bring out the mutual conditioning of these twin trajectories, intellectual and spiritual. The risk of a vicious circle is avoided by the impossibility of stopping circulation once and for all, each of these two reasonings being continually reinvigorated by the other.

The first rule of the conferral of meaning turns on the correct articulation of the various intellectual movements involved in this act, the point accordingly being that of guaranteeing freedom (its modality non-necessary and non-arbitrary) without which there can be no meaning. A second rule concerns the form of the discourse of meaning. Let it be said right away: meaning expresses itself in a narrative. Why? Because to speak of the meaning of life in the universe, of human life in particular, is to engage with its historical destiny, it is to trace a path which runs from its beginning to its end, impossible of accomplishment without the recounting of a story, the composition of narratives; by degrees the discourse of meaning tends, in fact, to take a stance in relation to the totality of reality.

This seemingly extravagant assertion returns us to the question already touched upon concerning the relation between science and myth. Several indices, already mentioned, urge caution in respect of a too rigorous separation of domains which would risk reducing the empire of meaning to a few episodes in human history. But how should we seek to ground this apparently ineluctable bond between scientific discourse about the cosmos and life, and the narrative of a natural and human history? It is given us through the notion of *trace* – we have already noted it in connection with the first rule. It is its hybrid status which destines it for the role of mediation: it is of the order of a mark left, or of the effect of an event now irremediably absent; it is at the same time of the order of a sign to be interpreted by man. Consider, for example, certain cosmic events (meteorites) and their effects on the evolution of mammals. We realize immediately that history is not played out merely among human persons but that it has been and remains affected by natural events, events which, in the case of the more crucial among them, are now lost in the mists of time. The trace is thus the 'locus' of this impact on human life, lending itself to mathematico-scientific analysis while raising at the same time our question of meaning. Here, then, is the principal reason why the scope of the narrative cannot be limited to human history but remains indispensably within the description of the evolution of the universe and of life. The duality of mathematico-scientific discourse and of narrative discourse cannot in effect be overpassed because the existence of science presupposes once and for all the primordial fact that we and our historical destiny are affected by the history of nature and of life, a fact that can only be narrated.

But how, in this articulation, do we safeguard the critical element which prevents scientific discourse about the universe and about life from surreptitiously turning into myth? P. Ricoeur distinguishes in every narrative two temporal dimensions: the 'episodic dimension' which 'draws narrative time towards linear representation' and the 'configuring dimension' which transforms the succession of events from the perspective of the 'final point' into a meaningful totality, making it possible to 'read the end in the beginning and the beginning in the end' (Ricoeur 1983, 103–5). We find here, at the level of discourse, what was said above of the 'hermeneutical circle' linking the different steps entailed in the conferral of meaning. The discourse of meaning is of the nature of 'configuration': taking off from a contingent point – the singular position of the person undertaking it – it displays a meaningful totality. To be sure, I can forgo giving meaning to my existence, or can even limit myself to merely concatenating episodes of life and history, contenting myself with these fragments of meaning without ever pronouncing on their global bearings. But if I want to give meaning to human life in the universe I am obliged to offer an opinion on the whole of reality, also involving my entire life. The genre of mythic narrative is here both touched and at the same time avoided. It is precisely the function of the second rule to obviate this confusion. On the one hand, the positing of meaning is always a risk-laden anticipation because the 'final point' – the point of departure for all meaningful configuration – is not at anyone's disposal; the meaning given is thus of the nature of a postulate (to speak with Kant) capable of structuring a human life. On the other hand, the rule of meaning prohibits the conflation of the two temporal dimensions of narrative, of making use, for instance, of the episodic dimension of the history of the universe and of the geo- and biosphere to extract a *compelling* argument in favour of *one* position regarding meaning.

Avoiding mythic discourse is thus acting with freedom as concerns meaning, by pointing out exactly where the narratives of evolution risk concealing alternatives. It is on this essential point that we must undertake to rework the theology of an entire tradition. Placing ourselves within the framework of the model of critical articulation which has just been traced out, we now engage ourselves in the Christian mode of giving meaning to experience and to the concept of 'life' at the heart of the universe of which faith confesses the 'messianic opening'.

III. The Messianic Opening of the Universe

If we take to heart the two rules just mentioned and the circular structure of all discourse about creation, we must begin our theological endeavour with the 'configuring dimension' of the 'postulation of meaning'.

The Finitude and Uniqueness of Life

The distinguishing feature of the biblical tradition as compared to other traditions (Hindu and Buddhist traditions, for example) is an insistence on the *uniqueness* of life which implies a certain understanding of finitude and death. Indeed, as biological entities, we are completely embedded in the evolution of life and cosmogenesis. Death, in the proper sense of the term, appears at the same time as 'sexuality'. (So long as creatures are reproduced by fission or budding, one cannot yet really speak of death: the generation of living beings continues and death is the condition of this process.) Now, what distinguishes the human person is that he or she *knows* he is mortal even if he only knows it through others or through anticipation (certain drawings in prehistoric caves bear eloquent witness to that). Our consciousness is, as it were, two-fold: on the one hand, we know that we are different, 'more than' biological life, because aware of our mortality (and this is the point at which our desire emerges, making of us beings of flesh and blood); and on the other hand, we know, too, that life would lose all its import if it could be indefinitely recommenced, the counter being continually reset at zero. The exemplar that I am exists only once, it is unique; birth and death are like a seal upon it, according it – jointly – the significance of uniqueness which, when suddenly realized, communicates to us the paradoxical experience of life as a maturation process at the heart of the ordeal of decay. If the first side of the mortality of individuals (some speak of 'avatars'), once it is realized, motivates the emergence of the *word* 'God'[8] and its equivalents, the other side, the experience of the maturation process of our

---

[8] The emergence of the term has been analysed by religious studies and the philosophy of religion.

uniqueness, is perceived by the biblical tradition as the 'trace' of a creation, or as gift.

There is no denying, however, the pervasive ambivalence of this elemental experience of life. Instead of being experienced as a gift, the awareness of finitude and the call to let one's own uniqueness unfold are often the points where what is manifested is a 'fear of being' on the part of the subjects, prompting jealousy and even violence. This 'infernal' concatenation is a theme whose many variations are displayed in biblical tradition. We would like to compare our lives, something which presupposes a common 'measure'. Although such comparison should lead us towards a dimension incomparably 'beyond measure' that the uniqueness of each individual represents, it slides constantly towards jealousy and ends in violence, in the laying hold of the life of another to the advantage of one's own; an obscure process, indeed, where the uniqueness of the one can unwittingly elicit jealousy of the other, and the fear of the being of the other, his violence which relentlessly assails the uniqueness of those around him. At the root of this terrible confusion one finds what scripture castigates as a lie: the suggestion, the persistent insinuation of some connivance between the 'boundaries' of life – death – and an underlying jealousy of the living world, its profound egoism, in relation to those who are its beneficiaries and bearers.

Given this confusion it is understandable that, according to the Scriptures, it is not enough to narrate the genesis of the universe and life; it is necessary to go on, to attain a discernment or an appraisal which will lead to the 'postulation' of a meaning, to an act of faith in respect to life. All these biblical attempts at evaluation are ultimately drawn together in the Epistle to the Romans, in particular chapter 8: 'I consider that the sufferings of this present time are *not worth comparing* with the glory that is to be revealed to us' (Rom 8:18). The issue of suffering – the irresolvable crux of theodicy – is introduced here in a sort of 'ponderation'. To try the weight of something is to compare the qualitative weight of things, of experiences. It is the work of an *entire* life and, most crucially, in the face of 'thresholds' to be crossed, whether felicitous or a trial. This process results in the discovery of a 'without measure', a 'beyond measure' as was suggested above; the discovery of the incomparable in life which has its times and demands time: the sufferings of life are to be interpreted, lies to be detected. Interpretation is accompanied by sighing and is not the capacity to sigh already a sign going beyond? Sighing establishes, in effect, solidarity with all of the living world and with the universe; for all that, only the compassion of the Spirit of God which sighs within us is decisive enough to make itself credible in our eyes. It leads to the astonishing inversion of perspective that occurs when the heart and mind suddenly adopt – as in verse 28 – God's own appraisal of life recorded in the simple 'anthropic' saying: 'to them that love God, all things work together for good'. Does it not become clear why it is impossible to reduce this *experience without guarantee – the* prerogative of human life in relation to all the rest – to a 'principle of sufficient reason',[9] subject to the jurisdiction of the sciences?

What Meaning should be given to the Programme and to the Law?

We have just anticipated somewhat the end of our journey. It passes, in the Epistle to the Romans as in other biblical texts, through a decisive crossroads where what is at stake is a critical articulation of cosmology, biology and theology. Life presupposes a separation, a structuring, a putting in place of programmes, the setting up of rules of the game or the institution of a law. This last protects humanity against chaos, confusion and violence; it is like a 'house' at once cosmic and historical which surrounds human life, furnishing it with a frame of reference.

An analogy presents itself here whose heuristic force may challenge both the theologian and the scientist. Just as the latter is prompted today to distinguish more clearly, in the analysis of the human genome, between the classic metaphor 'DNA-*qua-programme*' and another metaphor 'DNA-*qua-data*' (cf. Atlan 1999, 768f.), so too the exegete and the theologian are increasingly sensitive to the difference between the law and the contingent act

---

[9]　In the philosophy of Leibniz the 'principle of sufficient reason' offers a response to the question: 'Why is there *something rather than nothing?*'

of living, between the respect for a shared structure and the human person's historical access to his or her uniqueness which is an integral part of the path taken by each, relating to others and to the whole of his or her environment. We are indeed speaking of an analogy so as to preserve the differences of scale and perspective and, in particular, the emergence of human freedom. The programme and, certainly, the law, are always signs of something incomplete, a possibility that only the individual (the avatar?) can achieve. In this sense it functions as a factor representing permanence (at the level of reduplication or reproduction) or protection (at the historical level) when jealousy and violence manifest themselves as signs of the fear of being but also, and simultaneously, as assurances of an ever greater profusion of singularities.

One perceives here a crucial *bifurcation* that may be encountered in the entirety of the Scriptures, in both the Old and New Testaments: every programme, every structure or law can, as can their defenders, identify itself with 'life' and thereby nullify the promise inscribed in the profusion of variations and abolish, ultimately, the promise of free access, autonomous and without guarantees, of individuals to their own uniqueness. Law and its defenders are equally able to contribute towards dissipating this lie and pointing out the 'source' of life which is situated at once before and beyond programme, rule and structure.

The 'Source of Life'

Without disavowing the deep continuities between the three levels of the inanimate, the animate (animal life in particular) and human life – cosmology and the theory of evolution contribute powerfully to putting continuities in relief – one may, in line with biblical tradition, mark out *thresholds* and indicate their salient features: the idea of structure, programme, rule must be attributed to the inanimate world; with life, in particular the animal world, sexuality emerges as mode of reproduction but also as variation or differentiation and, hence, as relational interplay – to the human actors of the Bible the animal world offers a picture of violence (including their own) but also one of the 'political' utopia of an ultimate pacification (Is 11: 6–9 and 65:25) in the care of a peaceful and peace-loving 'shepherd'; finally, with the human world – man and woman – the possibility emerges of an experience of *uniqueness in relation*, a setting for desire, surprise and a maturing ever unforeseeable.

To deem with the Scriptures that this uniqueness, in an interactional relationship, is not only that of an 'avatar' transmitting genetic information, is to postulate, in other words, that the history of the human genome is not reducible to the destiny of 'DNA-*qua-programme*', it is already engaging with the meaning of life, imposing conditions for its possible understanding in terms of the 'trace' of a gift. In its accounts of creation the biblical tradition speaks here in terms of a 'messianic opening'. The use of this schema to interpret the individual and phylogenetic processes of the emergence and evolution of the interplay of multiple forms of uniqueness detracts not at all from their autonomy, the property of a free gift being precisely the withdrawal of the giver. He or she who postulates the gratuitousness of the gift of life for all, and in a unique manner for each, must nevertheless confront the contradiction imposed daily on this properly 'utopian' perspective and must situate him- or herself in relation to the 'sufferings of the present time' (Rom 8:18). The significance of the 'messianic opening', of evolution of the living world, is thus made clearer: it does not depend at all on the concept of finality but manifests itself at the moment where the experience of the gratuitousness of life makes the human person suddenly capable of assuming responsibility for his or her jealousy, violence and lies, and awakes in him/her the mysterious ability to transform the life he/she has been given into a life that he or she is ready to give. Scattered throughout the history of humanity are numberless examples of this fundamental stance that the biblical tradition has called 'holiness' or 'sanctification of life' and which ultimately characterizes the figure of the 'Messiah'.

This sanctification of life has its source in life itself; an affirmation which imposes itself on anyone who truly takes seriously the idea of creation as gift. It would even be necessary to show that the source of this possible sanctification goes back beyond human life and is rooted in the evolution of the living world which is not reducible to structures of reciprocity but manifests a generous profusion from the start. But the biblical tradition also attributes holiness, even primarily and pre-eminently, to the 'Giver of Life', who withdraws so that his gift may stand forth, all the while bearing it with patience. So it is we should understand, as in the Epistle to the Romans, the mysterious relation between the sighing of the Spirit, at the heart of a creation giving messianic birth to holiness, and Holy God himself.

Only a Trinitarian theology of 'life' – such as is suggested by the Nicene symbol of 381 – makes it possible to respect the autonomy of cosmological and biological approaches to evolution all the way down and simultaneously to perceive there the 'traces' of a messianic opening, *postulated* by the believer who, without denying the elemental mechanisms of reproduction does not solely see in it the effects of the need to survive but also, and above all, the emergence, owing to death, of a capacity to put at risk the uniqueness of one's own life for the benefit of that of another. It can only be a matter here of a *postulation without guarantee*, all other *form* of theological interpretation being in formal contradiction with *what* is postulated: a meaning of life accomplished through a gift of oneself fraught with risk. Thus the ultimate affirmation, in the Symbol, of 'the life of the world to come' is qualified very properly as 'expectation'. It would, however, be equally contradictory from the perspective of gift to want to introduce here *in extremis* an exteriority between 'terrestrial' life and 'eternal' life which would force us to abandon, ultimately, the 'model of critical articulation' of science and theology. *Given once and for all, the gift of life is, in effect – as gift – without repentance:* it is thus *in one and the same act* that the believer receives his life at the heart of the living world as gift of uniqueness (creation), which he relinquishes to the benefit of the uniqueness of others (holiness), and in which he discovers the work of the Giver himself who is also his own future (eschatology). Only this immanence, ever to come, ever imminent, of the Giver of life at the heart of the living world as a 'gushing source within eternal life' can, in effect, convince the believer of the groundedness of his appraisal of the significance of life.

Conclusion

Does creation theology need the concept of finality?

1. It certainly needs finality in the global sense of the term; this has been amply demonstrated by our reflections above. But we must make complete the affirmation of the First Vatican Council on the manifestation of the glory of God *through* the gifts that he has accorded his creatures – the doctrine of the two ends of creation – by introducing here the freedom to assign a meaning to life in the universe as the very conclusion of that same manifestation, involving the passivity, and even the self-effacement, of the Creator for the good of his creation.

2. This first affirmation presupposes an inalienable relation between the history of the universe and of life and human beings, between what is observed and the observer. This means that the cosmological principle which governs the constitutive opposition between the physical sciences (the standard model) and religious or mythic anthropomorphism and even anthropocentrism proceeds from a certain abstraction. The recognition of this circumstance does not bring in its wake an immediate re-evaluation of the teleological conception of the universe and life as mediated by the strong or enlarged strong anthropic principle. The counterpart of the recognition of the inevitable involvement of the observer in scientific method is critical reflection, both philosophical and theological, on the proper use of anthropomorphism in epistemology and creation theology; something which Kant achieved in a manner difficult to surpass.

3. Does the theologian ultimately need final causality to bring together the various levels of cosmic, biological and historical evolution? Our reply is negative to the extent that the three positions articulated in our first part – agnosticism, reference to contingency and anthropic finalism – are the expression of an authentic engagement concerning meaning that leaves open the question of the cause of our admiration of that

which, in the uniqueness of the life of each human being, is the manifestation of the Incomparable.

References

ATLAN, H. 1999. 'Le génétique n'est pas dans le gène', in *Etudes* 3906, 763–74.

BÜHLER, P. and KARAKASH, C. (eds) 1992. *Science et foi font système. Une approche herméneutique*, Geneva: Labor et Fides.

COURNOT, A. [1851] 1912. *Essai sur les fondements de nos connaissances et sur les caractères de la critique philosophique*, Paris: Hachette.

DEMARET, J. and LAMBERT, D. 1994. *Le principe anthropique. L'homme est-il le centre de l'Univers?*, Paris: Armand Colin.

DENZINGER and HÜNERMANN (= DH) 1966. *Symboles et définitions de la foi catholique*, Paris: Les Editions du Cerf.

DUBARLE, D. 1972 and 1973. 'L'historique des rapports entre physique et biologie', *Revue des questions scientifiques*, 143: 4, 461–77 and 144: 2, 141–67.

GANOCZY, A. 1995. *Dieu, l'Homme et la Nature. Théologie, Mystique, Sciences de la Nature*, Paris: Les Editions du Cerf.

JACOB, F. 1981. *Le jeu des possibles. Essai sur la diversité du vivant*, Paris: Fayard.

KANT, I. [1781–1787] 1980. 'Critique de la raison pure', in *Oeuvres philosophiques 1*, Bibliothèque de la Pléiade, Paris: Gallimard, 705–1470.

——. [1929] 1982. *Immanuel Kant's Critique of Pure Reason*, English trans., N. Kemp Smith, London and Basingstoke: Macmillan.

LACHIÈZE-REY, M. 1993. 'Les origines', *Recherches de Science Religieuse* 81:4, 539–57.

LADRIÈRE, J. 1987. 'Le principe anthropique. L'homme comme être cosmique', in *Cahiers de l'Ecole des Sciences Philosophiques et Religieuses*, 2, Brussels: F.U.S.L., 12.

REEVES, H., DE ROSNA, J., COPPENS, Y., and SIMONNET, D. 1996. *La plus belle histoire du monde. Les secrets de nos origines*, Paris: Seuil.

RICOEUR, P. 1983. *Temps et récit*, Vol. 1, Paris: Seuil.

RICOEUR, P., MCLAUGHLIN, K. and PELLAUER, D. 1984–88. *Time and Narrative 1–3*, Chicago: University of Chicago Press.

SERTILLANGES, A. D. 1945. *L'idée de la création et ses retentissements en philosophie*, Paris: Aubier.

8

Design in the Universe and the Logos of Creation: Patristic Synthesis and Modern Cosmology

ALEXEI V. NESTERUK

Introduction

The theistic argument from design in the universe is still a very popular topic in science–religion discussions. It has recently been argued that cosmological fine-tuning points towards the divine purpose behind the fruitful and beautiful universe and that an argument for theism is the best explanation of some fundamental scientific findings of the last decades (Polkinghorne 1998; cf. Nesteruk 1999). In a systematic book on physics and theology, M. Worthing analyses the meaning of the argument from design, reincarnated by modern cosmology, and its implications for theology and is cautious about making any straightforward theological inferences from physical arguments (Worthing 1995).

Design in modern cosmology is often associated with the fine-tuning problem, or with the anthropic principle. The argument from design is especially amplified when the fact of man's existence is considered from the perspective of the vastness of the universe. What is the significance of man, whose typical spatial scale (let's say 100 cm) is hardly comparable with the 10^{28} cm which stands for the size of the observable universe? It is stated, nevertheless, in modern cosmology, that in order for biological life to emerge, the universe must be large and old; then the problem arises as to whether the whole universe really has a plan to evolve in space and time, in order to sustain life in a nearly infinitesimal island of physical being. In other words, does the physical universe indeed bear the pattern of design at its ontological level, or is it rather the design of our intellect? This dilemma will be addressed in the present paper by making a comparative analysis of the famous Kantian critique of the inference from design and some theological arguments which date back to patristic and Byzantine thinkers. As a result a methodology is proposed for detecting the presence of genuine theological inferences in modern scientific theory. Finally, this methodology is tested using as an example a particular design-like model in modern cosmology, offered in 1979 by R. Penrose, such that the problem of design becomes a problem of special boundary conditions in the universe.

From Kant's Scepticism back to the Patristic Theological Synthesis

It will be recalled that, according to Kant, the inference from design is a natural tendency of human understanding to find order and harmony in a manifold of objects and events; where the order could not exist 'naturally' because of the vastness and a priori decoherence of existence. Kant himself described the attempt of this physico-theological proof of the existence of God in the *Critique of Pure Reason* as the oldest, the clearest, and the most accordant way of the common reasoning of mankind. This way suggests ends and purposes, value and meaning, where our observation would not be able to detect them by itself, and extends our knowledge of nature by means of the guiding concept of a special unity, the principle which is outside nature (Kant 1933, 520; A 623 = B 651). He demonstrated that the physico-theological argument appeals ultimately to the cosmological and ontological arguments for God. According to Kant, however, the *ideal* which is sought as an ultimate presupposition and the term of the empirical series of the world, reflects the integrity of human intelligence, rather than the integrity of the cosmos and that of God. In this sense, according to Kant, the argument from design cannot be a proper theistic argument for the God-Creator. There is no *substance*, or an *ontologically distinct* being, in that something which is called *ideal*.

Kant, in his negative assessment of the transcendental arguments for the existence of God, revealed a methodologically weak aspect of all theistic inferences from the contingent creation, namely their attempts to find a foundation for the world, that is, its *substance*, in the world itself; Kant demonstrated that this was impossible. The ground for the world-order can be found in the ideal, which according to Kant is intelligible 'reality'. Kant treated this reality as a subjective one deprived of an independent ontology. For Kant intelligible being was never an ontologically primary element of existence, and hence could not affirm, and hypostasize, the ideal as an ontologically distinct being.

In this Kant demonstrated that he was a strictly monistic philosopher. This prevented him from finding a theistic argument from design, namely that the foundation of the world has an absolutely distinct ontology; the ideal not being itself God indicates, however, the *principle of being* of God: the ground for the world's being is its non-being, and this is God.

One can state now that the problem of all 'classical' forms of the argument from design is connected with its attempt to justify the design of the world without breaking the closed ontology of the world. The breakdown of this closed ontology requires a philosophical change such that the foundation of the world must be sought in an otherness. This implies that the methodological approach to an inference of God from design in the science–theology dialogue must be radically changed in order to make possible the *demonstration* of the existence of the transcendent ground for the world from the design of the world.

The historical example of such a breakthrough from the closed, monistic ontology of the world, can be found in the Christian patristic theologians, who struggled with the monistic Hellenism of the surrounding culture and developed a theological synthesis between the Gospel message and Greek culture, which never existed before and which is, unfortunately, forgotten now in most discussions on science and theology.

The Greek patristics proposed a shift in understanding of the world ontology, such that the old Greek *substance* (Gr. *ousia*) was replaced by the relational notion of *hypostasis* and of *person*. It is a *person* who can know God from the world created by the Logos of God; for this *person*, being ontologically distinct from God, shares the same *logos* of the incarnate Logos of God, that is, Christ, who is the ground for both the World and Man.

We build our argument by employing the patristic theological notion of the Logos (Word) of God as it was used by St Athanasius of Alexandria. We also appeal to the concept of the *logoi* of creation (which are connected with the Divine Logos) as they were treated by the great Byzantine theologian St Maximus the Confessor. The concluding element of our methodology will require the employment of the concept of the basic, constitutive *difference* (*diaphora*) in creation. This last concept expresses a dualism in the created world between the *sensible realm* (the empirical world of phenomena in Kantian terms) and that of the *intelligible realm*.

Our intention is not to prove or disprove the intuition of design; it is rather a modest attempt to construct a theological methodology in order to *demonstrate* that the presence of the Logos of God can be detected through the *logoi* of things observed in the created universe, in a pattern of design.

Relational Ontology of Personhood versus Monistic Substantialism

Ontological 'substantialism' as a philosophical platform can be traced back to the Hellenistic culture of thought where the fundamental issue of any philosophical enquiry was *being*, which constituted a principle of unity of all things existing separately. The meaning of the word being can be connoted with such terms as *substance* or essence. Being according to the Greeks was a concluding term of the world, but at the same time it was a principle of harmony among existent things, the principle which is characterized by the word cosmos. Nothing, according to the Greeks, could escape from the ontological unity of being; even God was in the world. This was the manifestation of the closed nature of the Greek ontology, its fundamentally monistic character.[1]

Observed from this ancient perspective, the meaning of the Kantian critique of the arguments for the existence of God at the end of eighteenth century could be easily interpreted as a demonstration of the inability of human intelligence to break the closed ontology of the world (as in the Greeks), and to find the grounds of this ontology beyond the world, that is, in God; for Kant was arguing that any reference to an absolutely necessary being as the cause of the world was an unjustified transcendence of the understanding, beyond its legitimate realm of sensible experience, towards the world of intelligible forms, with no hope of hypostasizing ontologically (that is, not only in thought) that being which has been stated as God.

Kant's critique does not leave a chance to infer from design to God because his philosophy is a monistic transcendental phenomenalism: the phenomena are circumscribed by a transcendental experience that does not provide an access to reality as it is in itself, that is, to genuine ontology. Any attempt of the understanding to find *substance* behind the experiential data through an intelligible synthesis is, according to Kant, a vain activity; for there is no gateway to reality in itself apart from the way of experiencing the effects of this reality, as it appears to us through a 'prism' of transcendental human perception. According to Kant any claim about an ultimate reality, as inferred from experience, is an incorrect epistemological conclusion.

In spite of all this, modern scientific progress has on its agenda substance (matter, ultimate fields, particles, etc.); it rejects the Kantian critique. Science introduces the notion of ultimate reality on the level of 'constructs', that is, such conceptual realities which express rationally the aspects of observable empirical things which are not seen, but whose existence is inferred in the chain of logical causations. Scientists sincerely believe that there are objective

---

[1] For a concise account of Greek monism in early Christian times see a paper of G. Florovsky (Florovsky 1956).

entities corresponding to their concepts which, by construction, transcend beyond the experiential domain. This belief in the existence of entities, which stand behind scientific concepts, constitutes the difference with the Kantian position; for conceptual realities in science are considered ultimately as having the same ontology as empirical data.[2] One observes here a kind of extended monism, which incorporates intelligible realities. This, however, in contradistinction to Kant, makes the task of the separation of the worldly aspects of existence from those ones which are associated with the *essence* of God even more difficult; for there is a risk of the ontological identification of some aspects of the extended notion of the world, for example, its *intelligible* pattern and order, with the divine. The Christian theistic position would be threatened by this kind of 'theistic' insight.

The result is that the extended, but still monistic, scientific substantialism is not able to detect that the ontological basis of the world is beyond this world, that is, in its otherness, in the non-being of the world and in God-Creator. One is led to ask then for the place of the argument from design in modern scientific attempts to bridge science and Christian theology.

We believe that in order to make the concept of design a useful instrument in the science–religion dialogue one should adopt a different methodological approach. It is in patristic thought that the idea of Greek substantialism was eventually removed from the search for truth and ontological monism was broken. This shift was associated with two fundamental steps: the first was the employment of the concept of *hypostasis* as *ousia* and the second the identification of the *hypostasis* of a being with *person* (Gr. *prosopon*).[3]

---

[2] It is assumed in cosmology, for example, that the Big Bang has the same ontology as the observable universe; in all theories involving the idea of the plurality of worlds, the ontological status of all worlds is assumed to be the same as it is for our universe, in spite of the fact that all other universes are not observable in principle. The list of these examples can be continued further.

[3] The term *hypostasis* marks a concrete being, that is, every particular realization of this being, its concrete independence and intrinsic constitution. In the *hypostasis* of being we find the incarnation of all its essence or common features, but in an individual, distinct and unrepeatable way. See Prestige (1952).

The introduction of the *hypostasis* into the heart of being makes this being an existence; the ontology of being becomes an existential ontology based on the relationship of those *hypostases* which are involved in this being. But this implies the whole transformation of the idea of substance; substance acquires a relational character (Zizioulas 1997, 83). The difference between the substantial and hypostatic properties of God made it possible to break the closed ontology of Greek philosophers. The break was explicitly achieved by St Athanasius, who made a distinction between the notion of *substance* and *will* in God. He argued that to be, that is, to exist, does not mean to *act*. In the context of the trinitarian discussions of the fourth century this distinction had a fundamental implication: the ontology of God as Trinity with its internal life is based on the *substance* of God, whereas the ontology of the created realm, of the world, is based on the *will* of God. Because the substance of God and His will are distinct in God, the ontology of the uncreated realm and that of creation is different (Florovsky 1975).

The fundamental and final step in setting up the ontological priorities in the Christian concept of God was made by the Cappadocian fathers who identified the hypostatic properties of God's existence with personhood. The ontological primacy of person over substance shaped Christian ontology in a way which never existed before, and which is largely forgotten in science–theology discussions today. The person in his created existence is hypostasized by an unrepeated and unique existential link with God. It is through this link that the life of persons, understood as the image of and likeness to the communion of love in the Holy Trinity, becomes the definition of humanity (Zizioulas 1997; Ware 1995).

It is the person, through its ability to be in communion with God, via its spiritual intellect (granted as a gift to know God from within the created world), who establishes the meaning of reality and the criteria for truth. For without communion with God the reality hypostasized by persons in the created realm, as knowledge of events and objects, theologically speaking, has no being at all. Using Kantian language, knowledge is possible only because of man's ability to sense, to think and to contemplate. The difference of the patristic vision of knowledge from that of Kant's is, however, of an enormous extent. For the knowledge achieved by the person (under-stood patristically) is in its content a hypostasized form of ontological reality, not subjective impressions and mental con-structions; whereas, according to Kant, the knowledge of the appearances of things does not guarantee that these appearances bear any ontology.

Patristic theology confesses a two-fold ontological dualism: between God and the world, and in the created domain between the sensible and the intelligible.[4] It means that the ideas, which are the subjects of human reflection, do possess an independent ontological reality which, however, is different from the ontology of sensible things.[5] It is only the person, who can mediate between these two realms in creation, because it is only through personhood that one can hypostasize the sensible domain and intelligible domain in creation, as distinct ontological realms.[6]

For Kant intelligible forms are not objective, because they are beyond space and time and hence have no ontological significance. It is clear therefore that, for Kant, the argument from design could not have any profound theological meaning: design is a construct with no ontological content, and hence does not provide a base for a theistic inference to God; whereas for the patristic mind the design argument can have an ontological significance in the domain of intelligible forms which have an independent ontological mode of existence. The fundamental result which follows from the latter, is

[4] The latter dualism is named by some patristic and Byzantine writers as the basic dichotomy in creation.

[5] It is worth mentioning that R. Penrose is nowadays an enthusiastic proponent of Platonism in modern theoretical physics. He explicitly states that the physical laws which we observe on the level of their empirical appearance have an underlying ontology which is rooted in the world of Platonic ideas. In spite of the interplay between ideas and facts their ontologies are different. See, for example, Penrose (1997).

[6] This argument is based on the Christological dogma that the *logos* of humanity as a composite hypostasis of body and mind is similar to the *logos* of Christ who can mediate between sensible and intelligible. In fact the composition of man does reflect the composition of the created being. But it is humanity, being an image of God, who can mediate between the two realms. See the account of theology of mediation (Thunberg 1995).

that the design argument cannot provide any evidence for God as He is in Himself (this is similar to the Kantian claim), because God as substance (*ousia*) is separated from the creation, but it can be used for evidence of the willing activity of God in the creation. The ontology of this activity is based on the *uncreated energies* of God, or the *uncreated logoi* (underlying and forming principles), which not being themselves from this world, do form and sustain the existence of all 'things visible and invisible' in the world. The evidence of this divine economy is gifted to man-person who is, through his possession of the spiritual intellect (*nous*), capable of transcending beyond the empirical and macroscopic Earth into the vastness of the *intelligible* cosmos, covering all imaginable spatial scales from 10^{-33} cm to 10^{28} cm. In this transcendence the person, as a primary ontological element of the created world, becomes aware of the design in the world, and hypostasizes this invention as an intelligible entity. Because of being created through Christ, that is, having a similar *logos*, man is able to mediate between the sensible and intelligible universes, between things which are seen and the order among them, which is intelligible. It is through this mediation that the person can contemplate the *logos* of creation, that is, the common principle of order and harmony among sensible things, as well as things intelligible (Thunberg 1995). The contemplation of the *logoi* of created things in their unity, through faith, allows one to ascend to the awareness of the Divine Logos.

St Athanasius of Alexandria and the Argument from Design

St Athanasius, the Bishop of Alexandria (AD 328), in his fundamental Christological writings, was arguing for uniformity in the created world, that is, for the principle which makes it possible to apply the same method of knowledge to objects on different scales of space, time, complexity and order. For, according to his theological vision, the world was created by the Word-Logos of God and everything exhibits His presence, because of the Incarnation of God in flesh, that is, the principle of Christ Who is God and man.

Athanasius argues that it is through His Logos that God gave such an order to the universe, which is comprehensible by man, and through this comprehension man can know God from within creation:

> God knew the limitation of mankind, you see; and though the grace of being made in His Image was sufficient to give them knowledge of the Word and through Him of the Father, as safeguard against their neglect of this grace, He provided the works of creation also as means by which the maker might be known. (Athanasius 1996, 39)

Athanasius uses astronomical examples, for example, regular motion of the sun and the moon, regular sunrise, etc., in order to infer to a *consistent order* in the universe, when opposite motions and differentiated objects 'are not ordered by themselves, but have a maker distinct from themselves who orders them' (*Contra Gentes*, 35:4). He insists that the order among things is not self-produced. He affirms that the order is maintained by God, by means of uniting, balancing, administrating, ordaining, reconciling things (ibid., 36:1–3; 37:1). He claims that if things in the universe would exercise the power of ordering themselves, we should see 'not an order, but disorder, not arrangement but anarchy, not a system, but everything out of system, not proportion but disproportion' (ibid., 37:3). In another passage Athanasius uses the fact of the existence of life on Earth in order to conclude, in a similar fashion, to the existence of the principle of 'arrangement and combination' in the world, which is ultimately granted by God (ibid., 37:4).[7]

The inference which is implicit in Athanasius' arguments is that from the order in the world one can conclude to the existence of the maker of this order. In modern parlance it sounds like an argument for God from design. As we have seen above, fourteen centuries after Athanasius, Kant tried to reproduce a similar argument philosophically, but his conclusion was rather negative. The genius of Athanasius affirmed (speaking on the order in the universe, by

---

[7] The argument from the fact of life in the universe to its special order, and then to the maker of this order, can be compared with modern versions of the Anthropic Cosmological Principle, see for example, Barrow and Tipler (1986), which was used by some scientists and theologians as an argument for theism, see for example, Polkinghorne (1998).

which he did not mean the order or design from the already created matter) that this order is supported and sustained by the Word of God as a transcendent creator.[8] For Athanasius means by the order in the universe not an epistemological construction (this was what Kant affirmed later) but an ontological rational order, whose existence, however, has its ground in the *otherness* of things which are ordered, that is, in the ontology of the Reason or Word of God (*Contra Gentes*, 40:1). This is a fundamental argument in favour of a rationality of the universe which proceeds not from the *principles of existence* of the created things,[9] which just provide for the manifold existence of particular things, but from the Word of God, His Logos, Who unites all *logoi* in Himself in a harmony which penetrates into creation and is contemplated by man as the order and rationality of the universe. Athanasius writes:

> But by Word I mean, not that which is involved and inherent in all things created, which some are wont to call the seminal principle,[10] which is without soul and has no power of reason or thought, but only works by external art, according to the skill of him that applies it, nor such a word as belongs to rational beings and which consists of syllables, and has the air as its vehicle of expression, but I mean the living and powerful Word of the good God, the God of the Universe, the very Word which is God, Who while different from things that are made, and from all Creation, is the One own Word of the good Father, Who by His own providence ordered and illumines this Universe. (*Contra Gentes*, 40:4)

Athanasius foresaw a possible scepticism in the belief in the existence of the Word of God. He gives a characteristic answer to this by appealing to the fundamental Christian stance that every particular existence, considered separately by a naive mind as self-sustained and self-sufficient, is contingent upon God; in doing so, Athanasius exercises an argument from the *creatio ex nihilo*, which

---

[8] Kant argued that the inference from the order of the universe can only prove an *architect* of the word 'who is always very much hampered by the adaptability of the material in which he works, not a *creator* to whose idea everything is subject' (Kant 1933, 522; A 627 = B 655).

[9] That is, their *logoi* of creation.

[10] Athanasius' usage of the term 'seminal principles' is probably similar to the Stoic 'seminal reasons', which mean literally 'reasons', in the sense of rational plans. The abbreviation for these terms is *logoi*, see Wolfson (1976, 277).

was an important Christian dogma. It is this scepticism that caused so many problems for Kant at the end of the eighteenth century when he argued that no demonstration of the existence of creator of the world from order and design in the universe was possible. Athanasius insisted that such a demonstration was possible:

> And if a man were incredulously to ask, as regards what we are saying, if there be a Word of God at all , such an one would indeed be mad to doubt concerning the Word of God, but yet demonstration is possible from what is seen, because all things subsist by the Word and Wisdom of God, nor would any created thing have had a fixed existence had it not been made by reason, and that reason is the Word of God, as we have said. (ibid., 40:6)

It is through the inference for the Word of God from the created order that one can know that God *is*; for it is the Word of God Who *orders* the universe and reveals the Father. Athanasius makes at this point a clear link between the order in the created word and the concept of the Incarnation of the Word of God. It was not enough for God just to create an ordered world in order to teach men about the Father. 'Creation was there all the time, but it did not prevent men from wallowing in error' (Athanasius 1996, 42). It was the part of the Word of God, His Logos and the only Son who by ordering the universe reveals the Father, 'to renew the same teaching' (ibid.) through the Incarnation in the body, using these other means in order to teach of God to those who would not learn from the works of His creation.

There is one particular aspect of the Incarnation of the Word of God which can justify a principle of uniformity and order in nature, and thus make the earthly science applicable to all aspects of the cosmos. Indeed Christ, being incarnate God in flesh at a given point of the history of salvation and at a particular place of the physical universe, did not cease to be the Word-Logos of God who controls the whole of the creation:

> The Word was not hedged in by His body, nor did His presence in the body prevent His being present elsewhere as well. When He moved His body He did not cease also to direct the universe by His Mind and might. No. The marvelous truth is, that being the Word, so far from being Himself contained by anything, He actually contained all things Himself . . . Existing in human body, to which He Himself gives life, He

is still Source of life to all the universe, present in every part of it, yet outside the whole; and He is revealed both through the works of His body and through His activity in the world. (Athanasius 1996, 45)

This affirmation of the unique position of Christ in the World, when Christ-man, being in a body locally at a given point of vast cosmic space, is coinherent to all places in space, because He is in everything as the Word of God, provides implicitly a principle of the order in the universe such that every place in the universe as a place of the 'presence' of the Word, is coinherent with the place where God is incarnate in body, that is, at the Earth.[11] This implied, in the view of the Christian scientists of the time, that there was a uniformity in the laws of nature (which were known from the earthly experience) in the whole cosmos. This *intrinsic rationality* in the world, Athanasius argued, is held by the creative Logos, which is not the immanent principle of the World, but the transcendent artificer of the order and harmony in the created existence contingent upon the *transcendent rationality* of God.

We see here the fundamental difference between the view formulated by Athanasius and that of the Hellenic vision of the cosmos as partially ordered; for Athanasius both realms in creation, that is, empirical (visible) and intelligible (invisible), are part of the creation; the common principle of their creation, order and harmony is encoded in the Word-Logos of God. This view rejects the Hellenic idea that there is only a partial order in the world (*Contra Gentes*, 3:44).

It is interesting to mention briefly one implication of this theological development in physics as was realized by the Christian physicist John Philoponus of Alexandria (d. *c.* 570) who recognized that a true order in the universe must be universally valid (see, e.g. Jaki (1990, 69)). Philoponus was directly influenced by the Christian concept of contingent creation of the world out of nothing. For him the cosmos has no inherent principles of existence, it is not a necessary state of affairs from within, and at the same time the cosmos is endowed by the Creator and through the Logos with a

---

[11] The full account on the interplay between the concept of the Incarnation and space, see Torrance (1997).

distinct reality and intelligible order. How did this understanding of the creation influence Philoponus in his scientific views? T. Torrance gives an interesting example of this influence (Torrance 1999, 207–10). Philoponus tried to understand the created order from the distinction between the uncreated and created light in theology of creation. According to him we explain the visible order (empirical things) in terms of the invisible (intelligible), that is, in terms of laws either physical or moral. But the laws involve the intelligible order in the created world, which is derived and points back to the ultimate foundation of order in God (1999, 209). This last example is indicative for our further argument; for we will argue that the *demonstration* of the presence of the *logoi* of creation is possible scientifically by analysing the interplay in the order of things empirical and intelligible.

Demonstrating the Presence of the *logoi* of Creation in Scientific Rationality

The problem that arises is how to *demonstrate* the presence of the Logos from within the created realm. The clue to this demonstration can be found in the theology of the *logoi* of St Maximus the Confessor (*c.* 580–662). According to Maximus, the Divine Logos – Word of God – holds together the *logoi* of things (that is, their immutable and eternal principles).[12] Maximus considered the contemplation of the *logoi* of created things as a mode of *communion* with the Logos, which leads ultimately to the mystical union with God.

The fundamental aspect of this *communion* is that, in spite of the fact that it is exercised through the intellect purified through virtuous life, the *contemplation* of the *logoi* is not similar either to empirical perception or mental comprehension; it is a mode of the spiritual vision of reality, where the ontological roots of things and beings are seen as having their grounds beyond the world. This Christian contemplation of creation as it were from above, or from within, not through an external sensible or mental impression, may be treated as significantly different from what is accepted now in

---

[12] On Maximus' theory of the *logoi* see, for example, Thunberg (1985, 134–43; 1995, 64–79).

scientific experience. Indeed science starts with experiments and measurements, which in fact constitute our sense of reality, although mediated by apparatus. There is, however, an aspect of all scientific investigation, which shapes some contingent findings of empirical science into a theory: this is an access to symbolic language, for example mathematics, which makes possible the talk about entities standing behind the outcomes of measurements, for example, elementary particles, fields, global geometry, totality of the universe, etc. All these 'objects' are known to us only through their effects, and are representable in our mind only by means of symbolic images; their physical existence is affirmed in terms of their symbolic images. We understand at present that this way of looking at reality corresponds to what we call human *rationality*. The source of this rationality is hidden in the mystery of the *hypostasis* of man whose *logos* is Christ – the incarnate Logos of God. It is because of the latter that we can hope to unveil the divine intentions behind created things through principles and ideas involved in science through human rationality.[13]

According to Maximus, the Logos is present in all things, holding their *logoi* together, so that the world is filled with the divine reality, and man, according to his *logos* can have knowledge of the *logoi* of things. Maximus expresses this thought in a characteristic way, using terms, which sound quite appropriate to the contemporary quest for the divine:

> Indeed, the scientific research of what is really true will have its forces weakened and its procedure embarrassed, if the mind cannot comprehend *how* God is in the *logos* of every special thing and likewise in all the *logoi* according to which all things exist.[14]

---

[13] One should mention, however, that the natural contemplation which St Maximus used for description of knowledge of the *logoi* in their unity, which provides an access to the Logos of God, being organically a sort of communion with God, assumes that the Holy Spirit is present in this communion. This means that God opens His mystery not to those who only speculate abstractly about the high being and origin of the world, but rather, to those, for whom the communion through the works of the Logos in the world is accompanied by the gnostic communion through Scripture as well as by the sacramental communion with Christ. See, for example, Zizioulas (1997, 191).

[14] St Maximus the Confessor, *Ambigua*, 22 (Patrologia Graeca (PG) 91, 1257 AB); I use the translation from Thunberg (1985, 140).

In spite of the fact that natural contemplation of the *logoi* is not entirely based in the discursive thinking, it is important to make an effort to formulate an algorithm for the demonstration of the presence of the *logoi* in a purely intellectual analysis of scientifico-philosophical affirmations about created nature. In a way this task is quite paradoxical; for what we are trying to discover through the analysis of worldly things is their *logoi*, the principles which are uncreated in their essence, that is, such principles which manifest that the ontological grounds of things, which are affirmed in science, are beyond the world in their *otherness*. That is why these trans-cendent principles are present in scientific or philosophical argu-ments only in a hidden, mystical, way, and can only be conceived from an a priori theological perspective, that is, from a cognitive position which assumes belief in God, Maker of heaven and earth, and of all things visible and invisible.

A typical example of paradoxical thinking which points toward the transcendent source of that which is affirmed or negated is an antinomic proposition. It consists of a cataphatic (positive) pro-position (thesis) and an apophatic (negative) proposition (antithesis) with respect to the same notion. For Kant it was natural to claim that the presence of antithetical structures in thought indicates that this thought is in trouble, that is, it thinks of notions which are beyond the legitimate sphere of application of the categories of the understanding. Kant denied the ontology behind the notions which are affirmed or negated in the antinomy and thus claimed that the source of the fallacy is in the mind, but not in the nature of things. For Kant, any notion which was not experiential, that is, empirical, was a product of intelligible causations and was not ontologically real. That is why any transcendence of the understanding beyond the sensible domain was suppressed – no principle of existence transcendent to the world of phenomena was possible.

Theology, in contradistinction to Kant, offers a different under-standing of the antithetical structures of knowledge, based on a dualistic ontology in the created realm. The thesis and antithesis of the antinomy demonstrate that the ontology of the empirical domain cannot have its ground in the intelligible domain, and, vice versa, the ontology of the intelligible domain cannot have its ground in the empirical domain. There is, however, a way for man to mediate between sensible and intelligible which Maximus considers as an element of ascension to a mystical knowledge of God.

Performing the mediation between sensible and intelligible in our creaturely state of existence and with the whole human nature, we come to the conclusion that *there is a logos* of all creation. There is no way, however, to develop this principle further. To understand this principle man would have to be immanent to God. The transcendent gulf between God and creation prevents us from knowing why God created at all. The principle of why God overbridged the gulf between Him and all which can be created, is a mystery and is hidden from us in God-as-He-is-in-Himself.

There is nevertheless a way, suggested by Maximus, which allows us to express the mystery of creation in a quite extraordinary logical formula. As a microcosm, man 'recapitulates the universe in himself' (*Ambigua* 41, PG 91, 1312B, quoted from Louth 1996, 160), that is, he is able to communicate with the universal *logos* of the world at large, that is, macrocosm. It means that the universal *logos* must be accessible to man and at the same time it must remain a secret, the divine secret. Maximus treats this antinomy-like problem appealing to the principle of creation out of nothing in accordance with which 'the whole of creation admits of one and the same undiscriminated *logos*, as having not been before it is' (ibid.). L. Thunberg has reformulated this thought even more clearly: 'the divine principle which holds the entire creation together is that it should have non-being as the ground of its being' (Thunberg 1995, 401). This formula implies that the principle of creation is that which states the limit, which divides creation (in its being) from its non-being.

What kind of demonstration of the presence of the Logos can one offer following the theology of Maximus? The simplest idea is to construct antinomies in science, which will refer to the distinction between sensible and intelligible creation. Then, accepting a theological methodology of treating these antinomies, one will be able to conclude that their presence in scientifico-philosophical thought brings us to the common principle of existence of things scientifically empirical and things scientifically intelligible. This common principle is the *logos* of creation, that is, the principle of creation of the world out of nothing by the Logos of God.

In the next sections we will try to develop this theological methodology, applying it to a special model of creation of the universe with design, according to R. Penrose.

Design through the Low Entropy Initial Conditions in the Universe

The issue of design in modern cosmology is closely connected with the fundamental question of the nature of the observed post-collision correlations between 'particles' in the universe which, in our human comprehension, appears as a kind of order, or design. The nature of such correlations is related to the issue of the present-day value of entropy in the universe; for it is entropy which indicates quantitatively the extent to which the universe is in a state of order/disorder. It is known that this entropy (S) is measured as the number of baryons in the observed universe and its numerical value is $S = s*10^{80}$, where the specific entropy $s* = 10^8$ is the number of photons per baryon. $s*$ is a fundamental physical parameter which is critical for the existence of stable physical systems: a hypothetical variation of $s*$ by two orders of ten will break the condition for gravitational stability of the stars and galaxies and existence of life in the universe (Barrow and Tipler 1986). Our understanding of entropy is based on the second law of thermo-dynamics, which teaches that entropy is growing. This implies that the value of the present-day S is a result of irreversible evolution in the universe from some initial state with entropy less than S. This view implies that there is a universal irreversibility of processes in the universe; the specificity of the universe's present state is connected then with special initial conditions, rather than with any possible intrinsic mechanism, which drives the flow of time and gives direction to the evolution of the universe to its present *design-like* state.

There are two outstanding attempts to solve the riddle of temporal flow in modern physics. The first trend, developed by Prigogine's scientific school, tried to introduce irreversibility at 'local' level, that is, to claim that irreversibility is inherent in some underlying physical laws, which are to be discovered (Prigogine 1980; Prigogine and Stengers 1984). We have analysed Prigogine's programme elsewhere (Nesteruk 1999b).

An alternative approach to the nature of the present state of the universe, as being a state with a relatively low entropy and hence a state with a high level of post-collision correlations, dates back to the idea of Penrose; namely, that the present special state of the universe, which is associated with a kind of design, has its origin in boundary conditions in the remote past of the universe.

The dichotomy which we observe in these two approaches to explaining entropy and a specific arrow of time in the universe, which is observed by us locally, that is, 'here' and 'now', reflects a general difficulty in distinguishing whether this arrow of time is caused by local factors, or by the boundary conditions in the distant past or future. Because the universe is unique it is difficult to distinguish between laws of nature and boundary conditions governing solutions to those laws (any proposal in this regard is untestable scientifically) (Ellis 1990).

In this paper we discuss an attempt to catch the source of 'design', appealing to a starting point of its evolution. The approach, which is due to Penrose, is based on his firm belief that: 'If the important local laws are all time-symmetrical, then the place to look for the origin of statistical asymmetry is in the boundary conditions' (Penrose 1979, 586). The relatively small entropy of the present state of our universe, which is evidenced by the existence of stable structures, must stem from the low entropy conditions at its initial state, assumed to have been a 'Big Bang'. It is assumed sometimes that the state of matter near the Big Bang is approximately in thermodynamic equilibrium with a maximum of entropy. However, at present, the state of the universe displays an entropy whose value is not high enough to prevent the emergence of states showing precise macroscopic after-collision correlations. These correlations, observed in a variety of structures, are evidence that a state preceding the present one must show a lower entropy; this contradicts the hypothesis of maximum-entropy at the Big Bang.

To overcome this paradox Penrose pointed out that one should take into account the gravitational degrees of freedom of the universe (Penrose 1979). He proposed to ascribe to the gravitational field some new property, indicating an entropy later called the gravitational entropy (*GE*). Evaluating the possible amount of entropy which can be produced in the universe, during the whole period of its evolution from Big Bang to Big Crunch, he discovered that there is a tremendous lack of entropy in the baryon universe we observe now, namely 10^{88} as compared to the possible value 10^{123}. The reason for this was thought to be found in the low *GE* condition at the Big Bang.

To express this condition in geometrical terms it was noticed that the growth of *GE* corresponds to a clustering of matter that is accompanied by an increase in the degree of anisotropy of the gravitational field which is itself described by the so-called Weyl Curvature (*WC*). This led Penrose to propose a scenario for the development of the universe in which the evolution begins from a low *GE* state corresponding to weak gravitational anisotropy and evolves to a high *GE* state marked by strong gravitational anisotropy, presupposing that *WC* is a possible measure of *GE*. A more precise statement of this idea is his well-known Weyl curvature hypothesis (WCH): the Weyl curvature tends to zero at all past singularities, as the singularity is approached from future directions (Penrose 1979; 1989).

The physical implications of the WCH for the present state of the universe can be expressed as follows: we regard the character of the actual state of the universe, assuming that it began with a Big Bang and *WC* = 0, as being more and more of the 'precise-correlation' type and less and less of the 'low-entropy' type as time progresses. It is consistent with Prigogine's ideas that the complexity of the universe is due to a steady flow of correlations among particles that can explain a very special state of the present universe. The WCH is local in time and cannot be derived from macroscopic dynamics. According to Penrose 'there are in fact . . . laws which only become important near spacetime singularities, these being asymmetric in time and such as to force the Weyl curvature to vanish at any initial singular point' (Penrose 1979, 632). This implies that there must be some laws, local in time, which are responsible for macroscopic irreversibility but, in contradistinction to the ideas of Prigogine, these laws are important only at the singularity, that is, in the remote past. As a result, according to Penrose, 'the problem of time's arrow can be taken out of the realm of statistical physics and returned to that of determining what are the precise physical laws' (Penrose 1979, 633).

These laws have a fundamental importance since they pre-determine the entire thermodynamical evolution of the universe, and the result of this evolution, which we contemplate as the design. From a methodological point of view such an approach presupposes the search for hidden (unknown) 'laws' existing at the singularity which we can guess at only by observing their macroscopic effects in the present-day universe and which we associate with design, and with the entropy $S = 10^{88}$. This means that what is assumed as a hidden physical law at the cosmological singularity is, in fact, the law for design itself, as extrapolated from the present-day universe backward to its beginning.

We observe here an interesting shift of the problem of design, as order and harmony in the present-day universe, towards that in the remote past, the moment of origin of the universe. This means that the issue of design acquires the colours of the special original 'creation' of the universe. This way of thought is reminiscent of the Kantian treatment of the physico-theological (that is, teleological) argument of God, based in fact on the ideas of design; namely his demonstration that the design argument, in order to become a theistic argument, assumes its foundation in the cosmological argument – in the idea that God is the source of the totality of the world in space and in time. This is exactly the way of Penrose's logic when the problem of 'special entropy at present' is treated as a problem of a special temporal origination of the universe.

Penrose's Model and its
Transcendental Philosophical Interpretation

In order to illustrate that WCH implies such atypical conditions in the early universe, Penrose appeals to the idea of 'phase space' of different initial conditions for all possible universes (Penrose 1989, 344). Taking the figure 10^{123} as a maximum potential entropy for a universe of our type, he estimates the phase-space volume corresponding to its possible initial conditions to be $V = 10^{10^{123}}$. But our actual physical universe corresponds to a phase-space volume of size $W = 10^{10^{88}}$. This shows that the initial conditions of the universe we live in, constitute an infinitesimal part of V, namely $W/V = 10^{-10^{123}}$, that is, the precision with which the Big Bang must be set up, is nearly infinite.

Since there is no natural foundation for this kind of event Penrose introduces the idea of a god powerful enough to 'create' all kinds of worlds: only an omniscient Creator may possess the knowledge of that infinite amount of information necessary to pin-point that tiny part of phase space which describes the initial conditions of our own universe.

The function of this creator is only to launch the universe but not to govern it. According to Penrose it is governed by the time symmetrical laws of physics. The universe W where $S = 10^{88}$, which we associate with the presence of design, appears only because of the very special type of 'creation' which is formulated geometrically as the condition $WC = 0$.

In the rest of this paper we discuss this idea from a philosophical and theological perspective. First of all, let us realize that Penrose introduced the world W as a concept of our universe, which indicates the pattern of design, associated with the entropy S. The universe W has to be explained. The explanation of the universe W is not possible in terms of the state of affairs within the universe itself. In other words we cannot explain the specificity of W in terms of its various elements. It is because of this intrinsic contingency of the universe W and the number $S = 10^{88}$, that the metaphysical understanding jumps from the manifold of the universe in its varied content and unlimited extent to the assumption that the universe is built with some determinate purpose, that is, it is designed. From observing the order which science uncovers in the universe, such as, large-scale structure, cosmic coincidences, fine-tuning (see, e.g. Barrow and Tipler 1986), one comes next to the conclusion that this order and beauty must belong to the universe contingently, because it is hard to believe that the diverse things in the universe could co-operate among themselves in order to fulfil the formation of the order to which we attribute purpose and design.[15] At this point physical reason appeals to some wise cause, which could be the cause of the world.[16]

Penrose's intention is to remove the contingency of the state of affairs in the universe as it is now, back to the remote past, where, according to him, there was a 'law' which made the contingency, which is observed by us here and now, to be a necessary contingency. In other words, the universe which we observe now as a contingent, was not such in the past, because there was an original necessary law which caused the further development of the universe. This 'law', however, does not belong to the empirical series of causations, it transcends beyond the universe W itself. It was necessary for Penrose to introduce two more super-natural ingredients in his explanation, namely a plurality of the universes with different initial conditions V and the 'Creator'. The V plays a role of the substratum which is necessary for the 'Creator' to be able to design our universe W. The 'Creator' therefore is not a creator at all: it is an architect of the world (demiurgic god) who is not the creator of the world out of nothing, for V is not 'nothing', but rather the potentiality of all possible states of affairs, that is, the maximal symmetrical state of undifferentiated being.

We observe here an analogy with the Kantian criticism of the physico-theological argument for existence of God. The problem of the physico-theological argument is that one cannot achieve an understanding of the wise cause of the universe W on purely empirical grounds; one should appeal to the cosmological argument, that is, invoke the concept of the world as a totality of the series of alterations. But the concept of the world in this sense does not deviate from the series of appearances, which regresses in

---

[15] Compare with the reasoning of St Athanasius which we considered above.

[16] The notion of *contingency* is applied only to the *form* of the world, not to its *substance* (Kant 1933, 522; A 627 = B 649). The *idea* of the wise cause of the world can not have its *object* (Kant 1933, 518; A 621 = B 649). Kant denies any causation between an *idea* and its hypothetical *object* because he denies logical predetermination or existence of forming principle of object.

accordance with the empirical laws of causality, and, therefore, it assumes that the world itself is a member of this series. There is no chance, however, to find any first beginning or any highest member (as a primary and/or ultimate cause) in the series of the world W for which a concluding term of the series will be in fact the world V.

Science always tries to discover the ultimate source of temporal series in nature by making some regress towards the fundamental but hidden physical law, or, alternatively, to the very first beginning of this series somewhere in the remote past. The inevitable consequence of this search for the believed existence of the absolute cause of design, is a departure from the field of empirical realities and the temporal series in the world W, and an appeal to theoretical models, or constructs, like V: this is the logic of the transition $W \rightarrow V$.

The striking thing, however, is that the constructs of such underlying reality like V, which is supposed to be the first beginning and the highest term in the series of reasoning based on the laws of empirical causation, are far away, by their epistemological nature, from the empirical domain of being; they turn out to be in the world of conceptual realities which itself does not bear any predicates of temporality, and that is why the very cause of design does not belong to the temporal series. In other words, this ultimate cause of the empirical appearances of design is not actually the cause of empirical series in a strict sense of empirical causation, because it does not belong to the empirical world. It means that we witness a typical transcendental jump in theoretical research from the series of empirical analysis to the series and causation of intelligible nature, that is, to a kind of regress in a conceptual space, where the highest term, or the very first 'beginning', is revealed not by the methods of empirical advance, but rather by purely logical formulations of the absolute necessity of such a being which is responsible for the temporal series in the world. One must admit that Penrose's mathematical model (WCH) gives actually an example of such a regress within conceptual realities.

The logic of an inverse transition $V \rightarrow W$, which describes the actualization of our world W out of V, is then understood from our W perspective, as a causation in the conceptual space. Whereas for 'the Creator', for whom the manifold of the worlds V, and the world W as a part of V, are given in their *actuality*, the transition $W \rightarrow V$ means a transition between two ontologically homogeneous objects V and W. This implies that a divine entity which actualizes the world W out of V is seen by us also as a construct from the conceptual space.

We observe here a kind of mental inversion from causation in the temporal series ($W \rightarrow V$), to causation in the purely intelligible series ($V \rightarrow W$), the completeness of which is based upon the existence of an absolutely necessary cause (that is, the creator). This jump in reflection is based on an inability to build the empirical content of the concept of the unconditioned condition (V + creator) in the series of empirical causes. According to Kant the design in W cannot bring us through an empirical analysis to the existence of a necessary cause which would not be contingent itself; and therefore one can state that there is not an absolutely necessary cause or being.

In Kantian parlance the idea of the ensemble of possible initial conditions V and the idea of Penrose's creator have no ontological reference in the empirical realm; they both exist in thought as empty logical forms which function only for the purpose rather of the logical justification of W as a contingent and temporal state of affairs with some pattern of design. Some physicists, however, being inspired by the idea of many worlds, which appears in different parts of physics, believe that V has the same physical ontology as W, and that is why the causation which brings W into existence out of V is sought as a physical law.[17] The same takes place in Penrose's argument when the WCH is formulated metaphysically as a law imposed by the creator by means of pinning out a 'point' in a set of all possible universes.

The clash between the realistic treatment of V and of the creator, drawn from Penrose's argument, and the negative result from the same treatment following Kantian analysis, leads us to the only justifiable formula for dealing with the situation; namely, to treat Penrose's statement about the transition $V \rightarrow W$ as an antinomy,

---

[17] For example, Strong Anthropic Principle, Many World Interpretation of quantum mechanics, Chaotic Inflation.

which is similar to the fourth Kantian antinomy on an absolutely necessary being (Kant 1933, 415; A 452f. = B480f.):

> *Thesis:* There belongs to the world the ensemble of all possible universes V with different initial conditions, whose existence is absolutely necessary for our universe W with low initial entropy to exist as a part of V; and this is a causal condition of design in W (there is causal connection between V and W).

> *Antithesis:* There nowhere exists the ensemble of universes V in the world, as the cause of our universe W with low initial entropy, as being the causal condition for design in W (there is no connection between V and W: they belong to different ontological realms – intelligible and empirical – correspondingly).

As we mentioned above, Kant would use this antinomy for a negative conclusion about empirical evidence for the existence of an absolutely necessary being as a cause of the universe W with design. His argument, probably, would be that the V and the *creator* both belong to the intelligible realm and have no independent ontological being, or *ousia*, apart from the thought, which brought the ideas of V and of the creator into being. This Kantian denial of substance behind the idea of a necessary being, that is, its ontological existence in the intelligible world, leads ultimately to a denial of God and the possibility to ascend to Him through the observation of his *economy* in the created realm. This is an inevitable result of the Kantian agnostic and monistic substantialism.

Accepting that the empirically assessable notion of substance is possible only because of cognitive faculties of man, Kant, in his transcendental vision of man, deprived man from being able to transcend the empirical realm, and, as a result, to hypostasize intelligible reality, that is, the world of ideas as ontologically distinct from sensible domain. It is Kant's monistic ontology, which prevented his transcendental subject from bearing the *logos* of Christ, that is, allowing man to belong to both sensible and intelligible realms and, at the same time, to possess the ability to mediate between them.

We see that the need to overcome Kantian scepticism leads us naturally to a change in the anthropology of a subject, understood now Christologically. This change implies that we should not think of antinomies as puzzles for human reason, as something which are fallacious in themselves, but rather consider an antinomy as a natural difficulty in relating the ontology of the sensible world to the ontology of the intelligible world and vice versa; the lesson which we learn from the Kantian analysis of antinomies, and his scepticism on the proof of God, is that antinomies reflect an epistemological situation when one cannot find the ontological ground of what is affirmed or negated by thesis and antithesis, in the created being. The resolution of the Kantian antinomies in a theological perspective comes from an observation that antinomy reflects the process of mediation between sensible and intelligible realms, which is exercised by man, and, as result, the process of contemplation of the common *logos* of two realms in creation, that is, the immutable and uncreated principle of their differentiated existence, which is the Logos of God.

We can conclude that the appeal to the Christological vision of man, and to the ontological primacy of person, and its ability to hypostasize both sensible and intelligible things, gives us a powerful tool in order to employ the Kantian methods of antinomies in order to detect the presence of the *logoi* in the created things. We try now to establish this conjecture by an application to Penrose's model.

Design and the Logos of Creation

According to the Orthodox Christian view God created the world in such a way that there was an initial dualism between two realms: the realm of intelligible forms and the realm of sensible reality. The intelligible realm is simply understood as the 'spiritual', 'intellectual' level of created being. A good way of referring to this realm is as the *noetic* level of creation (Ware 1995, 49). On this level God formed the angels, who have no material body. But this level contains also intellectual images of sensible reality, that is, ideas. This makes the noetic realm reminiscent of the world of Platonic ideas. Ideas as intellectual images of sensible reality are inevitable ingredients of scientific theories, so that we will argue that scientific ideas have an immediate relation to the noetic realm which complements the sensible realm, that is, the material universe with its physical, chemical and biological forms of matter and life.

In spite of the dualism proclaimed in the Creed there is a unity between the two realms of created being, which is explained by the mystery of creation as whole. It is only humanity who exists on two levels of reality, and can be a mediator between these levels and hence a witness of their ultimate unity, as the unity of God's creation.

We see that the concept of *creatio ex nihilo* bears a kind of structure, which is primarily imprinted in the created world through the *difference* between intelligible and sensible. This word, *difference*, is an important category in St Maximus the Confessor's vision of creation. It comes from the Greek *diaphora* and has theological reference in Christological discussions in contradistinction to the Greek word *diairesis* which means *division* (Thunberg 1995, 51–7). Maximus states that the *diaphora*, as a characteristic of created being is *constitutive* and distinctive. This means that the difference in creation will never disappear. It plays a constructive role in creation, because it provides a common principle of all created things: all things are differentiated in creation and at the same time the principle of their unity is that they are differentiated. In particular it provides a common principle for the unity of intelligible and sensible creation through its *constitutive* meaning in the *creatio ex nihilo*. From this perspective the issue of the *creatio ex nihilo* can never be separated from the issue of *differentiation* in creation between intelligible and sensible; the *diaphora* in God's creation is an established order, the principle of variety and unity in creation, which is distinct from the Creator. This principle as imposed on the created realm through creation by Word-Logos, is the *logos* of creation itself. This *logos* was confirmed in Christ.

The immediate implication of the ontological category *diaphora* in creation, as applied to a scientific quest for the *creatio ex nihilo*, is that any physical or cosmological model trying to imitate the *creatio ex nihilo* in scientific terms, should deal with the fact that it is not enough just to produce a mechanism of how our empirical (sensible) universe was brought into being from nothing; one should realize that there is a 'parallel' creation of the invisible world, the world of intelligible forms or noetic realm. But the theory of creation of the noetic realm would be quite problematic, because it assumes a theory of meaning, or a theory of the intelligence which is responsible for the models of the sensible creation in physics. But the creation of meaning for things sensible is the work of the Logos through His uncreated *logoi*, and is not a part of scientific enquiry. Science, therefore, can responsibly argue only for a 'half' of creation or, in different words, it can only claim that it found the mechanism of *differentiation* in creation as seen from the sensible perspective. In this the *creatio ex nihilo* is accessible through science only up to the extent of *differentiation* in creation, but not as ontological creation out of nothing.

This view explains to us, finally, what was really indicated in Penrose's model; definitely it has nothing to do with *creatio ex nihilo* taken in its pure affirmative form. For the world *V* (out of which the sensible realm *W* emerged), pre-existed before the actualization of *W*. The 'creator' also belonged to the same realm as *V* and its work was just mastering the *W* from the material given in the *V*. Both *V* and the 'creator' belong to the intelligible series of causation, as we demonstrated before.

The orthodox view, which we employ now, is that the *V* is an object from the intelligible domain. Whereas the *W*, in its appearance to us, can be considered as a part of sensible creation. What does, then, the transition *V* → *W* mean? It shows not the creation of *W* out of *V*, but rather the *differentiation* between the intelligible, potentially existing world, *V*, and the sensible world *W*. Indeed both *V* and *W* exhibit the fundamental *diaphora* in creation. The inference from design in *W*, as an attempt to find the foundation of the *W* in the non-being of *W*, led us to the scientific model of *diaphora* in the created world. Indeed the specificity of the Big Bang, discovered by Penrose, points, in fact, to the specificity of the *constitution* of the *creatio ex nihilo*. We contemplate these special *constitutive* elements of the *creatio ex nihilo* through the model of this *difference* between *V* and *W*. The *difference* between the worlds *W* and *V* is the presence, or absence, of design in the universe, that is, design itself can be treated as a *constitutive* element of the *creatio ex nihilo*.

The antinomy, formulated above in the context of Penrose's model, can be rephrased as an affirmative proposition on the constitution of creation: God, creating the world out of nothing, sets up the *difference* between *V* (plurality of conceptual universes with different initial conditions) as the domain of intelligible creation, and our universe *W* (with the low initial entropy, and hence design) as the domain of sensible creation. From this point of view the WCH of Penrose is an attempt to describe this *diaphora* between *V* and *W*, as it is seen from within the *W*, that is, in physico-geometrical terms. The presence of the *diaphora* in the created being, detected in the Penrose model, reveals thus the common *logos* of both *W* and *V*, that is, that they have non-being as the ground for their being (St Maximus the Confessor: see above). From here one concludes that the *logos* of design is a principle that there is non-being of design, which is the ground for its being. This was exactly demonstrated in the model of Penrose and that is why we conclude that the model of Penrose points towards the *logos* of creation.

Finally one can reaffirm that the positive evaluation of the Kantian critique, applied to the argument from design, comes from the observation that this method is suitable for identifying the ontological differences (*diaphora*) of objects which appear in antinomies. The antinomy itself, as an antithetical epistemological formula, becomes an explicit way of inference to the common *logos* of things which are affirmed or negated.

[Acknowledgement: I am grateful to George Horton for discussion, comments and for help with polishing the language of this chapter.]

References

ATHANASIUS, ST. 1991. *Contra Gentes*, in *Nicene and Post-Nicene Fathers of the Christian Church*. Series 2. vol. 4, Edinburgh: T&T Clark/ Grand Rapids: Eerdmans.

——. 1996. *On the Incarnation*, New York: St Vladimir's Seminary Press.

BARROW, J. D. and TIPLER, F. J. 1986. *The Anthropic Cosmological Principle*, Oxford: Clarendon Press.

ELLIS, G. F. R. 1990. 'Major Themes in the Relation between Philosophy and Cosmology', *Mem. Ital. Ast. Soc.*, 62, 553–605.

FLOROVSKY, G. 1956. 'The Patristic Age and Eschatology: An Introduction', *Studia Patristica* 235–50.

——. 1975. 'St Athanasius' Concept of Creation', in *Aspects of Church History: Collected Works of Georges Florovsky*, Belmont, MA: Nordland, 39–62.

JAKI, S. L. 1990. 'Christology and the Birth of Modern Science', *The Asbury Theological Journal*, 45:2, 61–72.

KANT, I. 1933. *Critique of Pure Reason*, London: Macmillan.

LOUTH, A. 1996. *Maximus the Confessor*, London and New York: Routledge.

NESTERUK, A. V. 1999a. 'Polkinghorne on Science and God: a Review Essay', *Sourozh 77*, 34.

——. 1999b. 'Temporal Irreversibility: Three modern views', in Mogens Wegener (ed.), *Time, Creation and World-Order*, Aarhus: University of Aarhus, 62–86.

PENROSE, R. 1979. 'Singularities and Time-Asymmetry', in S. W. Hawking and W. Israel (eds), *General Relativity: An Einstein Centenary*, Cambridge: Cambridge University Press, 581–638.

——. 1989. *The Emperor's New Mind*, New York: Oxford University Press.

——. 1997. *The Large, The Small and the Human Mind*, Cambridge: Cambridge University Press.

POLKINGHORNE, J. 1998. *Belief of God in an Age of Science*, Yale: Yale University Press.

PRESTIGE, G. L. 1952. *God in Patristic Thought*, London: SPCK.

PRIGOGINE, I. 1980. *From Being to Becoming*, New York: Freeman.

PRIGOGINE, I. and STENGERS, I. 1984. *Order out of Chaos*, London: Heinemann.

THUNBERG, LARS. 1985. *Man and the Cosmos: The Vision of St Maximus the Confessor*, New York: St Vladimir's Seminary Press.

THUNBERG, LARS. 1995. *Microcosm and Mediator: The theological Anthropology of Maximus the Confessor*, Chicago and La Salle, Ill.: Open Court.

TORRANCE, T. F. 1997. *Space, Time and Incarnation*, Edinburgh: T&T Clark.

——. 1999. 'Creation, Contingent World-Order, and Time: A Theologico-Scientific Approach', in Mogens Wegener (ed.), *Time, Creation and World-Order*, Aarhus: University of Aarhus, 206–36.

WARE, KALISTOS T. 1995. *The Orthodox Way*, New York: St Vladimir's Seminary Press.

WOLFSON, H. A. 1976. *Philosophy of the Church Fathers*, Cambridge, Mass. and London: Harvard University Press.

WORTHING, M. W. 1995. *God, Creation, and Contemporary Physics*, Minneapolis: Fortress Press.

ZIZIOULAS, J. 1997. *Being as Communion*, New York: St Vladimir's Seminary Press.

9

Disorder and the Ambitions of 'Science and Theology': Ten Theses

WILLEM B. DREES

Introduction

Order and design seem to go together in arguments about nature and its Author; disorder, diseases and imperfections seem to count against a religious view of life. Yet, many writings on science-and-theology argue that despite appearances to the contrary there is a good order underlying our world. In this context, biology (adaptations) and physics (e.g. anthropic principles) have provided most of the material. Chemistry, with its ambition to purify elements and to create new materials, and more general engineering attitude to improving the world, seems at odds with fundamental assumptions of natural theology and its under-standing of God as the Author or giver of Laws and the intelligent Designer. In this paper I will argue that disorder in nature calls into question a wide variety of projects in 'science and theology', as too many projects are based on mistaken assumptions of harmony. Disorder in nature is a reality which can be considered as if it were designed to call humans to responsibility, to serve God and each other with all our heart and soul as well as with all our power and mind.

I. The Appreciation of Reality

Thesis: The *appreciation* of reality is at least as important a topic when we reflect on religion in relation to our current scientific world view as debates about *explanations*.

An optimist and a pessimist come to discuss our world. According to the optimist this is the *best* of all possible worlds. The pessimist agrees: 'I am afraid you are right, *this* may well be the best of all possible worlds.' Optimists and pessimists may agree upon the facts, and even upon their explanations, and still come to different conclusions on the evaluation of reality.

These differences in appreciation are religiously relevant. In monotheistic thought the notion 'creation' is not only employed as a semi-causal notion about the beginning of the world or its ontological dependence (at all times) on a creator. The word 'creation' suggests also that there are purposes, intentions involved in the explanation of the created order – goals that are deemed valuable. In the story of the first chapter of Genesis it is said four times that 'God saw that it was good', and one time that God saw that it was very good. 'Creation' is not solely explanatory, but has many existential connotations. For instance, the conviction that their God is also the creator of heaven and earth has been for Israel a comforting message in difficult times.

The valuational dimension is not only typical of theistic views with an explicit volitional element (a creator intending, desiring, etc.). If the divine had to bring forth a world out of necessity, volitional terms are no longer applicable to the divine. However, in classical emanationist philosophies, of which the system of Plotinus is the prime example, the One which is the original supreme 'principle' is supposed to be perfect in many ways – and 'perfect' is a valuational predicate.

In alternative religious views, valuational elements are clearly present as well. Let us consider as an example the popular *A Course in Miracles*. The basic idea is that our world of death and suffering is not real but an illusion, created by our mind. We continue to create this so-called reality because we see ourselves as beings separate from others and from God. When we start to see that only love is real, and that everything that is not in accord with it is an illusion, we will be able to reach, along a path of spiritual exercises, true peace. The inner voice that gave Helen Schucman these insights is presented as the voice of Jesus Christ. The view presented is, however, radically at odds with Christianity – as the world of creatures, of time and matter, is not genuine, not a divine creation, but a human illusion. The world-view of the *Course* is a modern variant of an old rival of Christianity, gnosticism. Good and evil are understood in terms of having more or less knowledge; evil is a necessary preliminary stage that will be overcome by the acquisition of knowledge. This world is a world of suffering; there is no room for trust in the meaning of ordinary life, but only the call for a total conversion, which dispels the illusion we have created. The *Course* offers a view of reality which burdens us mercilessly with the responsibility for all our failures (e.g. Van Harskamp 1998).

William James wrote in his *The Varieties of Religious Experience* ([1902] 1958, 49) on the difference 'whether one accept the universe in the drab discolored way of stoic resignation to necessity, or with the passionate happiness of Christian saints'. The evaluatory dimension was characteristic of what religion is about: 'At bottom the whole concern of both morality and religion is with the manner of our acceptance of the universe. Do we accept it only in part and grudgingly, or heartily and altogether? Shall our protests against certain things in it be radical and unforgiving, or shall we think that, even with evil, there are ways of living that must lead to good?'

Thus, as a heuristic formulation which may help to clarify and explore a complex area of discussion I suggest the 'formula':

$$a \text{ theology} = a \text{ cosmology} + an \text{ axiology}$$

with the + sign not being a mere addition, but the crucial issue: how the two are brought together. 'Cosmology' is not understood here as a branch of astrophysics, the study of the universe at large, but as a view of the way the world is, and thus a philosophical (one might even say metaphysical) position which can be more or less in line with scientific insights. Some theologies are struggling with the way science suggests a cosmology, and thus run the risk of coming up with cosmologies that are at odds with contemporary science (e.g. in magical understandings of reality, with disembodied ghosts or almost disembodied morphogenetic fields, or in 'scientific creationism'). In my perception, one can also accept the way science shapes our understanding of reality, and thus a naturalistic cosmology, and still struggle with the way our understanding of 'what is' can be combined with our sense of 'what should be'. That places all the emphasis on the '+' sign; one might consider such a theology existential rather than magical.

Some readers may think of resemblances with a scheme proposed by Nancey Murphy and George Ellis (1996). However, my scheme, which I published in Dutch in 1990, is a heuristic for exploring the field rather than a substantial thesis about what one holds to be the proper view of the relationship between theology, ethics and the sciences. Besides, I do not want to pronounce in this context on 'the moral nature of the universe'; my scheme can be used also to describe the positions of those who consider the universe to be amoral, whether indifferent or evil (e.g. T. H. Huxley, G. C. Williams) – such a position would be understood as offering a different view of the '+' sign. Unlike Murphy and Ellis, for whom each level of understanding requires a higher one until it finally includes a doctrine of God, I do not consider an atheist to be necessarily deficient in understanding; he, or she, rather holds a different existential position. Furthermore, I would not have that much continuity between science, metaphysical cosmology and theology, nor line up ethics with the social sciences as they did, as if ethics can be understood to be descriptive (the way things are) rather than transformative.

II. Marcion's Dualism

Thesis: Marcion's dualism is the deepest challenge to Christian theology.

Christianity has not been able to sort out in a logically consistent way its view of reality and suffering (and perhaps there have been good pastoral reasons for avoiding a rigorous logical resolution). An early attempt at greater consistency was that of Marcion, in the second century AD in Rome. He discerned a fundamental tension between our understanding of God as the creator of this ambivalent world, the God for whom justice seems to be fairness, 'an eye for an eye', and our view of God as the Redeemer, the Loving Father of Jesus Christ, in whom there is grace and abundant forgiveness. Marcion concluded that there were two gods rather than one – the Creator being distinct from, and lesser than, the Father of Jesus Christ. The Christian churches have rejected Marcion's solution. In all its creeds, Christianity has affirmed that it is the same God who is both the Creator of heaven and earth and the Father of Jesus Christ. In Catholic thought, this affirmation has often been developed in terms of a continuity of nature and grace. In Protestant thought, the distinction if not even tension between nature and grace has been more in the forefront. The tension also shows up in exegetical discussions. When Gerhard von Rad placed the Exodus events centre stage, while relegating Genesis to a place of secondary importance, he thereby provided exegetical support for those who – with Marcion – would look rather critically upon 'creation faith' as playing down the significant need for redemption, liberation, etc. In contrast, Claus Westermann in his exegetical studies on Genesis has argued that there are good grounds for appreciating the particular contribution of the creation narratives, which are not wholly subservient to the liberation ones. Creation narratives and other wisdom literature provides us with the message of God's blessing in all that is.

Ambivalence about the appreciation of reality is not just a matter for theologians. In European history disagreements on the 'evaluation of reality' have also been expressed in novels. A famous example is Fyodor Dostoyevski's *The Brothers Karamazov* (1879/80), especially in the objections of Ivan: 'If the sufferings of the children go to swell the sum of sufferings which was necessary to pay for truth, then I protest that the truth was not worth such a price.' One can also think of Voltaire's *Candide ou l'Optimisme* (1759). The philosopher Pangloss maintains that this is the best of all possible worlds. The more he argues his case, the less convincing it becomes.

Struggles about religious convictions in the world as we know it today are not just debates about the consistency of scientific and theistic explanations. Rather than confrontations over explanations, it may seem easier to allow room for a religious contribution to our evaluations of the world. However, one is then confronted with major disagreements within religious thought. Theists face a complex situation. Among themselves, they do not know how to handle the tension between emphasis on the goodness of creation and on the need for redemption. And furthermore, they are challenged by many others, such as those who argue as if there are two ultimate realities (good and evil, or, as Marcion, good and harsh); those who, like the gnostics, have only one ultimate reality, while abandoning our world with all its suffering as illusion; and the atheists who hold that there is just this world of mixed qualities.

III. Design Neglects Ambivalence

Thesis: The emphasis on design in science-and-religion neglects the ambivalence of reality and the importance of the religious dimension of transformation.

One area where the valuation of the world shows up in the religion and science discussion is in disputes on arguments from design, dealing with physics, biology and cosmology. There has been an optimistic, if not romantic, strand in design arguments at various levels – the universe is not only ordered in a useful way, but well ordered for our well-being. However, no strong arguments seem to be forthcoming. To the contrary, the more we know, the more we also know how inhospitable the universe is to life. That applies also to the future. There seems to be no guarantee that we will not bring the atmosphere of the Earth into a condition that is unfriendly towards our existence and that of many currently existing life forms. And when the Sun is through its stage of hydrogen burning, in some 5 billion years from now, the prospects will be even more grim. Science does not support the positive view of the world assumed in the design arguments, and it does offer some pretty good reasons to a more pessimistic view. As the cosmologist Steven Weinberg wrote, at the end of his popular book *The First Three Minutes* (1977): 'It is even harder to realize that this present universe has evolved from an unspeakably unfamiliar early condition, and faces future extinction from endless cold or intolerable heat. The more the universe seems incomprehensible, the more it also seems pointless.'

This assessment is a direct challenge to those who rely upon a design argument which seeks to claim that our world is a good place to be, and thus a good job done, indicating a good Creator. However, Weinberg's remark and similar considerations regarding the ambivalence of reality can also be a stimulus to reconsider what we see as the nature of religions. Religions are not just peculiar cosmologies, whether with a supreme Being or with demons, angels, and other spiritual entities floating around. Any proposal for a credible religion has to be not only intellectually coherent with our best knowledge; it also has to have the proper moral character. If one could make a convincing argument that there is 'a Maker' beyond the Big Bang, that would be fascinating – but it would not be religiously relevant if there were not also a moral dimension to it. In the New Testament we hear of two great command-ments, namely to love God and to love one's neighbour – with all the energy and knowledge one has. The commandment is not to believe in a certain explanation of the world or of phenomena in the world, but to live in a certain way, in a loving way. Similar calls can be found also in the writings of the prophets and elsewhere.

In religious life we respond to aspects of reality which we may not understand or control, but to which we feel positively related or for which we feel grateful. This dimension of religion I call *mystical*, since it has to do with a sense of being related to, or belonging to, something which surpasses us and our understanding. This is a dimension of religion with which many authors on the relationship between science and religion seem to identify when they emphasize elements which correspond to, affectively speaking, a positive view of reality, such as order, creativity, purposiveness, coherence, beauty, or mystery. It is such a religiosity which stimulates the quest for an implicit order which is meaningful and good. This is the background of 'natural theology'. By affirming reality to such an extent, the question arises whether such a natural theology is not too conservative, too much affirming the status quo, and insufficiently critical, failing to do adequate justice to suffering and evil.

IV. Prophetic Contrast rather than Natural Theology

Thesis: We need an 'anti-natural theology' with a clear sense of *discontinuity* between the natural (that which 'is') and that which should be.

Religions can be seen as human responses to experiences with aspects of reality which we do not understand or control, but to which we feel positively related. However, they also embody and articulate responses to aspects of reality we understand perhaps all too well, but nonetheless will not accept. In this case, we might speak of a *prophetic* religion, since it relates to the experience of a *discontinuity* between values and facts, between our axiology and our cosmology. To articulate this dimension of religion, we need a dualist element in religious language, articulating a contrast between what is and what should be. Such a dualism can be expressed in religious terms as the difference between earth and heaven, between the city of man and the city of God, between the present and the paradise, between the present and the kingdom of God, between nature and grace, and in many other ways. Thus, Gerd Theissen (1985, 4) wrote:

> Every faith contradicts reality in some way. That is inevitable, if faith is to be an unconditional 'Yes' to life. Think of all the horrors that could contradict this 'Yes'! Think of all the oppressive experiences against which it has to be affirmed: all the probabilities and certainties, including the certainty of one's own death!

The issue could perhaps also be argued in the context of the history of religions. John Hick (1989), following Karl Jaspers, distinguishes between the tribal religions which preceded the axial (transition) period around the middle of the last millennium BCE and the post-axial religions. The earlier religions located the individual within the social and cosmic order (and thus are typical examples of religions which stress continuity between cosmological and axiological aspects), whereas the later ones emphasized transformation, salvation, or redemption (and thus, in one way or another, a distinction between the actual social and cosmic order and the destiny of the individual). Platvoet (1993) offers a more elaborate analysis of the history of religions: according to him, the most recently emerged religions (e.g. New Age) have some of the characteristics of earlier types of religions.

The issue can perhaps also be formulated within the Hebrew and Christian traditions in terms of divine presence and absence. In his *The Elusive Presence*, Samuel Terrien traces the role of hiddenness through the whole Bible. One example is the story of Jacob wrestling with a stranger during the night; the stranger cannot be seen in the light of the day nor is his name revealed (Genesis 32). 'Thick darkness' characterizes the place of God, both at Mount Sinai and in the Temple in Jerusalem (Exod 20:21; 1 Kings 8:12; 2 Chron 6:1). The Ten Commandments prohibit the carving of images. According to Isaiah (8:17, 45:15), God hides himself. Job is challenged to tell where he was when God laid the foundations of the earth. Job places his hand in front of his mouth and is silent (Job 40:4). Job does not so much acknowledge moral guilt as hubris. In Jesus God's presence is not obvious. Is this not the carpenter? Do we not know his parents, brothers and sisters? (e.g. Mark 6:3). And he is not even able to save himself from the cross (Mark 15:29–32)! But then the centurion recognizes this man as the Son of God (Mark 15:39). Through humiliation comes exaltation (Phil 2:5–11).

The life of Jewish and Christian communities is not structured around a holy place, a temple where God would be present. Central to Jewish and Christian life are holy times of remembrance and expectation. The sabbath recalls the creation and the exodus and is a foretaste of fulfilment. The synagogue is a place of memory and hope, recalling God's great deeds in the past for the sake of the future. The hiddenness and absence can be seen mystically, in relation to God's holiness, but also in relation to prophetic engagement: this world is not as God intends the world to be.

Some contemporary theologians, sometimes under the influence of Karl Barth, are sensitive to such tensions within our world and within our faith. This may explain to some extent why so many theologians, at least on the continent, hesitate to follow old or new arguments of design that seek to establish that God shows through the processes of nature. There is implicitly not only a theology of divine presence, but also of divine absence – not merely as atheism, as non-existence, but as a way of being which is not in line with natural being.

Such concerns about the ambivalence of our world makes debates on order and design more complicated. Some theological writings on these issues are extremely hard to follow, if not outright obscure and incomprehensible. Sometimes an appeal to the moral-theological inadequacy of design arguments becomes a way of brushing difficult issues under the rug by abstaining from a genuine conversation with current scientific knowledge. But the reality of suffering, or evil – and thus of disorder, in a theological sense of the term – is a challenge to many of the science-and-religion arguments. I will briefly consider some terms that are commonly used in 'religion and science', but that seem to me to be problematic.

The first notion that is problematical is 'natural theology'. Natural theology with the interest of arguing from features of reality to the existence and nature of its Maker, seems to focus too much on that which 'is', thereby neglecting the critical dimension, our longing for this world to be better. Besides, arguments in natural theology are often quite selective, focusing on nice features of reality, but not the darker sides of nature.

V. Consonance

Thesis: *Consonance* seems to assume that harmony is there to be discerned.

In my opinion, the term 'consonance' assumes too much that harmony is something to be found. I suggest that it is something that needs to be constructed – both in the intellectual sense that we need to change our ideas in order to make them 'fit' together, but also in the ethical sense, that harmony needs to be constructed by changing this world, by changing our lives (see Drees 1990).

The term 'consonance' was used in passing by Ernan McMullin (1981), on the relation between the Big Bang theory and the Christian idea of *creatio ex nihilo*, or more generally, on a position which would be intermediate between, a positivist dismissal of cognitive claims in theology and the construal of a Biblical world-view:

> The Christian cannot separate his science from his theology as though they were incapable of interrelation. On the other hand, he has learned to distrust the simpler pathways from one to the other. He has to aim at some sort of coherence of world-view, a coherence to which science and theology, and indeed many other sorts of human construction like history, politics, and literature, must contribute. He may, indeed, *must* strive to make his theology and his cosmology consonant in the contribution they make to this world-view. But this consonance (as history shows) is a tentative relation, constantly under scrutiny, in constant slight shift. (1981, 52)

Whereas McMullin introduced the musical metaphor consonance mainly as a critical epistemic notion, arguing *against* too much confidence in the contribution theology could make to the appraisal of scientific theories, the term has acquired a more affirmative meaning in the writings of others. 'Consonance' has become a flag in science-and-religion, especially for some who claim that there are two independent sources of insight, which happen to be in harmony. Ted Peters, a Lutheran theologian associated with the Center for Theology and the Natural Sciences in Berkeley, gave a book he edited the title *Cosmos as Creation: Theology and Science in Consonance* (1989); more recently, another book he titled *Science and Theology: The New Consonance* (1998). Peters speaks of 'hypothetical consonance' on 'the domain of inquiry shared by science and theology' (1998, 1). Hypothetical, as:

> It would be too much to say that the current state of the dialogue between science and theology consists of total accord or total agreement regarding the role that God plays as the world's creator and redeemer. In its milder form consonance functions as an hypothesis: If there is only one reality and if both science and theology speak about the same reality, is it reasonable to expect that sooner or later shared understandings will develop? (Peters 1998, 1)

In my opinion, the term 'consonance' as it has come to be used in later years has various disadvantages. It assumes theology as a source of knowledge, on equal footing with the sciences, and thus assumes more symmetry in kind and standing than is warranted. But the more important problem is the assumption that we are looking for *harmony* between theological and scientific ideas. However, many theologies embody also a critical attitude towards reality – introducing a dualism of the real and the ideal, of the way things are and the way they should be, between the present and the Kingdom, etc. Arguing for 'consonance' risks becoming an argument that this is the best of all possible worlds, that evil is not genuine but only apparent evil, or at its worst justifiable evil, and so on.

VI. Building Bridges

Thesis: Neither is *building a bridge* a satisfactory metaphor for theology-and-science.

The image of a bridge assumes two sides where the bridge is based in the bedrock of particular domains; we are only to connect the two domains with an ingenious construction. It assumes that both sides are comparable as independent domains. Aside of assuming questionable symmetry, neglecting the challenges of historicity and cultural pluralism to religious traditions, the image does not capture the need to revise religious traditions.

The intellectual standing of both human endeavours is quite dissimilar. The natural sciences have been able to expand the domain covered from human-sized ranges to details within atoms as well as galaxies and even larger structures. They have shown an impressive increase in coherence across disciplines, as witnessed by the emergence of disciplines such as 'molecular biology'. They have shown an enormous trend towards unification at the level of ideas and explanatory schemes, both with respect to fundamental theories in physics as well as in the life sciences. They have proven to be extremely applicable, delivering us the power to manipulate individual atoms and genes. In contrast, neither at the level of ideas nor at the level of practices have religious traditions shown a similar record of convergence and fruitfulness.

The success of the sciences has been paid for, to some extent, by modesty in ambitions. In the present context, two kinds of modesty are especially important to consider. The sciences have, in general, intended to abstain from moral and other evaluatory judgements regarding reality. And they have focused on aspects of reality open to effective treatment, with operational definitions of concepts such as 'energy' or 'life', while abstaining from metaphysical, essentialist claims about such notions. In contrast, religious thinkers of various kinds have sought to articulate ideas about ultimate reality and the inner essence of things, transcendent explanations and the like, as well as on the meaningfulness of life or on absolute values. (Not that all scientists or all religious thinkers have kept clear to their side of the divide, but still, the difference in role indicated here is more or less mainstream understanding of science and of religion.)

Thus, both by success (science being more successful) and by scope (science being more limited in kinds of activities allowed) the enterprises of science and of religion are quite different. Another disadvantage of the 'bridge model' is that it treats the banks as given: the project is the building of the bridge. However, in doing religion-and-science we are engaged in disputes over the nature of religious convictions and practices; in the reflection on religions in an age of science, one has to be a revisionist if one is to recover some important elements of the traditions in the context of current understanding of our world. Thus, rather than assuming symmetry, it seems more adequate to me to acknowledge the asymmetry of religion and science in such intellectual pursuits.

Unlike those who seek to build bridges in developing a 'theology of nature', as a project that assumes a strong basis in a pre-given theological view, I am with 'natural theologies' in accepting asymmetry in the argumentative pattern, which runs from science to theology or metaphysics.

VII. Realism

Thesis: *Realism* too, is a problematic notion when it comes to theology and science.

Realism is a claim regarding the quality of our knowledge – that this knowledge is a good representation (of some sort) of the reality out there – and not about the existence of reality. In science, we become convinced in this respect when certain theoretical notions, such as 'electron', are well integrated into our theoretical web of beliefs and when they serve us well in practical contexts, for example, when electrons are used as tools in further research (electron microscopy, etc.). In theology we seem to lack a cumulative argument preserving previous results or practices or other indications of the fertility of particular ideas. Thus, the epistemic standing of realist claims in theology is more problematical. Furthermore, there are theological concerns regarding realism – whether we can positively claim knowledge of the divine, and whether this is knowledge of a detached kind similar to scientific knowledge. For many years, major authors in science and theology have emphasized critical realism and similarities between science and theology (Barbour 1974; Peacocke 1984). There is something attractive to such projects, but (aside of becoming sometimes an endless set of epistemic prolegomena on rationality) I wonder how they capture the particular inaccessibility of the Holy.

For a 'mystical' theology, which reflects a desire for unity, for a divine presence in continuity with our lives and our knowledge, awareness of the limitations of our models may do sufficient justice to its understanding of the otherness of the divine. However, the 'is not' is insufficient as an expression of the distinction between our models of the divine and the divine reality itself for a 'prophetic' theology, which is characterized by a sense of difference and contrast, of divine absence rather than presence, of contrast between what is and what should have been. On a 'prophetic' understanding of theology, there is a sense of 'and it is not' for which there is no analogy in science. In a prophetic theology, people also seek to articulate a sense of contrast between God and the world, between how humans behave and how God intended them to behave, or, more naturalistically, between ideas about 'what ought to be' and 'what is', as such ideas have evolved within reality. An 'is not' meant as a form of modesty about our language and knowledge is not enough to articulate such a sense of contrast.

VIII. Theological Dimensions of Technology

Thesis: To carve the field of discussions up in science-and-religion and, separately, ethics-and-technology, misses the theological dimensions of technological activity as contribution to trans-formation of reality.

The 'is-not' of religious language makes it hard to treat it just like scientific language. Such issues of disharmony are, however, not merely theoretical – they are related to our actions. When we get to issues of value, we also have to reflect on human action. It is that area, of technological activity, aimed at 'improving nature', which we will consider now.

Science offers more than understanding; it provides us with tools to change our world. Early technology was *imitating nature*, doing things which nature does well. At some point, we moved on to *improving nature*, making some things better than they would be without us. 'Better' is, of course, an evaluation – and thus invites the question what the standard is by which this is judged. Wheat is after millennia of human selection 'better' for producing bread, feeding the hungry. Sometimes we are even *correcting nature*, doing things differently, averting problematic consequences of nature. We humans cannot do without this side of science, restricting ourselves to the noble goal of understanding. The active attitude is deeply rooted in human nature; we are as much *homo faber* as *homo sapiens*. I also doubt whether a moral person should wish we would do without this active side. Not only can we not do without technology, we ought not desire to do without technology. There is, of course, the mythical image of paradise, of an effortless pastoral life with fruit in abundance. But if one is more realistic, we need technology for morally lofty purposes, to feed the hungry, to clothe the naked, to care for the sick. The lightning rod has led in some cases to negative religious responses, as if we would seek to deflect the wrath of God, but it would be immoral not to use lightning rods (Ferré 1993). Objections to technology surface again and again, and with them the warning that 'we should not play God' – not with medical technology, not in biotechnology.

Willem B. Drees

IX. Playing God

Thesis: 'Playing God' is negatively invoked when we are insecure about the distinction between that which is given and that which is open to human action. Implicitly, this assumes an understanding of God as creator, not as redeemer. Upon a different theological and anthropological view, transgressing such boundaries is called for.

Various notions are used in religious circles to describe the human role, both in relation to environmental concerns and in relation to modern biotechnology. Are we to be seen as stewards, or rather as co-creators?

Let me begin with a summary of the Bible, in a single sentence. The Bible begins on high, with paradise, which is followed by a long journey through history, with the expectation of final salvation. The liturgy is one of memory and hope. The sabbath recalls the creation and the exodus and is a foretaste of fulfilment. This U-shaped profile (Frye 1982, 169) implies that images of the good are present in two varieties, as images of the past (paradise) and as images of a City of God, a new heaven and a new earth, the Kingdom to come. If humans are considered stewards, one looks back in time, to a good situation which has to be kept and preserved. If humans are addressed as co-creators, the eyes are mainly on the future, on that which might come.

In relation to the use of human knowledge and power, some of the stories may be illuminating as well. In the synagogue Jesus meets someone with a withered hand. Will he heal on the sabbath? Then Jesus asks: 'Is it lawful on the sabbath to do good or to do harm, to save life or to kill?' The priority is clear. In this story of healing, from Mark 3, and in many other stories, a human is freed of the burdens of his past. A tax-collector and a prostitute are again on the way of life, the possessed relax and deaf persons hear. The social dimension which can also be found in the stories related to the prophets, is also found here. Especially those who have been less well off, get new chances, are seen in a new light. Discipleship as serving the poor and needy has often been forgotten, but it has resurfaced again and again in the history of Christianity. This resulted in particular in the care for orphans, widows and people who were seriously ill.

One parable is explicitly about stewardship (Matt 25:14–30). A landlord is to leave and entrusts his property to three servants. One received five talents, one two and the third only one talent, 'to each according to his ability'. The story is familiar. The one with five talents made another five; the one with two talents made two, but the one with only one talent buried it and returns it to his master. In the end, the landlord commands that the worthless servant be cast into the outer darkness; there men will weep and gnash their teeth.

From this brief tour of biblical texts and images I maintain that in biblical language the good is not only in the past but in the future as well, that humans – even when considered as stewards – can be active and even ought to be active although the initiative is with God, and that this activity is normatively determined as care for the weak and needy.

In speaking of *co-creation* one takes distance from the idea that creation is in principle finished and complete and from the idea that God will bypass humans in arranging everything. The history of humans is the history in which humans have responsibility. How this might be imagined, depends on the answer to the question whether one thinks of God and humans as similar or different. Is God's eternity a-temporal or everlasting? Everlasting fits better with the emphasis on history and growth, whereas a-temporality is a qualification that underlines the difference between God and the world.

If the difference is emphasized, the notion of co-creation fits less well. If God's mode of action is totally different from ours, we are not creators with God – as being creator, giving existence as ground of being, is something that can be said only of God. A similar problem applies to the notion of stewardship, which rests upon the idea that the steward takes on certain tasks of his lord, tasks that his lord could have executed himself. But emphasizing the difference also grants an enormous room for human responsibility, for human creative activity. For God has created the world with all its regularities and all freedom. God is not delegating power in some half-hearted way, intervening whenever things are different from God's intentions. There is not from time to time a shift to manual control, to correct the consequences of human free actions. In this perspective, humans are not co-creators in the sense in which God is a creator, but they are *creative creatures*, or perhaps one might say *created creators*, beings who genuinely act in creation.

When God is seen in temporal terms, the notion *co-creator* seems more appropriate. After the initial creation, God is thought of as working in the world in a continuing creative process, *creatio continua*, in interplay with humans. But if God is not only the initial creator but also one of the many actors on the stage, the question is how his activities relate to our knowledge. Would God act contrary to the laws he invested in the first place? Or in the room allowed for in those laws? And if we focus on humans: does God act through humans by overruling their own freedom, using them as mere instruments? Or by evoking a certain attitude, a particular vision? I only raise questions to emphasize a problem; even a long book would not solve these deep issues. My preference is to think through the case where God's mode of action is fundamentally not in competition with human actions and natural processes; either these processes are God at work, or God is the ground of these processes and of existence, but not an additional factor among other factors.

Stewardship has become prominent in reflection upon the ecological damage that we have done. In that context, stewardship has the connotation of nature conservation. It fits better reticence than actively changing nature. But human activity is not only a threat to God's good creation. It has also been seen as taking up the work God entrusted to us, to work for the good, under the guidance of the Holy Spirit – whether this work is primarily social or ecological engagement. Human creativity does not diminish God. To the contrary, the more one develops one's creativity, the more one surpasses current limitations, the more God becomes God. We cannot shift the burden of responsibility to God; we are responsible. Our task becomes to make God present in the world, or, as Isabel Carter Heyward (1984) puts it, with a verb which was new to me, our task is 'to god the world'. The issue is that in such theological projects we are not primarily doing theology on the basis of positive experiences of beauty and goodness, but rather out of engagement with justice, with love. This makes one focus on transformation as a central theological theme.

Transformation as personal conversion or social change is an important theme in many theologies, especially in evangelical and political theologies. Natural theologies arising out of experiences with the natural world mostly lack this; they tend to overemphasize the way things are as something deserving wonder. However, a theologically adequate view should, in my opinion, also attempt to disclose the possibilities for transformation of the natural order. Not only a natural theology, but also a theology with a strong liberationist tendency, requires a dialogue with the sciences, an appropriate metaphysics, etc. We do not have such a view in hand yet. I am at this moment only trying to understand the scope of the agenda that is there once one moves beyond simplistic debates on the Bible and scientific knowledge or proofs for the existence of God. In the dialogue with the sciences, all aspects of religious faith are involved – not merely creation, but also redemption, not only 'what is' but also 'what should be'.

Returning to the metaphors discussed, I would stress that neither the past (images of paradise) nor the future (a new heaven and a new earth) is acceptable as the sole point of reference. It seems to me to be far more fruitful to listen to the parables and pick up the sensitivity that can be found there for those in need. The questions then become not whether one should get involved but how – who will benefit and in what way? In that context it is important to be realistic about matters of power and politics, the inequalities within humanity, and the even greater asymmetry between humans and other living beings. We can serve God and our neighbour with all our heart, with all our soul, with all our strength and with all our mind – and hence also with science and technology. With the reminder that this great commandment is immediately followed (Luke 10) with the story of the Good Samaritan – thus warning us against too limited a sense of who our neighbours might be.

X. Conclusion

Thesis.

(1) Disorder in nature calls into question a wide variety of projects in 'science and theology', as too many projects are based on mistaken assumptions of harmony.

(2) Disorder in nature is a reality which can be considered as if it were designed to call humans to responsibility, to serve God and each other with all our heart and soul as well as with all our power and mind.

References

BARBOUR, IAN G. 1974. *Myths, Models, and Paradigms*, New York: Harper & Row.

DREES, WILLEM B. 1990. 'Theologie en natuurwetenschap: Onafhankelijkheid en samenhang', in Hans Küng et al., *Godsdienst op een keerpunt*, Kampen: Kok Agora.

——. 1990. *Beyond the Big Bang*, La Salle: Open Court.

——. 1996. *Religion, Science and Naturalism*, Cambridge: Cambridge University Press.

FERRÉ, FREDERICK. 1993. *Hellfire and Lightning Rods: Liberating Science, Technology, and Religion*, Maryknoll: Orbis.

FRYE, NORTHROP. 1982. *The Great Code: The Bible and Literature*, San Diego: Harcourt Brace Jovanovich.

HARSKAMP, ANTON VAN. 1998. 'Een mirakel van onze tijd. Of: De meedogenloze logica van A Course in Miracles', *In de Marge* 7 (3), 7–21.

HEYWARD, ISABEL CARTER. 1984. *The Redemption of God: A Theology of Mutual Relation*, Lanham: University Press of America.

HICK, JOHN. 1989. *An Interpretation of Religion: Human Responses to the Transcendent*, Basingstoke: Macmillan.

HUXLEY, THOMAS H. [1893] 1989. 'Evolution and Ethics', in James Paradis and George C. Williams (eds), *T. H. Huxley's* Evolution and Ethics, *with New Essays on Its Victorian and Sociobiological Context*, Princeton: Princeton University Press.

JAMES, WILLIAM. [1902] 1958. *The Varieties of Religious Experience: A Study in Human Nature*, New York: Mentor Books.

MCMULLIN, ERNAN. 1981. 'How should Cosmology relate to Theology?', in A. R. Peacocke (ed.), *The Sciences and Theology in the Twentieth Century*, Stocksfield: Oriel Press.

MURPHY, NANCEY and ELLIS, GEORGE F. R. 1996. *On the Moral Nature of the Universe: Theology, Cosmology and Ethics*, Minneapolis: Fortress Press.

PEACOCKE, ARTHUR R. 1984. *Intimations of Reality: Critical Realism in Science and Theology*, Notre Dame: University of Notre Dame Press.

PETERS, TED (ed.). 1989. *Cosmos as Creation: Theology and Science in Consonance*, Nashville: Abingdon Press.

——. 1998. *Science and Theology: The New Consonance*, Boulder: Westview Press.

PLATVOET, J. G. 1993. 'De wraak van de "primitieven": godsdienstgeschiedenis van Neanderthaler tot New Age', *Nederlands Theologisch Tijdschrift* 47, 227–43.

TERRIEN, SAMUEL. 1978. *The Elusive Presence: Toward a New Biblical Theology*, San Francisco: Harper & Row.

THEISSEN, GERHARD. 1985. *Biblical Faith: An Evolutionary Approach*, Philadelphia: Fortress Press.

WEINBERG, STEVEN. 1977. *The First Three Minutes*, New York: Basic Books.

WILLIAMS, GEORGE C. 1989. 'A Sociobiological Expansion of Evolution and Ethics', in James Paradis and George C. Williams (eds), *T. H. Huxley's* Evolution and Ethics, *with New Essays on Its Victorian and Sociobiological Context*, Princeton: Princeton University Press.

Index